Collaborative Planning, Forecasting and Replenishment

Dirk Seifert

Collaborative Planning, Forecasting and Replenishment

How to create a Supply Chain Advantage.
Preprint Edition

Galileo Business

Die Deutsche Bibliothek – CIP-Einheitsaufnahme
Ein Titeldatensatz für diese Publikation
ist bei der Deutschen Bibliothek erhältlich

Corrections by Elsbeth Kearful, Cologne, Germany

Typeset by reemers publishing services, Krefeld, Germany

Printed and bound in Germany by Bercker Graphischer Betrieb, Kevelaer

Inhalt

Foreword of the VICS-CPFR® Committee

We want to express our sincere gratitude to Dr. Dirk Seifert and the Harvard Business School for conducting research on CPFR[1] and for writing this book. The endorsement of CPFR by a research project conducted at the Harvard Business School is a major step in the acceptance of CPFR as a creditable business process reflective of emerging global trends and the impact of technology on efficient business processes.

This book describes a practical, yet intensive, thought provoking business process that demonstrates how to implement CPFR and gain quantifiable results, to be enjoyed by all parties to the value chain. It promotes an understanding of how to overcome the barriers to CPFR, which are primarily cultural, ignorance and a desire to maintain the status quo. It will become clear that technology is not a barrier to implementation and that CPFR is in fact flexible and adaptable to various business conditions and circumstances.

Supply chain management has been evolving for the past 25 years, beginning with the traffic, order management and warehousing departments. They were ultimately brought together under the umbrella of physical distribution. Subsequently inventory management and customer service were included, enabling integrated logistics, followed by production planning and procurement. Today we have Supply Chain Management, which is rapidly emerging into Value Chain Management which recognizes the importance of demand in addition to supply.

In this continuum, sales forecasting may be the responsibility of one department or be shared by several departments, generally operating in an information stovepipe. The mission critical information is given little, if any, import and consequently drives the supply chain with incorrect and/or untimely information. Current, fresh, visible information is a key ingredient to realizing value chain excellence coupled with defined agreed business processes. CPFR clearly identifies the need for collaboration among trading partners through-

---

1 CPFR® is a Registered Trademark of the Voluntary Interindustry Commerce Standards (VICS) Association.

out the value chain and identifies the financial and operational results that can be expected.

If the evolution of the supply chain has moved at the speed of sound, CPFR has evolved at the speed of light. Companies, who are in retail, technology, textile, automotive, drug and other industries across the globe, are rapidly adopting CPFR. The case studies and other information in this book will prove to be invaluable to the practitioner and to senior leadership. We wish Dr. Seifert and the Harvard Business School the best of luck and much success as they continue their important work.

Rita Marzian, Co-Chair VICS CPFR, Metro AG
Jim McLaughlin, Co-Chair VICS CPFR, Gillette
Joe Andraski, Vice-Chair VICS CPFR, OMI International

Preface of the Author

This book is a pre-print version of Collaborative Planning, Forecasting and Replenishment – How to Create a Supply Chain Advantage. The English and German full versions will be published in Fall 2002. The full version will include additional material and case studies.

Collaborative Planning, Forecasting and Replenishment is a determinant theme in the consumer goods economy worldwide. The prospect of enormous potential savings on the one hand, and growth through the avoidance of out-of-stocks on the other fascinates manufacturers and retailers equally. CPFR is a further development of ECR on the supply side. It represents the **second generation of ECR**. Through planning and forecasting, there are clear interrelations between the supply side and departments like Marketing and Sales Management, which until now were strongly attached to the demand side. This interdepartmental working relationship is typical of second generation ECR. The boundaries between strategy on the supply side and the demand side are becoming more permeable.

The Globalization of CPFR

Since the emergence of CPFR in the mid-nineties, the implementation of this new strategy has expanded rapidly around the world. *The Voluntary Interindustry Commerce Standards (VICS)* and *Global Commerce Initiative (GCI)* together with some of the most important companies in the North American consumer goods industry have laid the cornerstone for the success of CPFR. In Europe, *ECR Europe* and the national ECR organizations, *ECR Belgium, ECR Czech Republic, ECR Denmark, ECR D-A-CH, ECR Finland, ECR France, ECR Italy, ECR Hellas, ECR Irleland, ECR Italy, ECR Nederland, ECR Spain, ECR Sweden* and *ECR UK*, recognized early on the necessity of adapting CPFR to the specifics of the European market. They have done important work in recent years in developing standards for and knowledge exchange on CPFR. In Germany, for example, the *CCG's* (Centrale für Coorganisation) annual ECR-Conferences have become a national forum where state-of-the-art information on CPFR from manufacturing and retailing is presented and exchanged. It is an ideal national complement to the pan-European conferences such as that in Barcelona in 2002, organized by ECR Europe.

CPFR has also expanded in South America, Africa, and Asia. Retailers and manufacturers in Brazil, Columbia, South Africa, and Japan are successfully using CPFR in their business processes, adapting it for their own market conditions, and creating best practices which can be used by other countries in the respective regions.

CPFR Knowledge Transfer

The systematic transfer of CPFR knowledge will be an important task worldwide in the coming years. Creating CPFR expertise for large, medium and small companies allows them all to enjoy the sought after efficiencies. This is also the goal of a new CPFR educational initiative. *Joe Andraski* and *Tom Friedmann*, both CPFR veterans, have created a forum with the newly grounded *CPFR Institute* that will enable CPFR knowledge transfer on a variety of levels. The newest CPFR-findings will be adjusted to the needs of various target groups, senior management, middle management, and operations staff. The research group responsible for this volume identified itself with the goals of the CPFR Institute and supports them.

Structure of the Book

The book is intended to give the reader insight into the current use of CPFR in the consumer goods economy through case studies and contributions by experts in the field.

The **first chapter** describes Efficient Consumer Response as the starting point for the development of the CPFR concept. Both main components of ECR, Supply Chain Management and Category Management, are introduced here. The chapter covers not only the tasks and objectives of the individual ECR strategies, but also detailed explanations of things like the nine-step Category Management process and approaches to the reengineering of the value chain.

The **second chapter** begins with the value proposition of CPFR. It explains why this new management concept represents second generation ECR. Further, the CPFR process model is introduced and its potential efficiency advantages shown. The first section also contains a description of the first CPFR project by Wal-Mart and Warner-Lambert, which signaled the dawn of CPFR in the consumer goods industry. Afterwards Prof. Dr. Gerhard Arminger, Professor of the University of Wuppertal and Chief Scientist of SAF-AG provides insights on Sales and Order Forecasts in the CPFR Process for Retail. The contribution by Joseph C. Andraski, Vice Chairman of VICS-CPFR and Senior Vice President of OMI International, explains CPFR as an evolutionary step in Supply Chain Management. Julie Fraser of Industry Directions presents the most important results of a CPFR study done in collaboration with Syncra Systems. In it are data on actual CPFR use and the gain in utility obtained through CPFR in areas like forecast accuracy.

Chapter Three introduces the use of CPFR in the US. Tom Friedman and Greg Belkin of MoonWatch Media discuss important trends and experiences in the use of CPFR and present two brief case studies on Wal-Mart/Sara Lee and Schering Plough. Lawrence E. Fennell, Vice President at Wal-Mart, provides the reader with background information on the current retail environment. He writes about how to get started with CPFR and suggests methods for the intelligent implementation of consumer-centered CPFR. In conclusion, Christopher A. Brady, who is working in the Supply Chain Management at Safeway, describes the experiences and perspectives of Safeway with CPFR. He explains where the biggest benefits are coming from and also provides insights on implementation issues.

Chapter Four switches the focus to the implementation of CPFR in Europe. The introductory article explains the differences between the North American and European consumer goods markets. Furthermore, one receives an overview of selected CPFR projects in Europe. Saskia Treeck and Michael Seishoff of the Centrale für Coorganisation (CCG) present CPFR events they have coordinated in Germany, Austria and Switzerland. In particular they make reference to the CPFR management guidelines intended to ease the implementation of CPFR in the German-speaking economic regions of Europe. Gunter Baumgart, Dr. Birgit Ester and Christian Schick present the use of CPFR by dm-drogerie markt and Henkel in Germany. The implementation of CPFR by Henkel in Spain with two trade partners is the topic of Sergio Duque, Esteban Garriga und Hans Teuscher's contribution. The Chapter is concluded by an article by Peter Hambuch on the experience and perspective of Procter & Gamble in Europe.

The **fifth chapter** shows the possibilities for the implementation of CPFR. Georg Engler of Accenture discusses the development of a CPFR project from pilot to scalable implementation. Robert Bruce and Ron Ireland, two former Wal-Mart executives and current senior executives at VCC Associates identify important features of successful CPFR management and four fundamental strategies for the use of CPFR. Afterwards Ralph W. Drayer, former Chief Logistics Officer at Procter & Gamble and currently Chairman of Supply Chain Insights writes about the quiet revolution taking place in the industry right now. In the last article of this chapter, Christian Koch of SAP AG and Gerhard Hausruckinger of Roland Berger Strategy Consultants lay out the roadmap to the network economy and offer their prognosis of the future of the consumer goods economy.

The book is to be viewed as a platform for the expression of the opinions of different important players in the field: manufacturers, retailers, consulting companies and IT-solutions providers. The opinions expressed by contributing authors do not necessarily reflect those of the editor. The articles distinguish themselves through different styles and approaches, offering the reader varying perspectives on CPFR.

Acknowledgements

The book would not have been possible without the help and the inspiration of many people and companies.

I would like to thank Accenture, JDA, and SAP AG, who sponsored our research on CPFR.

Special thanks in particular to the contributing authors: Joseph C. Andraski, Prof. Dr. Gerhard Arminger, Gunter Baumgart, Greg Belkin, Christopher A. Brady, Robert Bruce, Ralph W. Drayer, Sergio Duque, Georg Engler, Dr. Birgit

Ester, Lawrence E. Fennell, Julie Fraser, Thomas H. Friedman, Esteban Garriga, Peter Hambuch, Dr. Gerhard Hausruckinger, Ron Ireland, Christian Koch, Christian Schick, Michael Seishoff, Saskia Treeck and Hans Teuscher for sharing the knowledge and experience of their companies.

I would like to thank the members of my research team: Alexander Adler, Mark Cicirelli, Kirstin Hornby, Julian Kurz, and Michael Lark. Heartfelt thanks also to those whose personal involvement facilitated intensive debate on many ideas contained in this volume Fred Baumann, Claudia Beckers, Rudolf Behrens, Roland Bertsch, Steffen Bundesmann, Prof. Clayton Christensen, Hans-Gerhard Degen, Richard Downs, Eli Fel, Berthold Figgen, Dagmar Fischer-Neeb, Dr. Stephan Friedrich, Prof. Janice H. Hammond, Prof. Dr. Hans Hinterhuber, Kathrin Holling, Steffen Jaeckle, Prof. Dr. Alexander Kracklauer, Dr. Jürgen Kohr, Dr. Peter Linzbach, Ronald Margulis, Graham Newland, Dr. Heiner Olbrich, Dr. Olaf Passenheim, Willibald Poplutz, Achim Pütz, Brigitta Rodens-Friedrich, Uwe Rosik, Wolfgang Runge, Christopher Sellers, Silke Slootz, Dr. Andreas Oetting, Jim Uchneat, Jürgen Weltermann, Prof. Sean Willems and Prof. Dr. Michael Zerres.

And finally, my thanks to Prof. D. Quinn Mills, Prof. Michael Y. Yoshino and the Research Division of the Harvard Business School, who all helped pave the way for the work presented here.

If you have questions, comments and criticisms regarding this book you may contact the author via e-mail: *dseifert@hbs.edu* or *seifert-d@gmx.de*

Boston, March 2002

Dr. Dirk Seifert
Harvard Business School

1 Efficient Consumer Response as the Origin of CPFR

Dr. Dirk Seifert, Harvard Business School

In the early nineties, the American retail and consumer goods industry was confronted with massive problems. An increase in productivity was hardly to be realized, revenues stagnated at the same time as costs were rising. Competitive advantages, and thereby an increase in market share were only to be achieved through aggressive pricing politics. The consequences of this were a negative effect on margins, contribution margins, and profit on sales. Retailing and manufacturing had to recognize that real gains through differentiation were only going to be achieved through open cooperative partnerships with one another.

The success of the retailer Wal-Mart made the consumer goods industry aware of the outstanding potential for rationalization and the possibility of improvements in productivity. Wal-Mart had concentrated on a more close-knit cooperation with its suppliers, in order to offer its customers quality products more quickly, efficiently and at lower cost. Wal Mart's strategy is based on a concept called Efficient Consumer Response (ECR). The result of these efforts are evidented in the store-wide records for inventory turnover, revenue per unit sales area, and operating profit.

ECR implies two essential components:

▶ **Consumer:** An orientation towards the needs of the consumer

▶ **Efficient Response:** A process oriented optimization of the supply chain, dovetailing individual elements (orientation to value added processes)

The deciding factor for ECR in the US was a number of projects and studies in 1992, which were initiated by the Food Marketing Institute in Washington and affiliated work groups like the Joint Industry Project on Efficient Consumer Response. The consultancy Kurt Salmon Associates had already done a landmark study in 1985, analyzing the supply chain in the textile and garment industry, and thereby developed the Quick Response Concept for that industry.

ECR is a comprehensive management concept for retailing and manufacturing based on a **value-adding partnership** between the participants. The strategy is made up of several different basic strategies. Accordingly, retail and manufacturing work together to make the supply chain efficient, rational, and oriented towards the needs of the consumer. The point of departure and likewise the foundation for ECR has been partnership and cooperation oriented thinking of retail and manufacturing. With ECR, it is about shifting from **intra- to inter-organizational process organization of corporations**. The following figure gives an overview of both main parts of the ECR concept and the associated ECR basis strategies.

Efficient Consumer Response-Concept	
Supply Chain Management (SCM)	Category Management (CM)
Efficient Replenishment (ER)	Efficient Store Assortment (ESA)
Efficient Administration (EA)	Efficient Promotion (EP)
Efficient Operating Standards (EOS)	Efficient Product Introduction (EPI)

Exhibit 1.1 The ECR concept and its basic strategies.
Source: CCRRGE (1994), Seifert (2001)

On the supply-side, cooperation in logistics between manufacturers and retailers should result in optimal **supply chain management**. On the demand side, collaboration in marketing via **category management** and the exchange of customer data make it possible for all parties to achieve a more efficient **marketing mix**. All efforts should stand against the backdrop of improved customer satisfaction. This can result from the increase of product availability and of quality, (freshness of product through more efficient logistics) or through customer oriented assortments, which offer optimal pricing (marketing cooperation). The objective of both aspects of ECR is the reduction or elimination of all activities which do not add value, and the concentration on factors which maximize value and productivity. ECR is an interdisciplinary marketing and logistics and management task between manufacturing and retailing companies.

Definition: Efficient Consumer Response

ECR is a comprehensive management concept based on vertical collaboration in manufacturing and retailing with the objective of an efficient satisfaction of consumer needs. The main components of ECR are Supply Chain Management and Category Management.

1.1 The Goals and Tasks of the ECR Concept

The primary goal of ECR is to transform sub-optimal individual solutions of individual links in the supply chain into a comprehensive solution. The concrete goal, in the realm of cooperative logistics and thereby in supply chain management, is the elimination of inefficiency which occurs through uncoordinated sequences in the supply chain: e.g. inventory or information which lies idle for long periods or the warehousing of unnecessary safety stock.

In cooperative marketing agreements, the objective is to rectify erroneous trends in promotional activities, assortment decisions and product introductions. The problems are rooted in non-existent or insufficient information on the customer and his needs. It is category management's task to offer a platform to retailers and manufacturers which supports the exchange of consumer data and tactics for a successful entry into the marketplace of the value adding partners.

The goal of ECR is to allow manufacturers, retailers and consumers to participate in the creation of value and thereby a **win-win-win situation**. The following figure shows the gains for each group with an example.

The consumer profits from ECR above all through an optimized cost-benefit ratio. Consistently low prices help maintain a constant and thereby cost effective flow of goods, reinforcing lower prices. Basic ECR strategies like efficient replenishment assure fresher products and higher availability. Measures like efficient store assortment bring about a customer-oriented range of products and an improved shopping experience.

Consumer	Retailer	Manufacturer
Fresher products	Quicker and more efficient system	Quicker and more efficient system
Greater and more consistent value for money	Reduced inventory and capital invested Lower depreciation Fewer promotion handling	Reduced inventory and capital invested Optimized production planning and use of capacity
More shopping satisfaction through improved product avaliability	Reduced out-of-stocks Greater customer loyalty	Reduced out-of-stocks Greater brand loyalty
Easy shopping experience (optimized categories)	Customer oriented assortment	Customer oriented assortment
Genuine innovations	Greater customer awareness through innovative assortments	Increased market share/ competive advantage
➡ Greater customer satisfaction	**➡ Lower costs and higher revenue growth**	**➡ Lower costs and higher revenue growth**

Exhibit 1.2 The creation of a win-win-win situation as the goal of ECR. Source: Seifert

Suppliers and retailers benefit through the cooperative implementation of ECR primarily through higher profits. This is made possible through the cost reductions in the supply chain and increases in revenue through an optimized marketing concept.

1.2 The Reversal of the Push Principle to the Pull Principle in the Supply Chain

ECR represents a reengineering of the supply chain in the consumer goods industry. Until now, the process flow in the supply chain was dominated by the push principle. That meant that in the traditional supply chain of manufacturing and retailing, product volume was pushed into the pipeline, regardless of retail sales. This tendency can be seen in the following facts.

1. Production is not synchronized with demand and thereby overburdens the warehouses of both manufacturer and retailer. The manufacturer's own production costs are minimized; however they cause higher costs at other stages of the supply chain.

2. Buyers from the retailer's side increase the volume of their purchases to obtain discounts and are measured by the success of these efforts. These savings are often lost though through higher overall costs in the supply chain.

3. Within retail organizations, there is seldom coordination between the sales and purchasing departments directed towards meeting consumers' needs. This unsatisfactory relationship leads to missing information at all stages of the supply chain and large swings in the demand for product in the trade channel. The consequences of extreme surges are overly large inventories in the supply chain, suppliers with capacities which are too low or too high as well as uncertain production planning and a low service level on fast turning SKU (stock keeping units).

The problem becomes more acute especially when the manufacturer is continually trying to increase deliveries of product. This leads to exorbitant deliveries of product and to cost intensive production peaks and a taxing of capacity. The large inventories are 'pressed' into retail outlets through the retailers' warehouses. Because of limited retail space, a **high pressure to sell** the product exists, which can only be reduced through lower prices and the resultant increase in demand. The consequences are constantly **sinking promotional prices and reduced margins for manufacturers as well as retailers**. Consumers alter their shopping habits, and no longer buy products at regular prices, but rather are always on the lookout for special offers.

Through ECR, the relationship just described is reversed. The **Pull-Principle** is now the dominating idea in the supply chain. A supply chain organized according to ECR principles references itself to the consumer and does not attempt to pressure product through the channel. The consumer with his needs and his buying behavior stands in the middle of all considerations. Demand is determined through exact measurements obtained via market research and the analysis of scanner data. Production and distribution in the supply chain are synchronized on the basis of information from retail outlets. Distribution works as the link between the production of the manufacturer and the consumption of the customer. A seamless exchange of information operates between all participants in the supply chain. The following figure should serve to clarify the reversal in the prevailing attitude.

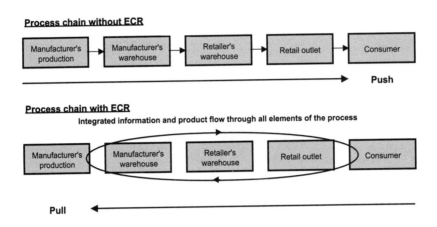

Exhibit 1.3 ECR-Reengineering the supply chain.
Source: KSA (1993), Zentes (1996), Seifert (2001)

The ECR reengineering process of the supply chain described above allows the vision of a **consumer driven supply chain** to become a reality. The model is based on the realization that multi-stage warehouse inventory systems function decidedly better when information on orders and stock on hand in all links in the supply chain is available.

1.3 ECR-Collaboration Field Logistics: Supply Chain Management

The work between participants in the supply chain historically has always led to conflicts in the trade channel. Every link in the chain was intent on minimizing its own costs. The optimization of logistics in a particular stage of production however often led to increased costs in preceding and following stages of the supply chain. The isolated optima of the individual stages did not lead to an overall optimum in the supply chain. Supply chain management, as the logistics foundation of the ECR concept, offers decisive differences for a **comprehensive optimization of the supply chain**. From SCM's perspective, the goal is a process-oriented overall treatment of the supply chain aimed at **total system efficiency**.

1.3.1 The Implementation of Supply Chain Planning

In the planning process of the logistics supply chain, manufacturers and retailers are supported by so-called supply chain planning (SCP) systems. Companies reach an optimal allocation of resources with these computer based applications. The following illustration gives an overview of the primary uses of SCP.

SCP-Application	Task
Demand Planning	Optimized quantification of demand
Distribution Planning	Demand-oriented demand management, e.g.: consideration of unexpected production gaps and late shipments
Constraint Based Master Planning	Constraint based master planning delivers real time planning in consideration of materials, capacities, and individual restrictions in integrated distribution, manufacturing and suppliers networks
Transportation Planning	Transportation planning that gives the necessary transparency and which can accommodate all movement
Manufacturing Planning & Scheduling	Detail planning of production. A precise time and dependencies plan is assured
Network Design and Optimization	Modeling of the entire supply chain and its business situation, in order to recommend the most economic strategy. Thereby, companies can quickly and easily see the course of the dovetailed process chain
Available to promise	Binding availability and delivery date agreements become possible though an integrated view of the supply chain. Thereby, all available inventory, orders, ressource availability (transportation, production capacity, personnel etc.) as well as alternate suppliers are considered

Exhibit 1.4 Primary Uses of the Supply Chain Planning System

1.3.2 The Goals of Retailers and Manufacturers bound to Supply Chain Management

Manufacturers and retailers have somewhat different objectives in supply chain management. The following diagram should serve to show the essential differences.

	Market position referenced goals	**Results referenced goals**
Retailer's objectives	Expansion of logistical competence through manufacturing partner Increased consumer loyalty Better understanding of actual demand behavior Improved image through fresher products Quick logistical realization of new product introductions	Increased revenue through reduction of out-of-stocks Increased turnover of stock Inventory reduction Reduced costs of capital invested Increased earnings Reduced logistics costs Lower depreciation through expired goods (expiration of 'use-by' date) Optimization of ordering and billing processes
Manufacturer's objecitves	Improved image as competence partner of retailer Quick logistical realization of new product introductions Ability to influence logistics chain Creation of a competitive advantage Better understanding of actual demand behavior	Increased revenue through reduction of out-of-stocks Increased earnings Optimization of ordering and billing processes Reduction of logistics costs Optimized production Reduced inventory of raw materials and finished product

Exhibit 1.5 SCM objectives of retailers and suppliers

1.3.3 The Cost-savings Potential of Supply Chain Management

In order to show the possible cost savings potential available through ECR cooperation in logistics#, a detailed cost structure analysis of the individual value adding operations in the supply chain is necessary. Significant in these calculations are the share of expenditures on logistics relative to total cost. In a **value chain analysis** by PriceWaterhouse Coopers, the essential cost components of retail and manufacturing in Europe were calculated. According to it, 21% of the manufacturer's total costs went on logistics. On the retail side, the study revealed that 44% of total costs were attributable to logistics and thereby that, savings in the supply chain tended to be potentially stronger for retailers.

A study of the Coca-Cola Retailing Research Group came to the conclusion that through supply chain management a cost savings potential of 1.5 to 2.5%

of end consumer prices is achievable. Before the backdrop of such figures, it is astounding that many companies in the consumer goods business are not doing more in the way of ECR cooperative logistics (supply chain management). In a study by the consulting firm KPMG (in collaboration with the Kellogg School of Management) done in 1998, 460 firms from 24 different countries were asked about the degree of integration in their supply chains. The results are shown in the following table.

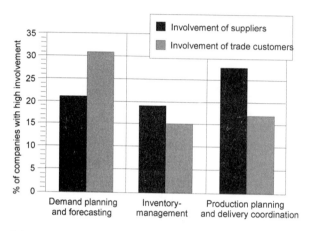

Exhibit 1.6 Degree of Supply Chain Integration

The study shows that the inclusion of suppliers (21% of those surveyed) in demand planning and demand forecasting is clearly less than those who include the customer (31%) in their decision making. The situation is reversed when considering production planning and scheduling. In this case consideration of the suppliers was a factor for 28% of those surveyed and only 17% referenced customer data. KPMG perceived that insight into the advantages of increased supply chain integration is present, but that an adequate implementation has not yet occurred.

1.4   ECR-Collaboration Field Marketing: Category Management

Category Management (CM) is defined as the joint process of retailers and manufacturers through which categories are managed as strategic business units in order to increase utility for the customer and thereby revenues. While in supply chain management, cost optimization in the supply chain stands in the foreground, in category management revenue optimization and the improvement of the gross margin are paramount. The full realization of cost reduction potential however is also the domain of CM. This comes about, for example, through more efficient structuring of promotional activities, efficient control of product assortment, or through the optimized development and introduction of new products.

1.4.1 The Goals of Retailers and Manufacturers bound to Category Management

	Market position referenced goals	results referenced goals
Retailer's objectives	Optimized assortment regarding target group and geographic position of the retail outlet	Profit optimization of the category through increases in revenue and earnings
	Improved image through consumer orientation, category performance and pricing	Increased revenue through reduction of out-of-stocks
	Gaining of new consumer segments	Reduced costs of capital invested
	Exploting of cross-selling potentials	Increased productivity of retail space
	Increased consumer loyalty	Improved reach of consumers
	Unique identity and positioning among retailers	Reduced costs through efficient promotions
	Price concept with higher value creation opportunitiy	Increased inventory turnover
	Early recognition of market and consumer trends	Increased profit contribution of assortment
	Acquisition of market- and marketing knowledge from manufacturers	Increased purchase intensity of consumers
		Cost optimization of new product introductions
Manufacturer's objectives	Acquisition of information about substitutions and complementary product relationsships	Profit optimization of the category through increases in revenue and earnings
	Strengthening of brand loyalty	Improved reach of consumers
	Price concept with higher value creation opportunitiy	Cost optimization of new product introductions
	Better understanding of consumer behaviour	Increased purchase intensity of consumers
	Access to POS data from retailers	Increased revenue through reduction of out-of-stocks
	Improved placement quality on shelf	Cost efficient use of advertising budget through efficient promotions
	Building of an image as a competence partner and preferred supplier	
	Early recognition of market and consumer trends	
	Gaining influence at POS	
	Test markets for innovative products	
	Creation of a competitive advantage	

Exhibit 1.7 CM strategies of retailing and manufacturing

The main idea of CM is a consistent orientation to the customer in product assortment and tender. The core of CM is, correspondingly, strategic control of product assortments. The goals of manufacturers and retailers in category management can be structured in terms of market-referenced goals (qualitative measures) and results targets (quantitative measures). The exhibit 1.7 systematizes the objectives of manufacturing and retailing.

1.4.2 The Nine Step Category Management Planning Process

The category management planning process has the objective of assuring a structured implementation of CM. The nine-step business plan describes a series of activities, the methodology and the responsibilities in the process. The initiation of the planning process includes the naming of clearly defined process owners with clearly laid out responsibilities in the execution of the individual steps in the plan. In such a cooperation, it seems prudent for the manufacturer and retailer to structure the steps in common. The category management planning process creates a balance between product and process investment and takes into consideration all required activities of the whole system from manufacturer to retailer to consumer.

Only when all partners have a complete understanding of the process can the details of the individual steps be adequately addressed. In the planning process, i.e. the definition, dimensioning, and structuring of the introduction of a category, one must always consider the demand structure and the buying behavior of the previously identified target group. In exhibit 1.8, the nine steps of the CM planning process are illustrated.

Strategy Analysis

The first step of the CM planning process entails a strategy analysis of the retail organization. Essential is an understanding of the firm's objectives, the firm's niche in the marketplace, and its image in the eyes of consumers. From that, strategies can be derived for a successful penetration and loyalty. These are for example the assortment, marketing and pricing strategies with quantitative measures like penetration rate and demand coverage quotas (loyalty). Particularly important for the strategy analysis is the identification of the retailer's target group.

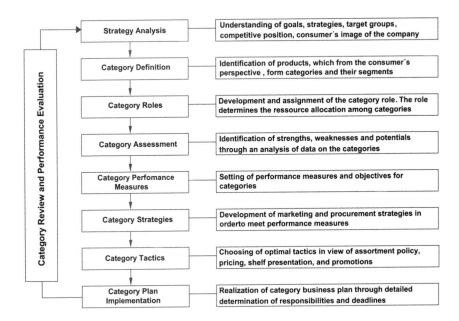

	Strategy Analysis	Understanding of goals, strategies, target groups, competitive position, consumer´s image of the company
Category Review and Performance Evaluation	Category Definition	Identification of products, which from the consumer´s perspective , form categories and their segments
	Category Roles	Development and assignment of the category role. The role determines the ressource allocation among categories
	Category Assessment	Identification of strengths, weaknesses and potentials through an analysis of data on the categories
	Category Perfomance Measures	Setting of performance measures and objectives for categories
	Category Strategies	Development of marketing and procurement strategies in orderto meet performance measures
	Category Tactics	Choosing of optimal tactics in view of assortment policy, pricing, shelf presentation, and promotions
	Category Plan Implementation	Realization of category business plan through detailed determination of responsibilities and deadlines

Exhibit 1.8 The category management planning process

The strategic framework consists of established corporate strategies and their connection to the category's business plan. The corporate strategy should embody the corporate vision and the resultant objectives in marketing and finance. Furthermore, a marketing strategy, a purchasing strategy and a strategy for developing relationships to suppliers should be generated.

According to the definition of the strategic framework at the corporate level, strategies for the individual categories can be derived and thereby support a comprehensive company strategy. On the basis of this result the business plans for the categories. In exhibit 1.9, the above-described connections are presented graphically.

Exhibit 1.9 Strategies of Rebildtailers and their connections to productgroup business plans

Category Definition and Segmentation

After strategy analysis comes the definition of categories and their segmentation. Vitek describes this step as follows: "Segmentation is the process where we take any category and break it down based on the consumer decision process. For example, we may see deli as a single entity but we could segment the category by flavor, pack size or even shelf life, depending on the consumer's shopping behavior." This step is critical in the joint efforts of retailer and manufacturer. This is where the basis for all following steps is established. One should pay particular attention to defining categories from the perspective of the user and not from that of the retailing or manufacturing partners.

The analysis of category structures consists of the identification of the most important categories, segments and sub-segments of the category. The deciding factor for success here is the most accurate possible reflection of how the target customer makes his purchase decisions in each of the categories. In the definition of categories, the retailers will profit from a reliable knowledge of the consumer and the market of the consumer goods manufacturer. Information on buying behavior is often presented in the form of buying decision trees.

The individual steps in the definition of categories should be correspondingly done on the basis of a thorough knowledge of the customer. In the following Exhibit, a model of the process of category definition according to McKinsey (Tochtermann/Lange) is shown.

	Understanding of the consumer's-attitudes and perceptions	Analysis of actual consumer behavior	Definition of consumer oriented categories	Evaluation of the new category concept	Execution market trials
Objectives	• Basic attitudes of consumer behavior • Behavior planning • Unfilled demand and first ideas on categories	• Connection between product/brand and buying-behavior • Actual buying process	• First hypotheses on new category definition	• Agreement on category definition and opportunities for improvement-	• Quantitative of new category definition
Tasks/ Analysis	• Analysis of the planning processes of consumers (Products, priorities etc.) • Determiniation of influences (occasions, etc.)	• Quantitativ/ qualitativ analysis basket analysis • Analysis of of the choice of outlet/channel • Investigation on purchase process and sequence	• Combination of attitude based and actual cosumer behavior • Determination of exceptions/ unfulfilled needs • Evaluation of new category definitions	• Creation of concept • Determination of panel size • Execution of surveys • Evalutation of data/discernment of trends • Optimization of category concept/ definition	• Evaluation of revised category definition • Generation of Key learnings and impact on sales revenues, margins etc.)
Instruments	• Comprehensive interviews • Fokus groups • Standard usage&attitude data	• Scanner data • Panel data • Participatory observations	• Expert workshops	• CHOICE test Evaluation of categories based on purchase readiness, personal relevance etc. of potential consumers	• Market tests test market simulations

Exhibit 1.10 The Process of category definition. Source: McKinsey

The Role of the Category

After the definition of categories and their segmentation, comes the fixing of the category's role. This third step is often discussed as the **core of CM**, while it is here that the desired high-level corporate and marketing goals, e.g.: market image of a company can be achieved. The determination of individual category roles offers the best approach to the differentiation from competitors. "Focus on how you will distinguish yourself from competitors and put the most thought into the selection of your signature categories."

The development of category roles is also of special significance in that it determines the priority of categories in the retailer's entire organization and its resource allocation. With the assistance of adequate resource allocation, the retailer optimizes his return on investment. In the following exhibit, examples of the four most important category roles are and their characteristics are shown.

Category-Role	The role of the category is:	Share of categories
Destination	• To be the *primary* provider of these products to the target consumer • To help *define* the profile of the retailer in the eyes of the target consumer • To deliver consistently *superior* value to the target consumer • To lead all retailer´s categories in the areas of turnover, market share, consumer satisfaction, service level etc.	• 5-7% of categories
Preferred	• To be the *preferred* provider of these products to the target consumer • To help *bulid* the target consumer´s image of the retailer • To play a *primary role* in delivering profit, cash flow and ROA (return on assets)	• 55-60% of categories
Occasional/Seasonal	• To be a *major* provider of these products to the target consumer • To help *reinforce* the consumer´s image of the retailer • To deliver *frequent, competitive* value to the target consumer • To play a *secondary* role in delivering profit, cash flow and ROA (return on assets)	• 15-20% of categories
Convenience	• To help to reinforce the target consumer´s image of the retailer as the place for One-Stop-Shopping • To deliver *good, everyday* value to the target consumer • To play an important role in the area of generation and margin enhancement	• 15-20% of categories

Exhibit 1.11 Category roles and their functions in the framework of CM

The concrete allocation of specific roles to the individual categories is based on, among other things, the results of quantitative and qualitative analyses, as well as market forecasting. An example for **quantitative allocation criteria** is the profit contribution of the category to the gross profit of the company. **Qualitative criteria** are for example shopping experience and other opportunities to create consumer loyalty. **Market forecasts** are made drawing on projected growth in revenues and market share.

In summary, it can be seen that the determination of category roles is the most meaningful step in achieving marketing goals and consists of three interdependent steps:

► The explicit determination within the retail organization of which category roles will be used.

► The assignment of category roles to each individual category.

► The allocation of the company's resources to categories corresponding to their roles.

Category Evaluation

The successful management of a category requires that its status be determined. Category evaluation entails an analysis of the relevant data on the category with a view towards the market and the customer. The goal is, on the one hand, to gain a clear understanding of the current potential of the category (strengths and weaknesses) and on the other to identify the corresponding revenue and profit potential of the category. This potential-analysis forms the basis for further advances in category management.

Category Performance Analysis

This step in the CM business planning process establishes the essential category goals and measurement criteria for the category in question. The following exhibit shows systematically chosen indices in external (consumer referenced) and internal (results based) measurement criteria.

Consumer Measures	Financial Measures
• Household penetration	• Turnover category
• Purchase frequency	• Days of Inventory
• Demand coverage	• Inventory turnover
• Purchase intensity	• Return on Investment
• Consumer satisfaction	• Gross margin
• Image of the retailer	• Net profit

Exhibit 1.12 Consumer referenced and results-oriented Measurement criteria for category performance

The sought after target values must coincide with the assigned category roles from step three. Typically, the objective of a high profile category is first and foremost increases in revenue and market share. In contrast, a supplementary category should make a contribution to profitability. As a rule, category performance criteria are developed on a yearly basis with possibility for corrections to and modifications of the business plan occurring on a quarterly cycle. The corresponding accounting can be aided with CM scorecards.

Category Strategies

In this CM planning stage, category strategies for retailers are developed. The strategies are drawn from the previously determined category roles. For example, a high profile category may offer the opportunity to aggressively position itself against competitors (defending turf). A seasonal or impulse category supports a strategy of building traffic. Finally, a supplementary category may support image building in that a broader assortment allows an easier and a more complete shopping experience (one-stop shopping). Accordingly, category strategies should always be in harmony with high level corporate and marketing objectives, e.g.: the sought after marketing image. The strategies generated set the framework for the implementation of the instruments of retail marketing.

Category Tactics

Category tactics formulate the specific steps for the realization of the previously developed category strategies. The tactical decisions support the best possible implementation of category strategies in order to meet the objectives of the category business plan. The core areas for the development of category tactics are assortment politics, in-store presentation, pricing policies, and promotions. The exhibit 1.13 shows the relationship between category tactics and category roles.

Implementation of Category Business Plan

The implementation of the category business plan occurs in the eighth step of the CM planning process. In this next to last stage, the concrete activities within the category, for example, assortment optimisation, promotion planning and shelf optimization, are finalized. The implementation plan includes a clear assignment of responsibilities upon activation and a precise schedule with set deadlines (milestones). These measures go a long way towards ensuring quality during the plan's implementation. In this phase, it is the practice to bundle the different resources of manufacturer and retailer to secure a quick execution in the retail outlets.

Category Role	Category tactics			
	Assortment	Shelf presentation	Pricing	Promotion
Destination	Complete variety • Best variety in market • Sub categories • Premium brands	Prime store location • High traffic • High exposure time • High space allocation	Leadership • Best value (per unit of use)	High level of activity • High frequency • Multiple Vehicles • Customized
Preferred	Broad variety - competitive in market • Major brands • Sub-categories • Major SKU´s • Private label	Average store location • High frequency • High space allocation	Competitive - consistent • Equal to competition (per unit use) • Major components of category	Average level of activity • Average frequency • Average duration • Multiple vehicles
Seasonal/ Occasional	Timely variety • Changing Suppliers • Sub categories • Changing themes	Good store location • High traffic • Average space allocation	Competitive - Seasonally • Close to competition • Some components of category	Seasonal/Timely • Multiple vehicles • Instore activities (Promotion teams)
Convenience	Select variety • Relevant brands	Available store location • Low space allocation	Acceptable • Within 15% of competition (per unit use)	Low level of activity • Selected vehicles

Exhibit 1.13 The relationship between category tactics and category roles

Measuring Results

The last step of the category management business planning process is the continuous control of the implementation and performance measurements. Continuous accounting of category results can be done with the help of a CM scorecard. Clearly defined polling parameters across several reporting periods enable comparative analysis.

The CM planning process offers a good basis for a structured approach to the implementation and use of category management in retail organizations. This model should not however be seen as a one-size-fits-all solution. The individual conditions and requirements must be adequately considered in the planning process. The efficient satisfaction of customer wishes in the framework of category management is supported by three fundamental ECR components: **efficient store assortment**, **efficient product introduction**, and **efficient promotion**.

1.4.3　The Management of Categories as Strategic Business Units

The task of highest priority in the competitive retail world is the development of unique characteristics and of barriers to imitation in order to be perceived as superior to one's competitors.

The key to success at the POS is a **new definition of categories** and their management as strategic business units, for which retailers and manufacturers are jointly developing new strategies. These new definitions mean a full retreat from traditional assortment structures. Until now, retailers have carried products with identical functions or homogeneous characteristics of production and materiality together as categories. The result is that, most retailers' assortments are nearly identical and take the "me too" approach as opposed to one of retail competition. In strategically arranged categories, articles are bundled according to functional aspects as perceived by the customer.

The conception of categories from the customer's perspective entails the coordination of categories according to demand scenarios and cross selling which "accommodate the satisfaction of additional customer desires" and which properly address the targeted market segment. This heightens the presence of an assortment amongst the competition and promotes a transition from **point of sale** to **point of difference** form the customer's perspective. Strategic categories for clearly defined market segments can be so conceived.

A concrete example of the strategically important target group of young families should make clear the revenue and profitability enhancing effects of newly defined categories. The products disposable diapers, baby carriages, toys for babies, and baby books which were previously considered individually can be brought together as a **baby care center** through their presentation as complementary articles in a common space. Unnecessary time for searching them out on the part of the customer is eliminated and impulse buying is encouraged. In addition, this arrangement creates a small world of its own which satisfies a clearly identified customer need. The presentation of products according to use scenarios offers the target group 'young families' real additional utility and creates thereby **customer loyalty**, which in view of future decisions on where to shop, is important. The retail chain Real, a division of Metro, has introduced the concept of baby care centers with notable success in numerous outlets.

The example of a strategic conception of a category just cited can be easily translated to other categories. Further themes for formation of categories might include wine, (targeted at high-income households), or ready-to-eat meals (singles).

The use of category management offers the opportunity, via the introduction of strategic, customer-oriented categories, for the retailer to distinguish himself from competitors in the market. This constitutes a comparative strategic advantage. Retailers have the opportunity, via the categories they create and their added utility for the consumer, to create barriers to imitation and to be rewarded with customer loyalty as a consequence. The example of Wal-Mart and its rapid growth in the last ten years is an impressive testament to this.

Quadrant Analysis as an Instrument of Strategic Investigation of Categories

An interesting approach to an appraisal of the strategic significance of individual categories is quadrant analysis. With this method, categories are evaluated according to the determinant's revenue share and gross revenue. The results testify to which objectives particular categories are well-suited. This is how one differentiates between the Dogs, which produce a small share of sales and low gross receipts from the Cash Cows, which have high values on both axes. The traffic builders, with their high sales volume, are good for bringing customers in the door. Because these types of items are typically sold at deep discounts, gross revenues are correspondingly low. Examples in Germany are Coca-Cola, and well-liked brands of coffee like Jacobs Krönung or Milka-Schokolade. The last strategic group is comprised of the so-called Sleeoers. They are identified by their high gross revenues and low sales volume. The expansion of the sales volume of this category represents the strategic direction. The following exhibit shows graphically an example of quadrant analysis. The arrows indicate the direction of strategic development in each case.

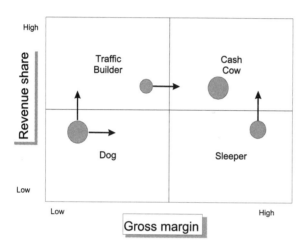

Exhibit 1.14 Strategic quadrant analysis for the evaluation of categories.
Source: Beckmann (1996)

Relevant Success Factors for ECR Implementation

Since the introduction of ECR in the early nineties, the new management concept has been implemented by most large concerns in the American consumer goods economy. With a delay of one to two years, top European retailers and manufacturers successfully began to integrate ECR principles into their business processes. Several companies were able to make the necessary changes rapidly, while others needed longer or are today still in the test phase of individual ECR components.

If one analyzes the successful use of this new management concept by pioneering firms, decisive factors for the successful implementation of ECR are revealed which are also of significance for the implementation of CPFR. The

ECR success factor study (Seifert 2001) identified and prioritized the most important ones based on a poll of experts. In this study, experts from consumer goods manufacturers, retailers, and consulting firms were queried on the utility of supply chain management and category management as well as the leadership competence of the firms interviewed.

In the survey, the experts were asked about the significance of nine different factors. Based on a scale of one to five (1 = very high relevance and 5 = no relevance) the factors were rated for their relevance. The following figure differentiates the statements according to respondents' background, showing the difference in perspective among the different groups.

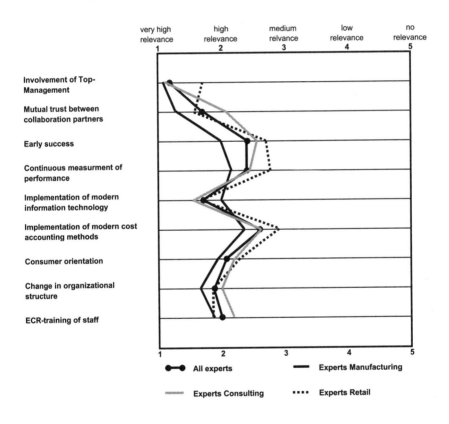

Exhibit 1.15 Significance of success factors by sector. Source: Seifert (2001)

The experts rated the 'involvement of senior management' as the most significant factor with an average score of 1.2. In addition, high-level sponsorship of ECR implementation by the board was clearly deemed the number-one requirement for success. This was however less pronounced in the opinion of representatives from retailing, who scored this factor 1.7 compared to 1.1 given by manufacturers and consultants.

Another salient factor was 'mutual trust between collaboration partners' with an average value of 1.7 for all participants. Manufacturers placed more emphasis here with a score of 1.3 than consultants, who gave it a rating of 2.1. At the same level of significance as trust was the 'implementation of modern information technology', receiving a 1.7 overall.

'Change in organizational structure' received a score of 1.9 from all participants. Manufacturing representatives gave it a 1.6, higher than the 2.0 given by consultants.

'ECR training of staff', 'consumer orientation', 'early success', 'continuous measurement of performance' all ranked high with values of 2.0, 2.1, and 2.4 respectively. 'Early success' had more significance for manufacturers at 2.0 than for retail at 2.7. Similar differences of opinion were apparent with respect to 'Continuous measurement of ECR performance'. Manufacturers rated it at 2.2 vs. 2.8 for retailers.

In comparison to other factors, the 'use of modern cost accounting methods' was considered secondary with a value of 2.6. In the poll, participants were asked to name other success factors for ECR implementation not listed on the questionnaire. Among those cited were 'consensus on joint marketing strategies', 'continuity in the business relationship/business partners', 'adequate incentive systems', and 'continuous market monitoring'. None of these was mentioned more than once.

Experience shows that the identified factors for ECR are also applicable to CPFR. Ralph Drayer, former Chief Logistics Officer at Procter & Gamble, supports this position in his statement, "The key barrier of CPFR and its implementation is a lot like we had found with ECR. It is that you have to have trust and leadership, understand the benefits and be willing to take the pain of transition, resource it and support it. CPFR is a new business model, it's a radical change from the way things are done today." The following section will introduce this new business model and will explain key benefits and implementation requirements.

2 The CPFR Concept

Dr. Dirk Seifert, Harvard Business School

2.1 The CPFR Value Proposition

The ECR concept presented in the first chapter ushered in a new era in the way of cooperation between retailers and manufacturers. The cooperation in marketing (category management) and logistics (supply chain management) paves the way for new strategic approaches. Collaborative planning, forecasting and replenishment (CPFR) represents a further quantum leap in the streamlining of business processes in the value chain.

2.1.1 Integration of CPFR in the ECR Concept

For most experts in the consumer goods economy, CPFR is an evolution and refinement of the original ECR concept. Volker Schröder, Director of Customer Logistics Management for Procter & Gamble, Europe, views CPFR as a "consistent and thereby more complex evolution of ECR... CPFR connotes a high degree of trust and a commonly held determination to not only share data but to achieve a measurable improvement in the quality of the data." Zygmunt Mierdorf, board member of Metro AG emphasizes, "The essence of CPFR is ECR, and the essence of ECR is the improvement of the relationship between producers and retailers. ... In addition, CPFR was developed, because of the opportunities afforded by the Internet and the B2B marketplace to better control and optimize the entire process. Common expectations and a continued sensitivity to the data direct the planning process."

In this book, and in the framework of the study of this topic at the Harvard Business School, CPFR is considered a further development of Efficient Consumer Response on the supply side. The intensified efforts in cooperative supply chain management like Cross Docking, Vendor Managed Inventories (VMI) and Continuous Replenishment in evidence since the early nineties find in CPFR a further development of collaboration. The demands on the quality of the partnerships are considerably higher than with the classic initiatives in cooperative supply chain management. The quality and the intensity of the information exchange (Info-partnering) demands a strong commitment to cooperation in the participating organizations. The exhibit below shows the integration of CPFR in the ECR concept.

Efficient Consumer Response – II. Generation

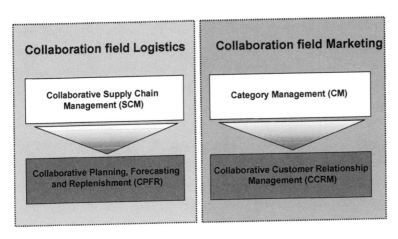

Exhibit 2.1 Integration of CPFR in the ECR concept. Source: Seifert

Collaborative Planning, Forecasting and Replenishment (CPFR) and Collaborative Customer Relationship Management (CRRM) represent **business concepts of second generation ECR**. Typical of CPFR is a strong relationship to the demand side of the equation. The components planning and forecasting demand intensive information exchange not only at the logistics level, but also in sales management, marketing, and finance planning. CPFR is thereby a tool for comprehensive value chain management of an organization. Senior management uses CPFR and its efficiency advantages in **Strategic Supply Chain Management**. The goal is an enduring improvement of the firm's own position in the market and the optimization of its own value chain.

Collaborative Customer Relationship Management as a further development of the demand side enables the coordinated management of all customer touch points (point-of-sale, TV, radio, call center, e-mail, Internet etc.). The intensive collaboration on the demand side beyond classic Category Management allows the exploitation of prominent synergy potentials in all aspects of customer management (customer identification, attraction, retention and development). CCRM represents another focus of the research group at the Harvard Business School. The topic however will not be discussed further here relative to CPFR. A paper on this topic by Seifert, Kracklauer, & Mills will appear in May 2002 in Germany and in the autumn in the US.

The CPFR Opportunity

Second generation ECR uses intensively the most modern information and communication technology. The inclusion of large B2B platforms (WWRE, GNX, CPGmarket, Transora) allows the use of state of the art technology in planning and procurement. The consistent use of modern data standards and computer languages like XML supports the exchange of complex quantities of data. CPFR brings the previously distinct experiences of sales planning of both partners together and simultaneously initiates a continuously improving understanding of the system.

> **Definition of CPFR**
>
> CPFR is an initiative among all participants in the supply chain intended to improve the relationship among them through jointly managed planning processes and shared information.

2.1.2   The Birth of CPFR: Wal-Mart and Warner-Lambert's first Pilot

The first CPFR project was begun by Wal-Mart und Warner-Lambert in the US. The IT companies SAP und Manugistics and the consulting firm Benchmarking Partners (now Surgency) supported the project with their particular know-how. The group defined Collaborative Forecasting and Replenishment (CFAR, the predecessor of CPFR), a process intended to reduce inventories across the supply chain. CFAR allowed comparisons of the sales and order forecasts of each trading partner and made visible any forecast differences early enough for the partners to resolve them. The CFAR model was first applied to Listerine mouthwash products supplied by Warner-Lambert. It included the sharing of forecasts and responding to inconsistencies between the collaboration partners' individual forecasts arising from events like Wal-Mart promotions capable of generating large swings in consumer demand. Prior to CFAR, Warner-Lambert was often caught unawares by these promotions. In order to prevent out-of-stocks they had to maintain substantial inventory as a hedge against such situations.

During the pilot, Wal-Mart and Warner-Lambert independently calculated the demand they expected six months in advance. The weekly forecast included data by week, by store, and by SKU (stock keeping unit). Both partners shared this information with each other as it was generated and they worked to resolve discrepancies between their forecasts on a weekly basis. Initially, the two companies exchanged forecasts on paper but the resulting manual comparison that allowed the process to be tested constrained any large-scale deployment. Eventually the Internet was used to exchange spreadsheets. As a result of the pilot, Wal-Mart began placing its order six weeks in advance to match the six-week manufacturing lead-time for Listerine. Previously, Wal-Mart had placed orders nine days in advance. By receiving an order six weeks in advance, Warner-Lambert was able to construct a smoother production plan since it could manufacture according to consumer demand for Listerine rather than manufacturing to maintain sufficient stock. Wal-Mart in turn saw that its in-stock position improved from 85% to 98%. The retailer also saw that sales increased by 8.5 million US-$ in one year with no new product introductions while inventories dropped over the course of the pilot by 25%. By the end of the experimental phase in fall 1996, Warner-Lambert's supply management had also improved substantially.

Over the course of the pilot, the **VICS Working Group** overseeing the project met every to two weeks to develop a widely applicable model for sharing and responding to forecast data, which later evolved into CPFR. The pilot of Wal-Mart and Warner-Lambert represented a substantial shift in approach since most retailers and suppliers were not used to sharing information, but Wal-Mart and Warner-Lambert had both realized benefits during the pilot. They had also developed a solid relationship in the process and continued to collaborate, paving the way for CFAR and later CPFR to be tested and improved in the future.

2.1.3   Institutions and Organizations of CPFR Development

Voluntary Interindustry Commerce Standards (VICS)

CPFR was conceived in the US and was first described and publicized by the Voluntary Interindustry Commerce Standards Association (VICS). VICS was founded in 1986 and is a voluntary, nonprofit organization. The mission of the VICS Association is to take a global leadership role in the continual improvement of the flow of product and information about the product throughout the entire retail supply chain. VICS members are key retail, manufacturing, and transportation companies whose highly influential executives collaborate to develop business process standards to improve the future of the retail industry supply chain for all its participants. Since the beginning VICS has worked to establish cross-industry standards that simplify the flow of product and information between supplier, manufacturer and retailers.

VICS CPFR Committee

VICS maintains its original CPFR-committee which is composed of retailers, e.g. K mart, Sears Roebuck, Walgreen, Wal-Mart, manufacturers like Gillette, Kellogg's, and Kimberly-Clark, Mars, Nestlé, Procter & Gamble, Sara Lee, Unilever, service providers such as Accenture, IBM, Syncra and Retek, and e-marketplaces like GlobalNetX-change, WWRE, CPGmarket and Transora. The mission of the CPFR committee is to create collaborative relationships between buyers and sellers through co-managed processes and shared information. The group aims to develop a set of business processes which entities in a supply chain can use for collaboration on a number of manufacturer/retailer functions towards overall efficiency in the supply chain. By integrating demand and supply side processes, Collaborative Planning Forecasting and Replenishment will improve efficiencies, increase sales, reduce fixed assets and working capital, and reduce inventory for the entire supply chain while satisfying consumer needs." This is an objective which clearly agrees with the principles of Efficient Consumer Response.

In the course of its work, the CPFR committee published the document, CPFR, Collaborative Planning, Forecasting and Replenishment Voluntary Guidelines, which describe the CPFR process, its technical support, and suggestions for implementation. The guidelines created received the approval of VICS board members in June of 1998. In November of 1999, the CPFR committee published the follow-up document, the "Roadmap to CPFR: The case Studies".

Global Commerce Initiative (GCI)

The Global Commerce Initiative (GCI) is a voluntary body created in October 1999. VICS was instrumental in creating GCI for the purpose of simplifying global commerce by establishing voluntary global standards. GCI operates through an executive board composed of senior representatives from more than 45 international companies drawn equally from the manufacturing and retailing sides of the consumer goods industry, together with eight sponsoring organizations. Four of the sponsoring bodies represent the interests of manufacturers and retailers (AIM, CIES, GAM and FMI). Two sponsors (the ECR movements and VICS) develop working tools for the collaborative management of the supply chain. The other two bodies are the principal standards organizations, EAN International and the Uniform Code Council, Inc. (UCC).

GCI has built a collaborative inter-business process that will endorse a recommended set of standards, enabling technologies and best practices with worldwide application, in order to provide benefits to all users, large and small, wherever they operate. This global approach will be developed and documented together with international standards organizations. GCI builds from a solid foundation created by the ECR initiatives in Europe, the US, Latin America, and Asia; the VICS Association in North America; and the work of the standards organizations EAN International and the Uniform Code Council (UCC). GCI is a global user group, not a standards body. Its job is to facilitate and encourage the best possible focused input on business needs on a global level, so that existing standards bodies can work with the confidence necessary to achieve true standardization.

From the initial release of the VICS CPFR guidelines at VICS 1998, The Retail Supply Chain Business Conference, this nine-step supply chain process model has moved rapidly beyond the pilot stage to full implementation by leading retailers and suppliers in the retail supply chain. It has also been adopted by leading retail and consumer goods Internet trading exchanges such as the

WWRE, GNX, Transora, and NovoPoint. In addition, UCCnet, ebXML, and the Global Commerce Initiative (GCI) have incorporated this collaborative commerce process model into their open standards infrastructure development. In June 2001 GCI published its CPFR-Recommendation. This recommendation for CPFR combines relevant portions of three previous VICS CPFR publications, along with new material. The process model is taken from the original *VICS CPFR Guidelines* document and advanced by the ECR Europe CPFR working group experiences and national ECR activities. Some technical information derives from the *Roadmap to CPFR* document published in 2000. Finally, the CPFR object model and XML specification come from the *VICS CPFR XML Messaging Specification*.

2.1.4 The CPFR Process Model

The CPFR Planning Process structures the relevant steps of the implementation-process of CPFR. The model is divided into three different phases. Phase one consists of **planning** (steps one and two), phase two is **forecasting** (steps three through eight) and phase three is **replenishment** (step nine). Exhibit 2.2 on the following page reflects the recommendations of VICS.

The following descriptions seek to explain the nine steps according to Voluntary Interindustry Commerce Standards.

Step 1: Develop Front-End Agreement

The first step of the CPFR model is to establish the rules and conventions of cooperation between retailer and manufacturer. The agreement sets the objective of both business partners. The pact also describes the actions and resources necessary for the successful application of CPFR. The jointly written paper defines the practical arrangement of the partnership, identifies the roles of the business partners involved and establishes how the performance of the respective parties will be measured. In total, the first step consists of ten individual actions:

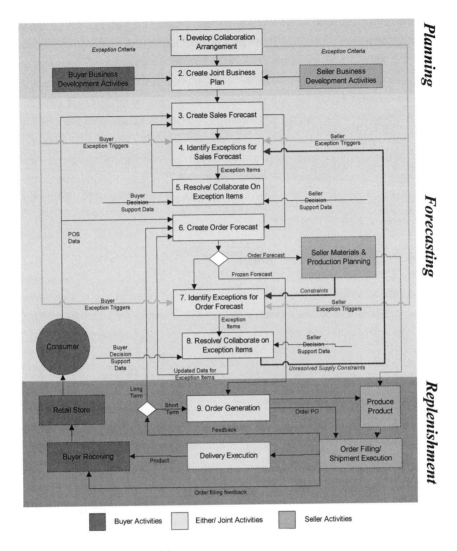

1. Develop Collaboration Arrangement

Exception Criteria

Buyer Business Development Activities

2. Create Joint Business Plan

Exception Criteria

Seller Business Development Activities

3. Create Sales Forecast

Buyer Exception Triggers

4. Identify Exceptions for Sales Forecast

Seller Exception Triggers

Exception Items

5. Resolve/ Collaborate On Exception Items

Buyer Decision Support Data

Seller Decision Support Data

POS Data

6. Create Order Forecast

Order Forecast

Seller Materials & Production Planning

Frozen Forecast

Buyer Exception Triggers

7. Identify Exceptions for Order Forecast

Constraints

Seller Exception Triggers

Exception Items

8. Resolve/ Collaborate on Exception Items

Seller Decision Support Data

Consumer

Buyer Decision Support Data

Updated Data for Exception Items

Unresolved Supply Constraints

Long Term

Retail Store

Short Term

9. Order Generation

Order PO

Produce Product

Feedback

Buyer Receiving

Product

Delivery Execution

Order Filling/ Shipment Execution

Order filling feedback

Buyer Activities   Either/ Joint Activities   Seller Activities

Exhibit 2.2 CPFR-Process Model.
Source: Voluntary Interindustry Commerce Standards (VICS) Association

1. Develop CPFR Mission Statement

The development of a mission statement creates a common basis for cooperation, trust, and availability of resources. The following components of Step 1 address in detail the content of the mission statement.

2. **Determine CPFR Goals and Objectives**

   Determination of concrete goals and tasks entails agreement on the appropriate indices for measuring performance. Additionally, the business practices and criteria for exceptions purchasing and the forecasting of orders is established.

3. **Discuss Competencies, Resources and Systems**

   The CPFR process demands a clear determination of the competencies, resources and systems of all parties involved and their capability to contibute to the process. Which departmental or functional groups are ready and able to contribute to the process long-term? Which additional capacities must be expanded or outsourced?

4. **Define Collaboration Points and Responsible Business Functions**

   Map the collaboration points to trading partner competencies and establish the responsible business functions. ("functional departments") that will be the key executors of the process.

5. **Determine Information Sharing Needs**

   The CPFR process requires information from both manufacturers and retailers. Identifying the demand for information determines which information will be shared, e.g. data on the identification of forecast anomalies. Furthermore, the frequency of the exchange, the medium of exchange, the allowable response time before information requests are honored and the forecasting method must be determined.

6. **Define Service and Ordering Commitments**

   This activity lays out the nature of order and delivery commitments in the framework of the CPFR process. This pertains especially to the phase in which collaboratively determined projections become firm orders.

7. **Determine Resource Involvement and Commitments**

   In this step, both CPFR partners establish which resources will be made available. This means for example how much time how many employees will devote to the CPFR process. This is true of resource allocation for the work process, agreements on process management and how initiatives like process improvement can be integrated in the system.

8. **Resolution of Differences between Partners in the CPFR Process**

   This activity comprises the standardization of rules for handling disagreements and differences between partners. Should something be contested, it is important to have measures for conflict resolution in place to which all have agreed.

9. **Regular Review Cycle for CPFR Agreement**

   This step is designed to establish a continual evaluation and to benchmark the success of the collaborative relationship. The agreement is modified whenever necessary.

10. **Publish Front-End Agreement**

    The jointly composed agreement becomes binding for all participants in the process. The agreement can be updated at any time to reflect new demands or developments.

Step 2: Create Joint Business Plan

In the second step of the nine step CPFR model, both partners work out a business plan taking into account their individual corporate strategies. This is comprised of defining product group roles, objectives, and articles.[1] Contract information for the products to be optimized is continually exchanged. This is for example the minimum order, necessary lead time for the order and the frequency of the order. The development of a common business plan improves the quality of projections in that available information from both partners is incorporated in the plan. Furthermore, this plan offers an appropriate platform for communication and coordination along the supply chain.

Step 3: Create Sales Forecast

The retailer's POS data and promotion planning provide the basis for the determination of sales forecasts. Sales projections become more reliable and convey thereby the intentions of the business plan at a higher level of detail.

---

1   The experience of Category Management business planning processes can be helpful in determining product group roles, objectives and articles. (See also part 1)

Step 4: Identify Exceptions to the Sales Forecast

In this step, all products are identified which represent exceptions to the cooperatively determined acceptance of the sales forecast. This can be seasonal products, for example. The exception criteria for each product is determined in the front-end agreement. (see Step 1)

Step 5: Resolve/Collaborate on Exception Items

The fifth step concerns the joint identification and clarification of exceptions to the forecast through real-time communication between the partners. Each change flows immediately into the new forecast. The accelerated communication and decision making by producers and retailers increases the reliability of the order which is generated later.

Step 6: Create Order Forecast

In this step, data from POS is linked to the individual inventory strategies of the partners to generate a specific order forecast. The preview represents a higher level of detail developed from the joint business plan (Step 2) and the sales forecast (Step 3). The order volume is based on the inventory targets per product and the destination of the goods. Consider the question: How much advance notice is necessary to transport the product its destination? Does the order information reflect temporal differences? The short term order forecast is used to generate actual orders. The long term order forecast flows into the overall planning.

Step 7: Identify Exceptions to the Order Forecast

In this step, all products are identified which represent exceptions to the cooperatively determined acceptance of the order forecast. The result is a list of those articles which on the basis of the criteria in the cooperation agreement represent exceptions.

Step 8: Resolve/Collaborate on Exception Items

The eighth step concerns the common identification and clarification of exceptions to the forecast through real-time communication between the partners. Each change flows immediately into the new forecast. The accelerated communication and decision making by producers and retailers increases the reliability of the order which is generated later.

Step 9: Order Generation

In the last step, an order forecast becomes a firm order. Order generation can be handled by either the manufacturer or retailer depending on competence in the process, access to appropriate technology and the availability of free resources.

Inclusion of Raw Material Suppliers in the CPFR-Concept

CPFR is a management concept that deals with the entire value chain as one entity. The optimization occurs not only at the intersections between manufacturer and retailer and retailer and consumer; it seeks also potential between supplier and manufacturer. Harmonized planning and production processes along the value chain offer considerable opportunities for cost reductions.

An example of a successful CPFR project comprising a supplier, a manufacturer and a retailer is the cooperation of Henkel with the Spanish retailer Condis and the packaging company Cartisa. The cooperation between partners is described in the following case study.

Case: CPFR Collaboration between Henkel, Condis and Cartisa

The consumer goods manufacturer Henkel, the Spanish retailer Condis (with 330 supermarkets in northern Spain), and Cartisa (International Paper) have collaborated on a CPFR project since the beginning of 2001. This is one of the few operating CPFR projects where not only the business process between manufacturer and retailer were optimized, but the packaging supplier as well. In this way, a CPFR optimization of the whole value chain becomes possible.

According to studies done by Henkel, Spanish retailers have a 10 to 18% out-of-stock rate, although the service level at the distribution center is 98.5 to 99.5%. This data indicates a considerable potential improvement in inventory management. According to Henkel, the problem lies in the area of promotions. The current project had already increased forecast accuracy 15% by May of 2001 and offered the participants to improve their out-of-stock situation.

Noteworthy in this example is the inclusion of the packaging supplier in the cooperation agreement. The case shows that the availability of goods, at the right time, in the right place, of the correct quantity and quality is decidedly dependent on suppliers of sub components. Planning, forecasting, and inventory control between retailer and manufacturer must be synchronized in the same way as between manufacturer and supplier.

2.1.5 CPFR and Value Creation

The use of CPFR makes it possible to take even greater advantage of the efficiency potential sought through ECR. The **CPFR Benefits Model**, developed by VICS-CPFR, allows it to quantify efficiency improvements. To a limited extent, CPFR connects completely new possibilities for rationalization in the value chain.

Typical benefits of CPFR are:

▶ **Drastically improved reaction times to consumer demand**
The systematic reduction of shortages and optimized turn-around times make for a more flexible and more reliable supply chain that ultimately improves product availability and customer satisfaction.

▶ **Higher precision of sales forecasts**
Through a cooperatively developed forecast, the forecast gains in reliability. The collaborative creation of the forecast along the supply chain enables everyone in the marketplace to profit from synergies. Independent of their position in the supply chain, or their activities there, the partners can bring their differing perspectives, consumer data, previous experiences, and research into the forecasting. This combined knowledge is the basis for high reliability in sales forecasting.

▶ **Direct and lasting communication**

The establishment of direct lines of communication raises the level of exchange between phases of the value chain. Next to the continual exchange of sales data, unique developments (increased or diminished demand due to weather or stepped-up advertising, etc.) can be readily considered.

▶ **Improved sales**

The cooperation of planning, forecasting and supply dramatically reduces out of stock situations. Previously lost income potential is regained. All partners profit.

▶ **Inventory reduction**

Imprecision in sales forecasts was the main reason for surpluses in the supply chain. Surpluses were kept on hand to even out inexact sales planning. Through CPFR, the safety stock can be reduced and availability increased.

▶ **Reduced costs**

The reconciliation of production plans with raw materials suppliers and manufacturers through optimized sales projections opens up further savings potentials. Set-up time, double work, and variability are reduced. A better use of production capacity means a more efficient production process. Reduced inventories mean lower capital, handling and administrative costs.

The CPFR concept can mean a dramatic reduction in the ramp-up time in supplying goods. Joseph C. Andraski, former VP Customer Marketing and Vice Chairman at Nabisco and chairman of the CPFR committee at VICS is designing a provocative vision with the statement: "Can you imagine the possibilities that exist when you begin production just two weeks before the product is needed?" According to Volker Schröder, director of Consumer Logistics Management at P&G, Europe, the current time required for replenishment is at least 10 to 15 days. The long-term goal of CPFR is to reduce this time to a mere three days, including production. Of the 130 replenishment process steps now in place, 40 should be made redundant through CPFR.

2.2 Sales and Order Forecasts in the CPFR Process for Retail

Prof. Dr. Gerhard Arminger, University of Wuppertal and SAF AG

The general process of collaborative planning, forecasting and replenishment (CPFR) is described in detail in other papers in this volume. The focus in this article is on two of the key elements in the CPFR process, namely on problems and possible solutions for the forecast of sales and the forecast of orders. The discussion is restricted to dealing with the problems of collaborative forecasting between individual retailers and manufacturers, the extension of the CPFR process to the suppliers of raw and half finished materials for the manufacturer is not considered here.

The second section gives a bird's view of the supply and demand chain management process for the retailer emphasizing the role of sales forecasts and orders for different hierarchies of the supply chain from the manufacturer to the individual customer. The third section considers in detail the requirements and possible solutions for good sales forecasts on the different levels of the supply chain. The fourth section focuses on order generation based on sales forecasts and shows how order restrictions may lead to orders that may be quite different from the forecasted sales. Consequently, the forecasting of orders can be done successfully only under fairly restrictive assumptions. The final section shows how some of these principles are implemented in a CPFR pilot project between an international retailer and an international manufacturer of consumer goods.

2.2.1 Integrated Demand and Supply Chain Management

Minimizing total Supply Chain Cost

A key objective of management in retail is the optimisation of the supply chain from the manufacturer through distribution centers (DC which may be include hubs, warehouses and cross – docking operations) and/or direct store delivery (DSD) to the store to fulfil the individual customer's demand. Overall objective is the minimization of the total cost of the supply chain operations which includes elements from the demand- and the supply side. The elements from the demand side are:

The lost profit per SKU per delivery period in any given store if an item is not available for the individual customer. Important measures for this loss are first, the number of items that are out of stock on any given day and second, the number of suppressed sales on any given day multiplied with the raw profit per SKU. These measures can usually be obtained directly or at least they can be approximated if the necessary support from the data warehouse, the transaction system and a computer-aided ordering system with simulation facilities are available.

The lost profit by losing a customer completely if a customer cannot find his or her favourite item in the store and therefore changes to another store or another retailer. This effect can usually not be measured directly and may only be approximated by market research or by educated guesses.

Typical elements of the cost for stores from the supply side are :

▶ The ordering and capital binding cost per SKU per delivery period in the store.

▶ The delivery rhythm or more generally the delivery plan from the manufacturer or the DC to the store generating necessary lot sizes for ordering.

▶ The minimal number of SKUs to be ordered by the store from the DC or the manufacturer.

▶ Logistic order restrictions on the number of SKUs to be ordered by the store from the DC or the manufacturer such as number of SKUs in a layer or on a pallet.

Typical elements of the cost for a distribution centre from the supply side are :

▶ The ordering and capital binding cost per SKU per delivery period in the DC.

▶ The delivery rhythm or more generally the delivery plan from the manufacturer to the DC generating necessary lot sizes for ordering.

▶ The minimal number of SKUs to be ordered by the DC or the manufacturer.

▶ Logistic order restrictions on the number of SKUs to be ordered by the DC from the manufacturer such as number of SKUs in a layer or on a pallet or the number of pallets in a truck.

▶ Bracketed conditions where the advantage of a lower price has to be compared with the additional capital binding, stock-keeping and handling costs.

On the DC level, the non-availability of goods corresponds to the out of stock situations in the store.

The manufacturer plays an important role in decreasing the costs on the demand and on the supply side. The manufacturer can help

▶ to lower the costs of suppressed sales by ensuring the availability of items in the store and in the warehouse by in-time delivery.

▶ to lower the capital binding costs by adapting to the retailer's needs for cost-optimal minimal ordering sizes, packaging, delivery plans and changing the bracketed conditions.

These effects can only be achieved by collaboration of the retailer with the manufacturer by sharing information about the specification of items, packaging, delivery plans, discount systems but most importantly by sharing information about future sales and future orders which is typical for the CPFR process. In exchange, the manufacturer may expect to have better forecasts for the demand of a specific retailer in order to optimise his own production process including the extension of the CPFR process to his own (pre) – suppliers.

Sales forecasts and order building play a central role in this process of minimizing the total cost of the supply chain. Sales forecasts and order building constitute a process that is reverse or dual to the physical process of delivering goods from the manufacturer to the DC and/or to the store. While the process of physical delivery constitutes the process of supply chain management, the demands of the individual customer at the individual store should generate the orders by the store from the DC and by the DC from the manufacturer. The customer's demand therefore constitutes the process of demand chain management by forecasting the future sales to the customers at store level and building adequate cost-optimal orders. Since in this forecasting and order building the pull from the customers demand and the push from the manufacturer and the retailer in form of promotions, advertising campaigns and special displays have to be integrated, the whole process is called integrated demand and supply chain management (IDSCM rather than SCM alone).

Integration of Forecasts for Different Levels of the Supply Chain

If fulfilling the customer's demand in the individual store is seen as the top – priority in retail, forecasting must start at the SKU level for the individual store. This priority has important consequences. The forecasting techniques that are employed on the store level must fulfil the requirements of micro-forecasting, that is a specific forecast for every SKU (item level) in every store. Aggregation across items and/or across stores is not meaningful in this case, on the contrary it may be counter – productive. The order building per store must be based on the individual sales forecast for the individual store. Since calendar events (Easter, Fourth of July, Thanksgiving Day, Christmas), advertising and promotional events may have very different effects in the different stores depending on the respective locations, the forecasting techniques should not be based only on the observed time series of sales but should be able to take this information about external influences into account. Otherwise, only trend and seasonal information can be extracted. Forecasts for sales and orders for stores are usually based on short term forecasts, that is daily or between 1 to 6 weeks depending on the delivery plans of the DC or the manufacturer.

The predicted demand and the orders generated by the sales forecasts for the stores should influence the forecast for the total shipments from the DC to the stores and the orders from the DC to the manufacturer. It should be noted that the aggregated sales forecasts per item from the stores should not be used as the forecasted number of SKUs to be shipped to the stores since the sales forecasts will not be identical with the cumulated orders from the stores. A better way of minimizing the total cost of the supply chain is to use either the shipments of an item from the DC to the stores or the cumulated orders of the stores from the past to the DC as dependent variable that is to be forecasted and then to use the aggregated sales forecasts from the stores only as an external information or input variable for the DC forecast. One should note that calendar events and promotion events are then automatically taken into account. Forecasts for shipments (or cumulative store orders) and order building for DCs are also usually based on short term forecasts, that is daily or between 1 to 6 weeks depending on the delivery plans of the manufacturer to the DC.

The sales forecast in the CPFR process is highly related to the shipment (or cumulative store orders) forecast for the DC. The order forecast is meaningful only under restrictive assumptions to be discussed later. The main difference between the sales forecasts on the store and/or DC level to the CPFR sales forecast is the time horizon. For the CPFR process, a mid-range forecast of 10 to 13 weeks is advised to enable the manufacturer to adapt the production process to the specific predicted demand of the retailer. However, like the sales forecasts on the store level and the shipment forecasts on the DC level, the CPFR sales forecast must take into account the basic demand of the customer (pull) as well as calendar events and the demand induced by promotional schemes such as different types of advertisement, displays and price reductions (push).

The mid-range time horizon may imply that other forecasting techniques should be used than for the short-time forecast in the sense that the highly adaptive forecasting mechanisms for the short-term replenishment in the store and the DC may have to be replaced by more structural models focusing on the question how much extra demand will be induced by specific promotional schemes. However, structural forecasting models rely even more heavily on external information than the adaptive forecasting mechanisms. Depending on way (DC or DSD) used for distributing the goods to the store, a mid-range forecast for the individual store (DSD) or for the DC should be used as an input variable for the sales and order forecast of the retailer.

Finally, a mechanism has to be found that reconciles the sales and order forecasts of the retailer and the manufacturer if they differ. This may be done by a rather time-consuming process of personal collaboration. A more effective way may be to use both forecasts as input variables for predicting the actual demand and then to weigh the retailers and the manufacturers forecast according to their respective ability to predict the final demand.

2.2.2 Sales Forecasts for Stores, Distribution Center and the CPFR Process

Sales and Inventory Forecasts for the Store Level

Presently, three distinct approaches to forecasting the large number of SKUs and store combinations required for store ordering are used in semi-automatic or automatic computer assisted ordering (CAO) systems: Aggregate, profile and micro-forecasting.

Aggregate forecasting manages sparse inventory and reduces processing time by grouping stores into store clusters and creating a single forecast for each item across the entire store group. This single forecast is then distributed based on each store's relationship to the store group. This method is as good, or as bad, as the quality of the group and never approaches the store-SKU as unique. Its specific characteristics are:

▶ Grouping stores into geographic or like-store clusters

▶ Create a single forecast for the store group.

▶ Distribute the forecast by volume ratio of each store to the total.

▶ Volume ratio is based on the total store to the total or a single category to the total.

The main problem of this approach is obviously that the forecast method never approaches the store-SKU as unique. Therefore the needs of the individual store may be highly over- or underestimated depending on how similar the needs of a specific store are to the aggregated demand in the store cluster. For all practical purposes, one can expect from this forecasting method for the same item many stock-outs in one store and more than necessary overstocking in another store. Also, in this approach it is practically impossible to take into account local effects such as local calendar events, local advertisements and other local promotions into account. In effect, computer assisted ordering in the store will be only semi-automatic rather than automatic and cannot utilize the benefits of full automatization which may be especially important if no qualified personnel is available in the stores.

Profile forecasting assumes that it can create a base forecast for each store/ SKU but manages sparse data by aggregating the sales influences. Therefore it creates seasonal profiles and promotion/price lifts across store groups. Its specific characteristics are:

▶ Forecast individual store items without external influences.

▶ Aggregate external influences by item and store groups (seasons, promotions).

▶ Create profiles from group aggregates.

▶ Create static weights for the application of multiple profiles.

▶ Apply various profiles to base forecast to produce actual forecast.

This approach generates three major problems:

▶ The results can only be as good as the quality of the cluster and the clusters will always include outlier stores.

▶ Whenever clusters are created the data must be transformed and assumptions made. These assumptions often skew the results.

▶ Marrying the various profiles such as seasonal profiles with promotion lifts is also based on assumptions. Often the forecast is not meaningful because seasons and promotions interact. The forecast cannot be unified.

The remarks about the quality of forecasts and the inability to achieve full automatization in the store made about aggregate forecasting also hold for profile forecasting.

Micro-forecasting creates a single unified forecast which takes into account trend and seasonality from historical sales as well as holidays, promotions and price. The weight and importance of each sales influence is considered at the same time and varies by the unique store-SKU. The specific characteristics are:

- ▶ Each store item is forecasted uniquely.

- ▶ Each item history and external influences are applied uniquely.

- ▶ Weight and importance of each influence varies by the store item.

The advantages of such a method are obvious:

- ▶ There are no separate profiles or promotional lifts to maintain or to merge.

- ▶ There is no clustering with its inherent problem of outliers and cluster quality.

- ▶ External information on promotions and price changes is automatically taken into account.

- ▶ The quality of the store specific sales forecast is much improved.

- ▶ Full automatization is achieved.

The disadvantages of micro-forecasting are twofold.

- ▶ First, the required data base implies that (daily) sales data are available for each SKU-store combination. In addition, if external information like calendar events, promotions and price changes should be taken into account, the store specific information for (local) holidays, promotion events and price changes must be available for future periods. This implies that sales, calendar, promotion and price information have to fed into the computer assisted ordering (CAO) system.

- ▶ Second, the functional requirements for the effectiveness and the speed of the forecasting and optimisation engine in such a CAO system are much greater than for aggregate or profile forecasting.

However, most large retailers have now either data warehouses and/or transaction systems that provide the required data base and automatic systems with the advanced features of forecasting and optimisation have been successfully installed by leading retailers in the store level. The functional requirements for a system adequate for micro-forecasting are given in the following subsection.

Requirements of self-learning Forecasting Systems

The retail user in the store should not be exposed to the complexity of the system. A self-learning or auto-adaptive forecasting system automatically selects the best model from an array of statistical models by classification algorithms and continually updates the forecast interrelationships. This process is repeated for each individual store-SKU with every forecast run. A complex set of models is maintained by a relatively simple set of user parameters. Additionally the system automatically balances the sales influences based on external information such as calendar events, promotion events and price changes in the past.

Learning from each new bit of history the system constantly improves its ability to predict future sales, rapidly recognize product trends, and build dynamic seasons. The retailer not only need not marry separate profiles and promotion lifts but the self learning system continually and automatically analyses the impact of each sales influence. In this way the influences of promotions, seasons, and events are considered at one time. The compound predictors can include price changes, sales promotions, event calendar, holiday information, and special circumstances depending on the availability of data provided by the client.

Optimal Inventory Forecast

Optimal inventory sets the target shelf inventory level in the store. There is an ideal shelf set that covers both presentation stock and the possibility of preventing lost sales without exceeding the costs of carrying surplus inventory. This optimal inventory in the store sets the lower limit for the ordering process. The ordering process must order at least such a great number of SKUs of one item that the optimal inventory for the first availability day of a new delivery is equalled or exceeded. Therefore, not only a forecast of the sales per SKU in a store is needed but also a forecast of the optimal inventory.

The retail industry has depended on three primary methods: minimum stock with safety stock, minimum stock with service level, and cost-based optimal inventory.

Minimum stock with safety stock is the most traditional and most manual of the methods used by retailers to set their target shelf set (or order up to level). The safety stock is either a fixed numerical amount or a calculated weeks of supply. This is a manually set stock that the retailer decides will cover their potential need and variable need. It is not dynamic and does not create a very accurate or cost-effective result.

Minimum stock with service level is the most traditional warehouse method for calculating the ideal stock with a dynamic safety stock. The service level is based on a symmetrical (bell curve) of inventory necessary to support the risk of being out of stock. The retailer sets a desired service level which is the percentage of time that they want to be in stock when the stock is needed based not only on projected demand but also on risk factors such as variability in forecasted demand as well as lead time variability.

Cost-based optimal inventory. The use of cost functions function redefines the traditional approach to service level and creates a shelf supply that covers volatility in forecast on a cost-optimum basis. It minimizes the total cost of lost sales and excess inventory. By recognizing the sometimes asymmetrical distribution of forecast error, especially for slow sellers, inventory more closely matches the reality of sales. This method uses the real costs associated with lost sales which may create a significant loss of a customer's shopping basket on the one hand and balances it with the cost of over-stocking on the shelf on the other hand.

Regardless of the method used, a forecast of the optimal inventory is needed and made. It should be noted that the forecast of the optimal inventory is based on the sales forecast but is not identical with the sales forecast. It will usually be greater than the sales forecast. Since the ordering is based on the forecast of the optimal inventory it us even more important than the sales forecast.

Sales and Inventory Forecasts for the DC Level

The remarks from section before about forecasting sales and optimal inventory for the store also hold in principle for the DC level of the supply chain. Before going into more detail, a word of caution about the variable that is to be forecasted is in order. In principle, there are two options. The first is to use as predicted (or dependent) variable the aggregated shipments of an item from the DC to the stores. The disadvantage of this approach is that an item may be not available because the manufacturer could not deliver in time. Therefore, the time series of shipments can be distorted which makes forecasting more difficult. The second option is to use the cumulated store orders as dependent variable. This option makes only sense if the store orders themselves are based on good SKU-store forecasts and have been optimised to fulfil logistic and other restrictions. In practice, usually only shipment data are available. However, this will quickly change, so that both options will be available in the near future.

Aggregate and profile forecasting were originally developed for application in the DC. Some of the disadvantages of these approaches for the store do not occur on the DC level. Micro-forecasting with self learning systems that utilize information about external influences is also available for the DC. The disadvantage of aggregate and profile forecasting is that there is no simple way of utilizing external information as input variables for the forecasting system. The advantage of micro-forecasting is that external information can be utilized easily.

If the dependent variable in the DC is the shipment from the DC to the stores then the aggregated sales forecast from the stores will be an excellent external information or input variable for the forecast of the shipments. It should be noted that the aggregated sales themselves should not be used as an input variable for the shipment forecast since the time lag between the aggregated sales from the stores and the shipments from the DC to the stores may already be considerable. In addition, the aggregate forecasts from the stores already take the effects of calendar and promotion events into account, so that there is no need to aggregate holiday events and promotion events on the DC level. The same remarks hold true for the cumulated store orders as dependent variable.

As on the store level, the shipment forecast is short-range and has to be complemented with a forecast of the optimal inventory to fix the lowest possible level of stock that has to be maintained through the ordering and replenishment process. Altogether, the micro-forecasting approach with self learning and inclusion of external information is much more promising than aggregate and profile forecasting.

Sales Forecasts for the CPFR Process

The sales forecast for the CPFR process follows in many regards similar considerations as the sales forecast for the stores and the shipment forecast for the DC. The main difference lies in the following points.

First, the time horizon for the sales forecast is mid-range that is 10 to 13 weeks ahead. This does not mean that the short-term forecasts are not made. It means that every week a forecast is expected, that covers each of the following 13 weeks. From the retailers view, these forecasts imply that a short-range forecast may be used for the first 4 – 6 weeks and that a mid-range forecast will be employed for the following weeks.

Second, the forecast of the retailer (FoR) is complemented by a forecast of the manufacturer (FoM). It should be noted that the forecast of the manufacturer relies on one hand on the data that are shared by the retailer with the manufacturer, for instance sales data, promotion data price data etc., on the other hand it may also rely on information that may not be accessible to the retailer, for instance national advertisement campaigns, information about the whole market of retailers since the manufacturer will supply many retailers and not one retailer exclusively, etc.

Third, the forecast of the retailer and the forecast of the manufacturer are both mid-range forecasts. While the short-range forecasts typically rely on the most recent information to adapt quickly to new developments, the mid-range forecast concentrate mainly on the effects of calendar and promotion events to improve production planning for excess demand. Therefore, the highly adaptive models for forecasting on the short-range should be replaced by more structural models for the mid-range. This implies that the possibility to include information on external influences should be used for forecasting. In turn, this implies that again micro-forecasting should be used rather than aggregate or profile forecasting. Again, the aggregate sales from the store forecasts could be used as an input variable for the sales forecast of the retailer for the CPFR process. The manufacturer may want to use his own information about market segmentation and national advertisement campaigns as input variables for his own CPFR forecast.

Fourth, the sales forecasts of the retailer and the manufacturer have to be reconciled if large differences between these forecasts exist. This may be done in the CPFR process by setting up joint committees to deal with these differences for each item. Such a process can be handled easily if only few items must be managed by such a process. It becomes ineffective and expensive if many hundred or even thousands of items and many manufacturers and/or retailers are managed in this way. Therefore, such a decision making process should be supported again by a self-learning micro-forecasting system where the FoR and the FoM for each item are considered as input variables for the mid-range forecast of each item.

Finally it should be noted that some retailers not only expect a joint forecast on the aggregate or on the DC level but also on the level of the individual store. In this case, the manufacturer has to undergo a similar forecasting process as for a vendor managed inventory (VMI).

2.2.3 Order Building and Forecast

While the integration of sales forecasts between the levels of store, DC and CPFR may be complicated in detail, but is rather straightforward in principle, the integration of order forecasts is much more difficult and can presently be done only when fairly restrictive assumptions apply.

Order Building and Forecasting for the Store

The order building for each SKU is based on the forecasts of the sales and the optimal inventory but it is also heavily influenced by the stock that is still on the shelf, by open deliveries, deliveries already planned for a latter time point, the delivery plan of the DC or the manufacturer to the store, presentation stock, minimal order sizes and logistic restrictions such as layers or pallets. However, all of this can be taken into account routinely by a good CAO and can even be forecasted if only the order for the first delivery period is used as dependent variable. The first delivery period is the time between the first day on which the goods from today's order are available and the day on which the goods from the next possible order day will be available.

It should be seen that this is a rather restrictive assumption because in practice, the determination of economic order quantities tries to optimise the logistic cost not only for the next delivery period but for a given series of successive delivery periods. Typical examples are the minimization of logistic costs for one supplier by looking at the predicted sales and optimal inventories for all items of a supplier for the next K delivery periods to fulfil restrictions such as the minimum order value (for instance 1000 US Dollars) across all items of a supplier or filling up a half or a full truck to lower transportation costs. In this general case, the building of the order is based on the predicted sales, but it will be almost impossible to predict how much will be actually ordered in detail with great accuracy.

Order Building and Forecast for the DC

The same remarks as for the store hold true for the DC. In the DC, the logistic restrictions will play an even greater role because the filling of pallets and trucks will be of great importance to minimize transportation and handling costs. In addition, bracketed conditions will have much greater influence than in the store. Altogether, the forecasts for the shipments to the stores and for the optimal inventory in the DC to avoid non-availability of items will again form the basis for the actual orders but the orders themselves may differ greatly from the shipment forecasts because of present stock, delivery plans and logistic and financial restrictions. A meaningful order forecast will only be available if only the next delivery period is considered as feasible.

Order Forecast for the CPFR Process

An order forecast for the CPFR process from the retailer's view is hampered by the same difficulties as an order forecast on the store and on the DC level. Again, under the restrictive assumption that orders are made only for the first delivery period, an order forecast can be achieved by looking at the one delivery period orders per item as dependent variable for the forecast and by using the same forecasting methods as for the sales data. The forecasted sales (and possibly) the forecasted stock at the beginning of the delivery period may be used as input variables if a self-learning system with the possibility to include external influences is used as the forecasting engine. However, if the orders are optimised for more than the first delivery period, the order forecasts will be fairly difficult to make. To the author's knowledge it has not even been attempted yet.

2.2.4 Issues in Practical Implementation

This final section discusses how some of these principles are implemented in a CPFR pilot project between an international retailer and an international manufacturer of consumer goods. The main goal of the CPFR process between these two partners is the joint sales forecast for items which will be specially advertised and promoted in the mid-range future. An interesting side problem is that the sales forecasts should not only work for the aggregate but also for the store specific level.

Both partners have powerful transaction systems for managing merchandise in place. They have also agreed on software which allows them to share information about the items that are used for the project, meaning that the sales and the forecasts can be accessed by both partners. The retailer also uses a microforecasting tool which allows to include external influences for sales forecasting and order building in the store.

The CPFR pilot process may be described briefly by the following steps:

▶ For each store, sales are predicted by the retailer for the all weeks in the short- and mid-range using historical sales as well as information on calendar and promotion events. These predicted sales are aggregated and shown to the managers in charge at the retailer and at the manufacturer.

▶ Retailer and manufacturer give their own forecasts on the aggregate level based on additional data or on their possibly superior judgement of external influences. These forecasts are broken down to the store level and serve as additional input variables for the forecasting tool.

- ▶ The process of forecasting on the store level is repeated with the additional input variables. The forecasts are again aggregated and sent to the managers in charge for checking and confirmation generating a collaborative sales forecast of retailer and manufacturer.

- ▶ Since the sales forecasts are available for mid- and short-range, the short-range forecasts may be used for order building at the individual stores.

This procedure combines some interesting features. First, it manages the CPFR process not only on the aggregate but also on the store level. Second, it lets empirical results decide how much weight should be given to the FoR and the FoM. Third, it still includes the element of personal communication between the responsible managers but it supports it heavily with IT tools. Fourth, the problem of order forecasting is pragmatically solved by using the short-range forecast to adjust for the most recent developments.

2.3 CPFR emerges as the next Movement in Supply Chain Management

Joseph C. Andraski, VICS-CPFR and OMI International

The advent of Supply Chain Management was a result of the development and implementation of a series of processes that began in the early part of the last century. It began with the development of Economic Order Quantity (EOQ), progressing through Material Requirements Planning (MRP), MRPII, Distribution Requirements Planning (DRP), Just in Time, Total Quality Management (TQM), Theory of Constraints (TOC), Time Based Competition (TBC), Supply Chain Management (SCM) and finally what some are calling Value Chain Management. Supporting each process was a philosophy that dealt with how to improve the effectiveness and efficiency of business.

It is fair to say that each process was flawed and consequently there was a natural evolution from one to the next, with each step bringing improvements. Innovators dealt with organizational and cultural barriers, as senior leadership demanded operational improvements. Technology played an important role as a key enabler. On the other hand, customers were demanding reliability and flexibility and customer service gradually became an important area of focus. It is important to note that each of the processes was essentially internally focused and the sharing of information for the most part was not considered as important or relevant.

Getting to Supply Chain Management was a journey that has taken some 85 years, since EOQ, nonetheless some 35 years since the introduction of MRP. Considered in the light of AMR Research findings that only 20% of all companies with sales of $500M plus, have invested in SCM. This is startling given the attention that SCM has received and considering the discussion of how companies will compete with their supply chains. Does this imply that senior management is not convinced that the investment in SCM will deliver on the promise? Enterprise Resource Planning (ERP) is a necessity for those companies who have multiple system platforms, multiple business components, and operate on a global scale; however, implementation for some has been a nightmare. We believe that this is the natural evolution of the supply chain, as flaws are found and improvements are made in process, technology, and business practices.

2.3.1   Studies Reveal Supply Chain Management Benefits – Opportunities and a Path Forward

Research recently conducted by Bain & Company indicates that the returns on software investments have been elusive. Forty-four percent of 300 executives state that they have little or only basic data; do not track forecast accuracy; do not track vendor performance, and do not communicate any of this information to senior management. They are essentially ignorant of how much supply chain inefficiencies really cost. They also reported that 80 percent of their efforts were focused within their own four walls, but that they intend to increase their external supply chain activity over the next two years.

In a recent study completed by A.T. Kearney, it was found that there are 5 companies who used operational excellence to help deliver value 2.5 times the average of all other participants in the study. In all of the metrics used, these companies excelled: e.g. 255 inventory turns of work in process, versus 65.

These companies have carefully designed and effectively managed formal programs, which generate continuous performance improvement.

Gartner Group reports that companies who believed that software deployment would lead to rapid ROI are in the "trough of disillusionment". Tales of failure were prevalent in 2001. The Gartner Group believes that there is a dearth of Supply Chain Planning understanding, with only a few pockets of educated individuals and a lack of good data to drive the planning engines. They report that the effort required for change management was greatly underestimated and that most employees felt victimized by a wave of technology. Vendors, it is postulated, were selling their vision rather than what they could actually deliver. They also found that there was a lack of good data to drive the software engines, i.e. enterprise data was often unavailable or too dirty to use.

Ernst and Young found, in a study conducted in 2000, that only 25 percent of those responding to the survey were satisfied with the results of their supply chain management programs. CSC found in their study that, all of their subjects were internally focused and in the first or second stage of a 4-stage model for supply chain best practices.

Considering these findings over the course of the history of supply chain management, one must acknowledge that there have been substantial gains in effectiveness, efficiency, customer service, cash flow, product quality, and availability of information. However, this is not about what was done yesterday, it is about what can be done today. Past successes are history, and expectations as to how supply chain management will contribute to the success of a company are what must be addressed both today and tomorrow.

Professor John Kotter of the Harvard Business School has done extensive research on companies who have succeeded through external orientation, compared to those who fail to look at factors outside their own organization. He has many examples of companies who have learned from corporations outside of their industry, who have reached out to their customers to create a tight bond that benefited both sides. In spite of the many examples identified by Professor Kotter, and the financial results those companies have enjoyed, we still find those companies who remain internally focused relative to their customers and suppliers. The philosophy of supply chain management is to reach back to the supplier of raw material and carry information and product to the point of purchase. Suffice it to say, however, that most businesses and supply chain management professionals are thinking about what transpires within their own four walls.

2.3.2 Progressing Beyond Supply Chain Management

Supply chain management must evolve, much as we have seen the evolution from EOQ to the present day. We have learned that the vertical silos within organizations must become horizontal and that the supply chain must evolve into a supply net, connecting all players in the game of satisfying the consumer. The critical functions within an organization must be integrated into the planning and execution process. For example, marketing has as much, if not more, influence on the success of supply chain management than as responsible. The timeframe in which products are promoted and consequently produced and distributed is a function of the plans that are developed by marketing. All customer plans are a result of the product plans created by marketing that are designed to meet company sales and financial goals. Marketing cannot be excluded from supply chain planning, but must be considered an integral part to be embraced and leveraged. This takes us to Value Chain Management, i.e. reaching out beyond those functions that are typically considered to be SCM and/or logistical.

One should consider for a moment some of the barriers to realizing the potential of supply chain or value chain management. Apparent thus far is that senior leadership has not provided direction or support, that adequate metrics are unavailable or unused, that silos and cultural issues still exist within companies, that information is either unavailable, untimely, or inaccurate; and that individuals and corporations are slow to adapt to new ways of doing business and the new demands of the market place. All are relevant and exert significant influence.

While not each of these barriers will be addressed here, a hypotheses is offered that suggests why companies have not realized the expected ROI from investments made in technology and business processes. Supply Chain Planning depends on primary information that is gleaned from a forecast, typically generated from historic sales and then run through triple exponential smoothing, various algorithms, etc. to arrive at a forecast for the out months. We have concluded that corporations are internally oriented and often operate within their organizational silos. In many cases, there are multiple forecasts within a company, each with built-in biases and safety stock calculations. The forecast used to drive DRP may not be the forecast used by the sales and marketing organization, or the forecast used by procurement, or the forecast used by the manufacturing organization. Obviously there are many opportunities for improvement, the hypotheses here will remain that if a forecast were developed in conjunction with a company's key trading partner, its accuracy would be substantially improved.

Collaboration leads to New Efficiencies

That leads us to Collaborative Planning Forecasting and Replenishment (CPFR). While in the evolution of Supply Chain Management, CPFR is still in its infancy the subject of collaboration has come to the fore. Practically every trade/business magazine refers to collaboration. The scientific community has embraced collaboration and the sharing of information across the Internet. Collaborative commerce is now being practiced in the chemical, automotive, textile, and pharmaceutical industries as well as in retail. This points to dissatisfaction with the confrontational business climate between trading partners and to the need to find another business model which will help companies meet the demands of their customers and of Wall Street.

There are now recognized business gurus espousing collaboration as a business practice and a mindset for companies to establish for internal and external relationships. Tom Peters, who wrote in *Search of Excellence*, now tells us that it is essential to collaborate with one's trading partners. Tom suggests that the new world will require companies to deal with their trading partners in a collaborative way. Well known global consultant, Michael Hammer, who wrote *Reengineering the Corporation* and several follow up books, including *The Agenda*, says "Knock down your outer walls, collaborate whenever you can". He goes on to say that, "the walls between the supplier and the customer equal costs and the higher the wall, the higher the costs. And the walls between companies are much higher that the walls inside companies." Here is a progressive individual, who believes that most companies have far to go in exploiting the potential of supply chain management. After strongly recommending that corporate structures and business practices be scrapped and rebuilt, he then advocates collaboration as one of the keys to success.

Reading Jack Welch's book, *Straight From the Gut*, one finds that GE was collaborating both internally and externally years ago. Welch believed in boundary-less Management, where different companies collaborated on best business practices and customer satisfaction was used to measure service. His approach however had a twist: He asked 'when did a part or product begin delivering a profit to the customer?, not simply whether or not it was delivered on time. In a recent conference, Welch gave a presentation on the importance and value of collaboration, a significant endorsement given the success he and GE have enjoyed over the last 20 years.

2.3.3   CPFR as a Change Agent

It is obvious that there is a strong movement to collaborative commerce independent of CPFR. This suggests an endorsement, albeit somewhat indirect. CPFR provides a framework within which trading partners can conduct collaborative business relationships with benefits to both players. There have been numerous surveys conducted by universities, trade associations and trade journals which have addressed the subject of CPFR, i.e. its current status, plans for future implementation, etc. Generally speaking, companies in the consumer products industry have indicated that approximately 10 to 15 percent of the respondents are engaged in CPFR, another 10 to 15 percent expect to implement CPFR in 2002 and 20 percent in 2003 or 2004. Of course, there are those who believe CPFR is all hyperbole and no substance. That is to be expected, as there will always be those who will resist change and find reasons to challenge the positive experience of those who have decided to venture forward. One must keep in mind that CPFR is new, for the most part misunderstood, and a step in the natural evolution that hits at the very heart of what most companies and individuals resist: *change*.

Gary R. Forger, editorial director of *Modern Materials Handling,* has said, "the real-deal companies are the engines driving supply chain collaboration forward," and "collaboration is a much broader partnership than simply talking or sharing forecasts." He went on the say "if the truth be known, collaboration is still in the early evangelical stages. That's fine. There's nothing wrong with patience for (and a little faith in) an idea this new and with this much potential. Because when collaboration takes off, any company that isn't up to speed hasn't got a prayer."

There have been companies who have announced CPFR pilots and unfortunately have fallen on hard financial times. To be clear, CPFR is not a magic bullet that can remedy poor business strategy, untimely events and unfavorable market conditions. One should consider that the retail industry has far more stores than are required to service the consumer. Retailers got caught up in the economic growth that took place over the last 10 years and built stores to meet competition on the one hand, and the expectations of Wall Street, on the other. The shake out has begun, with the bankruptcy of Kmart, the closing of Service Merchandise and the announcement of Toys-R-Us closing Kids-R-Us stores. The automobile industry can now produce approximately 18 million more vehicles per year than are needed in the market place. The excess capacity of the steel industry is greater than the production of the entire U.S. steel industry. This story can be told in sector after sector. To be clear, CPFR could not have avoided these calamities. However, if Cisco had stayed closer to its customers and in so doing understood that demand for its products was declining in early 2001, Cisco would have slowed down production and not built inventory for anticipated sales, which ultimately resulted in an inventory write down of $2.5B.

Cisco, Ford Motor Co. and Chrysler have all made great progress with supply chain management initiatives, reducing operating costs and inventory carrying costs by many millions of dollars. These industry leaders have all fallen on hard times because of a number of decisions or circumstances that were not directly related to supply chain management. CPFR can have very favorable results, but it cannot abrogate poor management decisions.

Vinod Singhal, at the Georgia Institute of Technolgy's DuPree College of Management and Kevin Hendricks, associate professor at the University of Western Ontario's Richard Ivey School of Business, researched supply chain management performance and shareholder value. They estimate that glitches (parts shortages, changes by customers, ramp-up/roll-out problems, production problems, development problems and quality problems; caused internally, by suppliers or customers) destroy about 7.5 per cent of a company's shareholder value at the time of its announcement. Another 9 percent is lost in the 120 days before the announcement of the glitch, and a further 2 per cent in the 120 days after the announcement. The total loss is 18.5 per cent of shareholder value. Examples of companies who have suffered such losses include Motorola, Hershey, Sony, Boeing, and Apple Computer, all of whom took major hits in market value as a result of supply chain glitches.

So while it may be difficult to specifically attribute stock growth to supply chain management improvement, the negative impact on shareholder value as a result of supply chain failures is clear. The CPFR Benefits Model however does point out the financial improvement that a company can expect by implementing CPFR. This model can be found on the CPFR.org and VICS.org websites. It is a tool which can provide guidance based on the experience of those considered among the best in their class. Experts in activity based costing have developed the standards. Any company considering CPFR should take the opportunity to explore this model, which is cost and obligation free.

2.3.4 Industry Standards are Critical

Assume there is a case for a new business process that advances the progress made in supply chain management. That business process is CPFR, a global, open, neutral business standard for value chain partners for the coordination of plans in order to reduce the variance between supply and demand, and to share the benefits of a more effective and efficient value chain. In every case study reported, trading partners have experienced an increase in sales, an increase in profits and improved utilization of working capital. Interestingly enough, these are some of the very measures on which CEO's find themselves held accountable by Wall Street. Since the completion of the Voluntary Inter-industry Commerce Standards (VICS) Associations Voluntary Guidelines for

Collaborative Planning, Forecasting and Replenishment (CPFR) Guidelines in 1998 and its sequel, the Roadmap to CPFR in 2000, there have been rapid advances in the application of the guidelines and the enabling technology.

Furthermore the Global Commerce Initiative (GCI), a group of international companies that has come together to endorse global communication standards and business practices, has endorsed CPFR. The EAN-UCC Global Standards Management Process (GSMP}, has recently approved the CPFR XML schema, providing a major step in the approval process that will provide the creditability the EAN-UCC. Given the size and influence of these companies and those that make up the Voluntary Inter-Industry Commerce Standards Association (VICS) and the VICS CPFR Committee, it is fair to say that CPFR has received global endorsement. This is also supported by the fact that ECR Europe as well as ECR Brazil, IAC/EAN Columbia and Japan have joined the CPFR Committee.

There is great interest in, and adoption of, CPFR in Japan by retailers, wholesalers, suppliers and public trading exchanges. Research on CPFR by the Distribution Economics Institute of Japan has been done for the last three years and is continuing. ECR Brazil and IAC-EAN Colombia are sponsoring educational seminars in response to the requests of their membership. Our global VICS CPFR committee members are learning from one another, collaborating on the exchange of information, and taking into consideration the specific business requirements of the countries involved. Rarely has a new business process been so embraced by countries across the globe, with companies working together in a spirit of cooperation and with the determination to develop universal guidelines for improving the performance of companies in all industries.

Soon a new release of CPFR Guidelines will be issued which incorporates the lessons learned since the release of the Roadmap in 2000. It includes practical information for companies using CPFR. For example, the Business Planning section is greatly expanded and provides specifics on making plans between trading partners. The information in the Technology section is excellent.

N-tier, i.e., taking CPFR beyond the basic buyer/seller relationship to other key players in the supply chain, e.g. deliverers of raw material, packaging suppliers, distribution service providers, et al, highlights another fertile area for finding significant savings. The CPFR Committee is committed to working with the public trading exchanges, which have expressed their commitment to CPFR. We expect to provide support to, and a venue for the exchanges to report the progress they have made with membership pilots to the VICS CPFR Committee. The importance of systems interoperability is clear and there is support by the Committee for the recommendations recently made by the Uniform Code Council (UCC) for using a third party to evaluate and certify compatibility among software.

The Committee strongly supports UCCnet, which is a not-for-profit subsidiary of the Uniform Code Council. The business vision of UCCnet is to provide an internet-based, easily accessible trading community, forming a cost-effective, nondiscriminatory universal platform for the synchronization of the "item information" among trading partners. The technical vision is to provide a "technology-neutral," open, scalable, distributed architecture that offers participants a secure, reliable mechanism for the synchronization of item content. Further, it is to encourage the voluntary participation of all solutions providers to develop service offerings and products consistent with UCCnet's open architecture and not inhibit competition in any way.

2.3.5   CPFR Addresses Several Key Pain Points

One of the problems with realizing the expected return on investment mentioned above, was the availability and accuracy of information. Incorrect product information has cost the retail industry dearly in incorrect invoices, returned products, lost sales, customer service problems, etc. This travesty exists because of the manual and error-intensive form of information sharing that characterizes the retail industry today. Perhaps it is not as serious in department store verticals, but is clearly a major opportunity in other retail verticals. *The New York Times* stated "Companies will work with UCCnet to agree on a single procedure for changing product descriptions...other online marketplaces may ultimately adopt the Uniform Code Council's standards as a way to make the ordering process between buyers and sellers more efficient." *Chain Store Age* says "The range of applications which could utilize UCCnet is nearly infinite. Pricing, promotions, logistics, scan-based trading, item movement, collaborative planning forecasting and replenishment (CPFR) and process modeling are all bases for potential programs... Retailers outside the grocery segment should get on board early as UCCnet expands its focus."

As CPFR is adopted and companies move to production and full scale implementation, the process it will be essential to use the clean information, resident in the data bases of trading partners. UCCnet will enable trading partners to reap the benefits from CPFR on the one hand, while significantly reducing the time consumed in category planning and essentially eliminating the unnecessary clerical effort expended on correcting invoices, prices, and promotions. Leading retailers, including Wal-Mart, Ahold, Shaw's, Wegmans and others have clearly stated their support for UCCnet and have encouraged their suppliers to participate with them and take advantage of the benefits to be realized by using UCCnet. Technology is only effective if the information used to drive the business processes is accurate and timely.

Continuing with technology, the advancement made in SCM could not have come about without the features and functions that have been used to improve effectiveness and efficiency. For example, there is integrated supply chain management: from supply chain planning for balanced time supplies expressed in case volume, to cubic space required for distribution, and dollars of inventory for cycle and safety stockall are based on the retail ship service level standard a company desires. And supply chain execution for the control of inventory replenishment, inbound management, real-time yard location control, real-time distribution center modeling and management, store order processing and store invoicing...with closure of the closed loop being the 3-way matching process for each vendor's freight and product invoice relation to the purchase order for both warehouse and store receipts and supply chain management and measurement for the integrated view of manpower utilizations, capital employed, equipment engaged, inventory effectiveness and key efficiencies gained by using software tools.

If the above were supported by CPFR, and conversely if CPFR is supported by these features and functions, the opportunities to increase sales and improve profits are compounded. Forward –moving, fledgling capabilities will mature and event management, exception processing, visibility, electronic tagging of product and the easy exchange of operational and planning information will pave the way for the web value chain built on the spirit of collaborative commerce and enabled by technology.

2.3.6   Implementation and Payback can be Quick

The time required to implement CPFR is dependent on a number of factors, which can be addressed by doing an internal assessment, outlined in the Roadmap to CPFR. The time required is also dependent on the company's decision to either start small and gain experience before moving forward, or to build the entire support infrastructure before engaging in the first CPFR relationship. Either approach is reasonable, however those who have been the innovators believe it is prudent to start small and build on experience. Total implementation time for some companies has been as short as 2 to 4 weeks. Retail buyers typically spend minutes per week with CPFR suppliers.

Resource requirements have varied, however it has been a reallocation of resources rather than a demand for additional headcount. In many organizations, the resources are now invested in the account sales team, the continuous replenishment team, the financial team, the marketing team, and the customer service team. With CPFR, there is a significant reduction in the number of "do-over's". On the playground, disputes were settled by calling a "do over." In business "do-over's" are expensive and require organizations to staff up to handle them, although the employees are never identified as " do-over experts". Most companies, although not publicly, state that some 50 per cent of their resources are used to resolve problems, correct errors, and handle the requisite communications. Imagine that if doing a better job of planning, through CPFR substantially reduces the "do-over's" and productivity will be improved.

The benefits of CPFR vary with trading partnership. Case studies presented in this document highlight the opportunities identified and exploited by companies willing to share their experience. However, it should be emphasized that one of the key improvements has been in increasing sales, which points out that CPFR is truly a holistic business process that touches on practically every element of the value chain. A significant benefit is the move from a push philosophy to a pull philosophy, i.e. a sales and customer specific plan that is driven up from the customer rather than down to the customer. It results in something unique, that is, producing what a consumer wants to purchase rather than what a manufacturer wants to produce. There is also the joy of seeing functions within a company begin to collaborate, to share plans, to understand the challenges that their colleagues face because of top-down versus bottom-up planning.

In the past, we have dealt with partnering, strategic alliances and other initiatives that were well intended, not well thought out, not equitable, or a combination of all three. There was never a true understanding of the benefits or of what partnership really means. While the golden rule still prevails: he or she who has the gold rules, CPFR will shift the paradigm to a more equitable sharing of opportunities because he or she will not be entirely focused on cost, but on an entire value chain, which includes sales growth and effective asset utilization.

Obstacles to Collaboration Persist

There are barriers to CPFR, which should be recognized and taken into consideration. There is, for example, the lack of internal alignment with regard to corporate goals and objectives that support a company's commitment to its shareholders and stakeholders. Other barriers include but are not limited to: compensation that promotes a silo mentality, non-existent change management skills, tunnel vision, the "not invented here mentality," internally focused organizational silos, legacy systems, and finally, but most importantly, leadership that is focused on Wall Street and making the numbers regardless of the expense to the long term prospects of the company. Just look at trade loading practices in the grocery industry as a prime example of leadership dictated by Wall Street.

There are other barriers, like the personal comfort zones which people choose not to leave, even if it means the demise of the company. Too often the argument is that "my business is different and its unique characteristics demand that the status quo must be maintained." There is nothing especially difficult about CPFR, it just takes a willingness to learn, assimilate, absorb and implement, and to maintain the attitude that only excellence will suffice.

CPFR is a keystone of collaborative commerce, which is destined to be found in the collaborative processes identified by AMR in their January 2001 Report on Retail E-Business.

▶ Collaborative Demand and Promotion Planning

▶ Collaborative Replenishment Management-supplier to shelf

▶ Collaborative Logistics Management

▶ Collaborative Product Lifecycle Management

▶ Collaborative Trade Funds Management

▶ Collaborative Product Item/Catalog Maintenance

▶ Collaborative Trading Partner Profile Maintenance

▶ Collaborative Consumer-Level Market Intelligence Management

▶ Collaborative Category Management and Merchandise Planning

The public and private trading exchanges, the development of technology, communications, interoperability mergers, acquisitions, etc will all influence the evolution of collaborative commerce. Nevertheless, the age of collaboration is here and the funeral of the age of confrontation is taking place. Much needs to be done, but the rewards will be great and worthwhile.

CPFR will last the Test of Time

The future will see innovative business practices and processes that will build on what we have learned through CPFR. Drucker says it takes about 10 years for a business process to become successful after going through the trials of innovation, experimentation, implementation, and failure. We strongly believe that CPFR will be the exception.

We will see change, because industry is under tremendous pressure, brought about by the options offered and the demands of the consumer for service, price, convenience and product innovation. In response to consumer and shareholder demands, industry will begin to employ the power of the infrastructure that currently exists, and become a very efficient and effective global delivery system.

Influencing factors will include the implementation of affordable technology, i.e. hosting, transaction based fees, "mini me" systems that provide basic functionality, with minimal investment in hardware that avoids the balance sheet. The economy will recover, and new ERP players will emerge. The problems related to the interfacing of best-of-breed systems will no longer cause service and operational problems.

The consolidation of retailers and wholesalers will continue, creating large companies that have a strong grip on their primary markets. Consolidation will also continue with manufacturers, third-party providers, and technology providers. This will result in a balancing of leverage and the use of collaborative efforts necessary to effectively and efficiently move products from the source of raw materials to the point of consumption. The use of statistical forecasting tools as we know them today will be replaced with interactive systems which exchange and interpret information, which will in turn drive the value chain.

Organizations and the skills which exist today will not be recognizable because of functions which will no longer be needed due to technological innovation and the use of third-party providers. Third parties, using the Internet and Collaborative Transportation Management, will manage transportation. Finally the dream of continuous movement and the intelligent use of motor carriers and their most important asset, the driver, will be realized.

The economy will rebound and the challenges brought on by a mobile work force and full employment will be met with the reengineering of business practices and the implementation of integrated and compatible technologies. Productivity will improve and corporations will use some of the gains realized in profitability to help the disadvantaged around the world. After all, the age of collaboration is intended to fulfill a greater calling than what can be found in the metrics used to measure business success, and it all began with Collaborative Planning Forecasting and Replenishment and VICS.

2.4 CPFR – Status and Perspectives: Key Results of a CPFR Survey in the Consumer Goods Sector and Updates

Julie Fraser, Industry Directions Inc.

2.4.1 Survey Background

Syncra Systems and Industry Directions conducted a survey of manufacturers, retailers, distributors and logistics providers among others – primarily in the consumer goods sectors in 2000. Our objective was to gain an understanding of whether or not and how companies are deploying Collaborative Planning, Forecasting and Replenishment practices, the results from those who have done so, and where the industry may need further education on CPFR and its benefits.

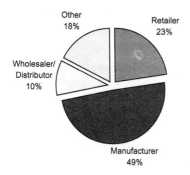

Exhibit 2.3 CPFR-Survey-Respondents by industry.
Source: Industry Directions/Syncra Systems

The survey respondent base includes many types of companies. About a quarter of the respondents are retailers, half are manufacturers, and the remaining quarter are other types of firms, including wholesalers and distributors, logistics and transportation providers, consultants, and systems integrators.

The organizations range from under $100M to over $5B, with 42% over $1B and 58% under $1B in revenues. Note that some respondents represent divisions of larger companies.

The respondent base consists of 130 individuals from 120 different companies. Many of the companies are household-name retailers and consumer goods manufacturers. They represent a range of job titles, as shown in the exhibit below. Most of these respondents have multi-departmental views because of their job functions – such as MIS, Management, or supply chain.

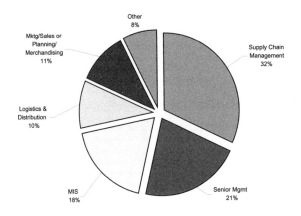

Exhibit 2.4 CPFR-Survey-Respondents by job type.
Source: Industry Directions/Syncra Systems CPFR: The Next Wave

Collaborative Planning, Forecasting and Replenishment is gaining momentum as more companies add it to their strategic initiatives and business improvement activities.

Based on the results of this and other industry data, it appeared many retail and consumer goods companies would have made significant progress in piloting or rolling out CPFR during 2000-2001.

▶ 68% of the participants were actively researching, undergoing pilots, or preparing to roll out CPFR.

▶ Only 32% had no plans.

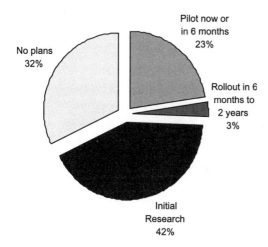

Pilot now or
in 6 months
23%

No plans
32%

Rollout in 6
months to
2 years
3%

Initial
Research
42%

Exhibit 2.5 CPFR stage. Source: Industry Directions/Syncra Systems

As major retail and manufacturing companies now in pilot mode expand their implementations, pressure will mount on other companies to begin collaborating as well.

Companies with CPFR pilots underway – both in our study and in the VICS *Roadmap to CPFR* – are already gaining significant benefits. These benefits include increased service levels and sales and at the same time decreased inventory as, highlighted in the next section.

While the publicity around positive results is helping to build momentum for CPFR, industry interest is propelled even more strongly by intense pressure on companies to improve their supply chain's business performance. For example:

▶ Increased retail consolidation and pressure from emerging e-retailers has put greater pressure on margins and same store revenue growth. Retailers need their suppliers to assist in lowering inventory while avoiding stock-outs.

▶ Consumer goods manufacturers recognize they need to better serve retailers and distributors, and need parallel improvements from their material suppliers.

▶ Participants throughout the extended supply chain are fighting to add value and avoid the "disintermediation" that e-commerce is widely believed to allow.

In a *Consumer Goods Technology* survey on priorities for 2000, reducing supply chain costs, compressing time to market, and collaborating more effectively with trading partners were ranked as the most important business initiatives. All of these are benefits of CPFR. Companies are realizing that collaborating with their trading partners may be the only way to achieve the performance levels they and their stakeholders expect.

Further, many are recognizing that they now compete as supply chains, not just as individual enterprises. CPFR is the first recognized industry standard to provide templates for supply chain partner planning collaboration.

CPFR Processes

The term Collaborative Planning, Forecasting and Replenishment makes intuitive sense. However, it's important to understand how it actually works. The starting point is an agreement between trading partners to collaborate – by developing and taking responsibility for plans, forecasts, and replenishment orders.

To collaborate, both the buyer and seller contribute to a single plan and forecast for what they will sell, and how, when, and where goods will be promoted. Each partner uses its own business systems (ERP, demand planning, forecasting, supply chain planning and execution) to develop and execute plans. The VICS CPFR communications standards – and supporting software – are the mechanisms that partners use to communicate plans and make subsequent changes. The result is a supply chain that is more efficient and demand-driven.

Because they are sharing a common plan and forecast, it becomes possible for the buyers' order cycles to be synchronized with suppliers' production cycles. Many companies are even taking it a step further and integrating their supply and demand planning processes, coordinating activities between replenishment and promotional planners, and jointly identifying and creating opportunities for additional revenues.

CPFR can also reduce costs. For example, once they agree, trading partners can safely freeze a forecast and automatically convert it into a shipping plan. This eliminates the order processing steps. Further, collaboration improves visibility of the constraints on both sides, allowing plan adjustments before, not after, plans and forecasts are finalized. Having reduced uncertainty, manufacturers and retailers alike can reduce safety stocks, stock to demand, and respond quickly to change.

2.4.2 Proven CPFR Benefits

The core objective of CPFR is to increase the accuracy of demand forecasts and replenishment plans necessary to lower inventories across the supply chain and attain high service levels of the right products in the right locations. This results in higher sales at both a category and brand level because consumers are then getting exactly what they want, when and where they want it. This is only possible when companies collaborate, sharing knowledge through a common set of processes.

Naturally, only the companies whose CPFR programs are underway can report actual benefits achieved. The results from the quarter of the participants who qualified are listed at the end of this section. However, we asked all of the respondents about what they expect could be achieved by implementing a CPFR program.

All of the companies in this study see the value of CPFR – both those currently involved in CPFR programs and gaining benefits, and those who have not yet begun. Eighty-nine percent of the respondents expect CPFR will provide:

▶ improvements in trading partner forecast accuracy;

▶ decreases in inventory and safety stock;

▶ reduction in out-of-stock and improved service levels; and

▶ increases in sales.

Specific expectations are based on where companies are currently operating, and those with lower levels of performance will generally have the greatest potential benefit. However, in this study, those with the best performance levels are well aware of how much further CPFR might improve their capabilities:

Forecast Accuracy Levels

Half of respondents whose forecast accuracy is 90% or greater predict that CPFR would improve their trading partners' forecasts by at least 20%.

Two-thirds of those with the highest level of forecast accuracy agree that their trading partners' forecast accuracy would benefit significantly from CPFR.

Inventory Levels

Two-thirds of respondents with the lowest inventory value today believe they would gain more than 10% in additional savings in inventory and safety stocks, as the exhibit below shows.

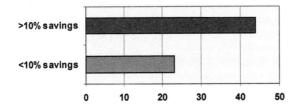

**Expected Inventory Savings from CPFR,
<$100M Inventory Currently**

Exhibit 2.6 Expected inventory savings from CPFR.
Source: Industry Directions/Syncra Systems

Service Levels

Half of those with over 98% service levels today believe they could significantly improve by using CPFR.

Sales Increases

Of those already piloting or expecting to pilot within the next 6 months, 35% expect sales increases of over 10%, and over 90% expect some sales increase.

The one-quarter of respondents to this survey who have gained some experience operating with CPFR report the following as among the greatest benefits:

▶ "Weekly downloads of promotion plans means we quickly caught changes to timing, codes, and/or quantity"

▶ "Accurate forecasts"

▶ "Grew sales and reduced inventory by double-digits"

▶ "Improved fill rates, reduced inventory, and shared the benefits"

▶ "Weekly downloads of actual retail sales [to a CPG company] allow us to see market reactions quickly and easily"

▶ "Business with the customer with whom we have CPFR in place was up 80% this past year"

▶ "Initial work improved sales $9M"

▶ "Began to use data to make decisions in a way that builds business for both"

▶ "100% service level over past 9 months and approaching 40 annual turns"

▶ "We have a successful CPFR process in place with our largest customer. This past year the customer's business with us was up 80%."

These results match the expectations and goals of CPFR. Until recently, early adopters of CPFR did not share their benefits or success factors because of the strategic advantage they were gaining.

2.4.3 Performance & Challenges

Forecast Accuracy

Greater accuracy in plans and forecasts is a major goal of CPFR. As such, it's important to understand where companies stand with forecast accuracy. Please see below data on forecast accuracy in the 2000 survey:

▶ 63% reported less than 90% forecast accuracy.

▶ 18% reported forecast accuracy of over 90%.

▶ 19% didn't know their organization's forecast accuracy. This high number suggests a lack of education about the critical nature of forecast accuracy to customer service levels and costs.

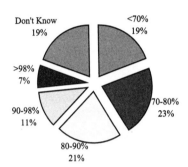

Exhibit 2.7 Forecast accuracy. Source: Industry Directions/Syncra Systems

This survey data shows the bullwhip effect. The bullwhip effect is where those partners more removed from demand have increasingly less accurate, more volatile forecasts. (The end of the whip near the "hand" of demand barely needs to move for a mighty lashing to take place at the far end of supply.)

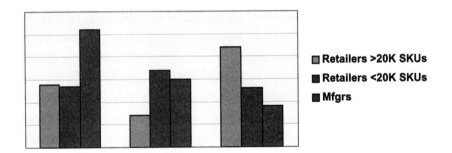

Exhibit 2.8 Forecast Accuracy by organization type.
Source: Industry Directions/Syncra Systems

Manufacturers – particularly those not currently involved with CPFR – have less accurate forecasts than the retailers. This common supply chain problem is particularly striking when comparing manufacturers to high mix retailers. Retailers with more SKUs tend to be more accurate than those with fewer SKUs. The retailers who handle fewer SKUs report a wide range of forecast accuracy, with no clear pattern.

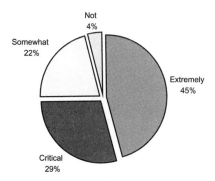

Exhibit 2.9 How critical is a more accurate S&OP forecast?
Source: Industry Directions/Syncra Systems

In this study, smaller organizations also had more accurate forecasts than larger ones.

▶ 20% of respondents under $1B and only 15% of those over $1B reported over 90% forecast accuracy.

▶ 26% of the over $1B firms have less than 70% forecast accuracy, and only 16% of the smaller size firms had such poor forecast accuracy.

Three quarters of the respondents believe a more accurate sales and operations planning (S&OP) forecast would be very important to their organization.

▶ 45% of the total rate this as extremely critical.

▶ 51% say it is critical or somewhat critical.

▶ Only 4% say it is not critical.

Impact of Inaccuracy

Companies in this survey were well aware of the problems that inaccurate forecasts cause in their businesses. They recognize that these problems directly impact their fundamental business issues of timeliness, market share, margins, sales, and customer service levels.

Most retailers consider stock-outs a major problem, and over 40% have issues with materials shortages, inventory costs impacting margins, lost sales due to inability to respond to market variability, and service level problems due to poor responsiveness to last minute changes.

The top issue with which manufacturers struggle is the high cost of inventory and obsolescence. They also have concerns about all of the difficulties listed by retailers. Others are most concerned about inventory costs, materials shortages, and poor responsiveness to change.

Customer Service Levels

An important area which forecast accuracy affects is customer service levels. For retailers, this represents having the right product on the shelf the moment customers walk in looking for it – at a price they're willing to pay. For manufacturers, it is delivering perfect orders, or delivering the right quantity of the SKU mix requested at the specified time. This is especially critical when items are on special promotion.

Among the retailers surveyed, there is a wide range of service levels. This may be because some interpreted service as incoming perfect orders, while others viewed it as in-stock levels.

▶ While nearly half the retailers reported over 90% service levels, a third have less than 80% service levels.

▶ In contrast, two-thirds of the manufacturers claimed over 90% perfect orders, and just 12% have service levels under 80%. This discrepancy could be the result of retailers failing to provide a buffer between demand and the manufacturers.

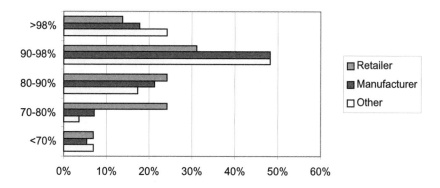

Exhibit 2.10 Current service levels. Source: Industry Directions/Syncra Systems

Of all respondents, 10% did not know their service levels – most of these companies have no CPFR plans. This highlights a group of companies that need internal education to understand the critical nature of service levels to supply chain success. Awareness of lost opportunity and supply chain inefficiency often provides the sense of urgency needed to spark companies to embark on CPFR.

Retail stock-outs can mean significant lost sales. Beyond the immediate loss from the out-of-stock item, customers often take their business elsewhere – for all of their shopping needs, not just for the unavailable item. Manufacturers who cannot deliver perfect orders similarly risk erosion of customer loyalty, as they may be the cause of these lost revenue opportunities – for their trading partners and themselves.

2.4.4 Leveraging Diverse Initiatives & Systems

There were multiple supply chain initiatives underway in 79% of the respondent companies, many of which leverage information technologies. To show them graphically, we divide them into initiatives and systems.

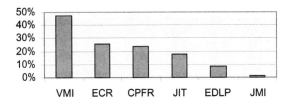

Exhibit 2.11 Supply Chain Initiatives. Source: Industry Directions/Syncra Systems

▶ Vendor Managed Inventory (VMI) is by far the most widely implemented supply chain improvement initiative, at 47% of those surveyed. However, of these, almost none have taken it to the next stage of shared responsibility or Joint Managed Inventory (JMI). This is where CPFR communication can facilitate the next step.

▶ ECR is the second most widely implemented initiative, and is relevant to those in consumer goods retail and their suppliers.

▶ Almost as many are implementing CPFR, which is impressive, given how recent the guidelines are.

▶ 18% use Just in Time (JIT), which is a similar concept to ECR but used primarily by manufacturers.

▶ 9% practice Every Day Lowest Price (EDLP) – a concept that some retail segments use, which would affect those retailers and their suppliers.

CPFR is the next stage in the evolution of supply chain initiatives. It goes beyond current internal system implementations and pushes the next level of information sharing out to trading partners. Using CPFR, companies are joining forces and taking responsibility for mutual plans that result in greater benefit than if they were to remain independent.

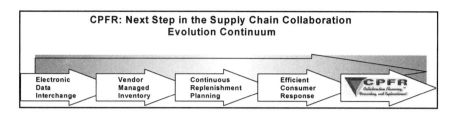

Exhibit 2.12 CPFR as the next step in the supply chain collaboration evolution.
Source: Industry Directions/Syncra Systems

CPFR is also an enabling process for all other supply chain improvement initiatives. To quote the VICS *Roadmap*, "CPFR is about setting common goals for organizations and builds on and extends other Efficient Consumer Response (ECR) successes, such as category management and Continuous Replenishment Planning (CRP). It pulls them into a cohesive plan, supports better execution of the plan, and invites improved planning in the next business cycle."

CPFR leverages current investments in database and applications software, including Warehouse Management Systems (WMS), Forecasting/APS, Enterprise Resources Management (ERP), Materials Requirements Planning (MRP), Distribution Requirements Planning (DRP), and Customer Relationship Management (CRM). All of these applications are widely used by the respondents, ranging from 46% using WMS and 41% using ERP to 9% using CRM. These systems store and execute plans and forecasts, or track customer preferences. Very often it is advantageous to link these systems, at the partner level, to CPFR. Generally, this is not a complex process.

What can be complex is the wide variety of systems in use by each of the partners. It is not uncommon to find unique ERP, supply chain, warehouse management or CRM system combinations in a supply chain – as we find in the respondent base. There are no single leaders in these software segments.

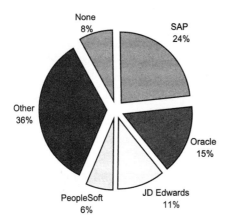

None
8%

SAP
24%

Other
36%

Oracle
15%

JD Edwards
11%

PeopleSoft
6%

Exhibit 2.13 Enterprise Resources Management in use.
Source: Industry Directions/Syncra Systems

Enterprise Resource Planning

▶ 50% use SAP, Oracle or JD Edwards.

▶ 42% are split among 22 other systems.

Supply Chain Planning/Forecasting

▶ 27% use Manugistics.

▶ 9% have deployed i2.

▶ Of the remaining 64%, no more than 6% use any one system.

Warehouse Management Systems (WMS)
WMS is the application most commonly implemented among the respondents.

▶ 7% use EXE and 6% use OMI.

▶ More than 60% use a WMS other than the seven provided in the survey.

▶ 16% use custom-built WMS.

The enormous variety of planning and execution software in use creates an interoperability puzzle for CPFR. As a result, CPFR initiatives must use fully open, vendor-neutral CPFR communications products to support deployment in one-to-many and many-to-many trading partner environments. Since the question of software neutrality is crucial to CPFR infrastructure extensibility, it is worth noting that most of the CPFR products available are from companies that also offer supply chain planning, forecasting, or execution software. To succeed over the long haul, CPFR will need communication products that are truly open and interoperable.

2.4.5 Sharing the Knowledge

As the term collaboration suggests, CPFR is all about sharing knowledge with supply chain trading partners. Companies start by implementing CPFR programs with their top tier partners, based on who is ready to participate. Companies who have begun to gain the benefits are beginning to roll out CPFR to more partners.

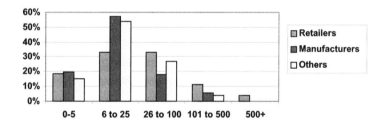

Exhibit 2.14 Expected number of trading partners in CPFR long term.
Source: Industry Directions/Syncra Systems

When asked how many partners they envision rolling CPFR out long term, most respondents indicate plans for 25 or fewer partners. However, more than half the retailers expect to roll it out to more than 25 partners, and 15% of retailers expect to roll out CPFR to more than 100 trading partners. Manufacturers are more likely to follow the 80/20 rule, and roll out to the essential customers that make up the bulk of their business. In this set of manufacturers, less than a quarter anticipate rolling it out to over 25 partners.

The limited number of partners planned for CPFR is due in part to how few share data with their trading partners today. Less than half of the companies in the 2000 survey share any data beyond promotional plans, and just 56% of the total share promotional information.

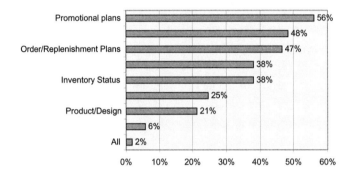

Exhibit 2.15 Information regularly shared with partners.
Source: Industry Directions/Syncra Systems

CPFR is a program designed to enable key trading partners to improve their sales while reducing inventory and overhead. There is some early indication that such benefits might drive companies into CPFR relationships with more partners than this group of respondents anticipates today.

There are a number of respondents who see the potential to roll out CPFR quite broadly. For example, one retailer that expects to roll out to over 500 partners is a well-known nationwide chain; another expects over 200 this year. Many of the larger companies (over $250M) expect to collaborate with over 100 partners.

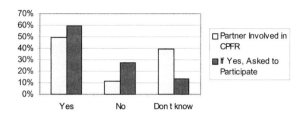

Companies Involved Invite Others

Exhibit 2.16 Partner involvement in CPFR. Source: Industry Directions/Syncra Systems

Often, CPFR initiatives are pushed by one of the partners or a central "hub sponsor." Of those who know about their trading partners' CPFR initiatives, most have been asked to participate. However, in the total respondent base, not quite half are aware that their trading partners are involved in CPFR, and nearly 40% don't know whether a partner uses CPFR.

Since many of the respondents are expecting to pilot or roll out CPFR programs in the next year (and even more are conducting research to embark on a pilot), the views on participation and number of partners for CPFR are sure to change. We expect that a year from now, respondents will expand their long-term vision for CPFR to include well over 25 partners.

2.4.6 CPFR Implementation

While the benefits of CPFR are impressive, implementation has its challenges. Perhaps the most significant issue revolves around making what VICS calls the Organizational Shift to a consumer-centric, inter-enterprise orientation.

The respondents agreed. Sixty percent indicate that, indeed, internal process changes are difficult. A lack of partner trust is another major cultural issue that companies must address.

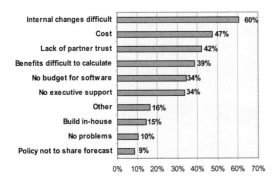

Exhibit 2.17 CPFR challenges. Source: Industry Directions/Syncra Systems

For those farthest along – in pilots or in planning to roll out CPFR in the near future – the top three issues are internal process change, lack of trust with partners, and cost of implementation. The other issues were not considered significant stumbling blocks by those experienced in CPFR. These companies have gained executive support and are further along in quantifying the benefits.

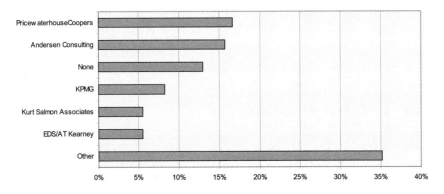

Exhibit 2.18 Consultant or systems integrator for ERP or supply chain. Source: Industry Directions/Syncra Systems

Many respondents are using a consultant or system integrator for their ERP and Supply Chain software implementation. The two most widely used firms are PricewaterhouseCoopers (16%) and Accenture (15%). The other firms called upon for system implementation support include KPMG (8%), Kurt Salmon Associates (6%) and EDS/AT Kearney (6%).

Several respondents have also turned to Arthur Andersen/ Senn-Delaney, Ernst & Young, and Deloitte and Touche – all grouped under "other". Since these firms have gained knowledge of the company's issues and IT infrastructure, including them in the CPFR implementation may make sense.

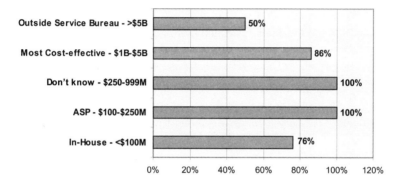

Exhibit 2.19 Approach to large-scale CPFR deployment by company size.
Source: Industry Directions/Syncra Systems

To reduce the cost of a CPFR implementation and accelerate its time to market, outsourcing is a viable option. Almost one in five of the respondents would consider outsourcing in their large-scale CPFR deployment plans. More (28%) would manage CPFR for a large number of trading partners in-house.

Interestingly, respondents in each size range had a different primary approach to how they would deploy CPFR to a large group of trading partners. The smallest companies would want to keep management internal. Organizations over $100M and under $250M are keenly interested in ASP's – perhaps because some of these companies are highly dynamic and growing.

Half of the largest companies expect to use service bureaus to manage large CPFR implementations. Even in the remaining half, outsourcing is often a key element. They showed interest in ASP's, as well as a combination using internal management for the major trading partners and outsourcing for less strategic partners.

Key Advantages of CPFR

The companies that have already undertaken CPFR are reporting some exciting benefits. Supply chain partners are finding collaborative planning can increase sales while reducing costs. The results include:

▶ increased sales of the products for which planning was collaborative

▶ reduced forecast error

▶ reduced replenishment cycle times

▶ visibility to better set store-level replenishment parameters

▶ improved in-stock rates for retailers

▶ reduced days of supply, lower inventory levels, and higher inventory turns

▶ smoother demand pattern for suppliers

▶ increased service levels from suppliers to retailers

▶ lower production planning and deployment costs for suppliers.

Even respondents now achieving excellent performance see opportunity for further improvements using CPFR. For example, half the companies with over 98% service levels believe they could achieve significant improvement in their service levels with CPFR.

Service Boost Expected; >98% Service

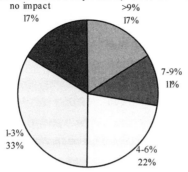

no impact
17%

>9%
17%

7-9%
11%

4-6%
22%

1-3%
33%

Exhibit 2.20 Service boost by CPFR. Source: Industry Directions/Syncra Systems

Progress since the 2000 CPFR Research Study

One of the developments which occurred since our initial CPFR research in 2000 was the emergence of widely supported Public Trading Exchanges like Transora and Worldwide Retail Exchange. The attraction of a public exchange is that a single communications mechanism can enable collaboration with many trading partners. To date, CPFR has consisted almost exclusively of one-to-one pilots and implementations between a single retailer and a single supplier for a defined set of products. Because of the nature of CPFR, each interaction must be narrowly defined – but manufacturers would prefer a way to leverage the infrastructure and business process of CPFR across several retail trading partners and suppliers.

Quite a few manufacturers find that the trading exchanges are a logical way to do business, but some exchanges are not yet fully equipped to handle CPFR. In other cases, questions arise about how the exchanges might work together to allow members of each to collaborate across those exchange boundaries. So while some companies have based their approach to CPFR on that of one of the major exchanges, quite a few others are finding that they must move forward without full confidence in how, when or even if public trading exchanges will fully support their efforts

What we have seen in working with U.S. manufacturers is that CPFR is starting to gain momentum. While retail customers generally provide the first impetus, manufacturers are starting to embrace this effort as they realize the benefits as well.

Larger manufacturers in particular appear to be taking CPFR seriously, and executives are placing priority on collaboration, particularly with retail customers. As with any major initiative for process and systems change, executive support and attention are critical to success. Our observation is that the manufacturers that have made CPFR a priority and proactively pursue it, rather than simply agreeing to a customer's request to participate, are having the most success.

CPFR in Practice

One of the interesting developments of the past few years – since the publication of the VICS CPFR Roadmap – is that to get moving quickly, quite a few companies are collaborating with critical partners in a manner that is less complete than the full CPFR process. This is a traditional sequence for manufacturers taking on new businesses processes: they crawl before they walk, and walk before they run. Taking it a piece at a time can ease the challenge of transition.

Initially, quite a few manufacturers gain significant benefits just from accessing one level of the retailer's forecasts or plans – and alerting him to issues in an informal process when they cannot meet expectations. Ongoing identification of exceptions and collaboration to keep fulfillment in line with the latest demand movements are processes that require even further internal process and organizational change.

Companies that are further along in their CPFR implementation are finding that the role of operations increases and that of sales decreases over time. This reflects the move from only reviewing customer forecasts and providing feedback – a sales function – to collaborative planning and replenishment, where operations and supply chain functions manage the processes.

Further, most CPFR initiatives are working at the Distribution Center level, not necessarily the store level. This is another level of detail that may be best achieved over a period of time for some trading partners. It is also important to recognize that the internal changes required for retailers to analyze and deliver store-level demand information to trading partners may continue to be a sticking point for some time.

Many applications software vendors have also announced or improved their support for CPFR since our initial research. As a result, more U.S. manufacturers are using commercial software for CPFR than before – and some of those use an outsourced or ASP rather than adding infrastructure and applications to support CPFR internally. At this point, many companies use a combination of mechanisms to support their CPFR activity, including Excel spreadsheets and internally developed software – or customer-specific software – along with these commercial products.

Today's technology would allow companies to exchange data via XML via the Internet, but our discussions suggest that many CPFR programs use EDI, flat files, and e-mail mechanisms for data sharing between partners. XML is just taking hold as manufacturers migrate from older enterprise applications to those that can transmit XML, so this transition probably will not take place any time soon for a number of the U.S. manufacturers we have encountered.

So while the VICS CPFR Guidelines outline a relatively comprehensive process for collaboration between trading partners, many companies are getting started with a more limited process. Similarly, the commercial software available that leverages XML and newer technologies is just beginning to be adopted. In practice, CPFR is being implemented and adopted incrementally.

Benefits Drive Adoption

In our initial study the respondents that had active or complete pilot projects reported stunning inventory reductions and gains in sales levels with the partner, and service level and fill rates. Our conversations more recently indicate that these benefits are still strong. Companies are also improving their forecast accuracy and, above all, their trading partner relationships. This bodes well for future expansion of CPFR activities.

Some manufacturers are finding it difficult to quantify hard benefits from CPFR because they see the largest gains in internal communications and process efficiency, as well as better trading partner relationships and becoming a pre-ferred supplier. However, those furthest along have improved – usually simul-taneously – in sales, inventory levels, and customer service. These are measur-able, and as companies recognize that metrics will be key to sustaining CPFR efforts and gauging success with each partner, companies are assembling scorecards to track gains.

It's not just the largest U.S. manufacturers that are participating and gaining benefits. Quite a few $500M-$2B consumer goods companies or divisions also have CPFR pilots underway or complete, and their results are at least as strik-ing. Some of these manufacturers are also very aggressive in pursuing expan-sions to their pilots and adding CPFR activities with more trading partners. This is a refreshing change from all retail-driven CPFR, and we expect those aggressive manufacturers to generate even greater results from their efforts than those who wait to be invited.

The benefits to manufacturers and their suppliers are that, with a more realistic view of demand as it changes at the retail level, they can stay synchronized and work to grow sales without as much risk of inventory overages or stock-outs. The good news for retailers is that their suppliers are increasingly inter-ested in working with them to keep the shelves stocked, and getting beyond the pain of some of the earlier VMI efforts. For U.S. consumers, all of this could add up in the long run to more pleasing retail shopping experiences – where the brands American shoppers prefer are easier to find and products promoted are more likely to be available in the local store.

CPFR continues to drive value for consumer goods manufacturers and their trading partners. U.S. Manufacturers are incorporating it into their larger sup-ply chain initiatives, and leveraging the power of collaboration with trading partners to further the success of their value networks. CPFR has its chal-lenges, and manufacturers are notoriously slow to change their processes, but CPFR is taking hold. In this environment, collaboration is creating win-win sit-uations for U.S. industry and consumers.

3   CPFR in North America

3.1   Major Trends in North American CPFR Adoption

Tom Friedman, MoonWatch Media Inc.
Greg Belkin, MoonWatch Media Inc.

The *VICS Collaborative Planning, Forecasting, and Replenishment (CPFR)* supply chain process initiative has become an adopted next practice globally. In its current phase of development the objective is to extend its process model to a retailer's or supplier's full range of trading partners. Within the last three years however, several discussions among top industry executives have occurred concerning best-practice procedures. To this end, we present analyses of five major trends involving CPFR adoption in North America, as well as some case studies.

3.1.1   Collaboration Means Restructuring Supply Chain Processes

CPFR and other collaborative processes provide true end-user benefits.

Supply chain collaboration is more than visibility, information sharing, and improved technology. It also involves changing the nature of trading relationships in order to add value for end users, as well as benefiting all participants in a collaborative value chain. For example, the nine-step VICS CPFR process standard replaces traditional customer and purchase orders with collaborative demand/order forecasts and an automated replenishment order flow. These steps allow buyers and sellers to redefine how they work together and leverage each other's resources.

Actions that rely on technology to transfer functions from one side of a transaction to another, or accelerate existing workflow processes, do not create significant added value to collaborative trading partnerships. Vendor managed inventory (VMI), for example, moves a retailer's inventory management and replenishment role to the supplier. The supplier's greater pipeline transparency and longer span of inventory control, from the sources of supply to the retailer's selling location, simplifies the coordination of product flow and workflow. However, due to a lack of shared perspective, this process creates several logistical problems. After the implementation of VMI, many retailers have discovered these hidden logistical problems, and have thus been required to make additional investments.

ACE Hardware is one such retailer who at first relied on VMI, but soon realized the extended benefits of CPFR. ACE's expanded single view of a supplier did not provide perfect transparency or a means of integrating retailer stock status, retailer promotions, new store openings, distribution center realignments, and total assortment management requirements into sales and order forecasts. Since each supplier used its own planning and execution processes, coordination of multiple product flows deteriorated, while competition for supply chain resources and scheduling grew exponentially as the number of VMI programs increased. As a result, inventory support for promotions was inconsistent, product shipments lacked coordination with total pipeline activity, and many independent reactive demand forecasts proliferated.

To solve this problem, ACE decided to add a single, shared demand forecast, based on the nine-step VICS CPFR model, and developed a single collaboration software suite, accessible to both supplier and retailer. The retailer and its suppliers used the CPFR process steps to jointly develop a front-end agreement and business plan to drive the supplier's planning and replenishment process execution. As an added benefit, ACE's small and medium-sized suppliers were able to participate in this new collaborative model without significant systems expense or operational overhead. Supplier forecasts were seamlessly coordinated with storewide promotions, total assortment planning, and other retailer data to optimize service levels. Most importantly, the supplier's uncertainty over competing priorities and objectives were kept in line by jointly reconciling this data with its demand and order forecasts.

Achieving effective collaboration is not a one-size-fits-all process. It is dependent on the identification of those business processes that offer the greatest opportunity for collaborative improvement. To this end, the CPFR Web site, www.cpfr.org, provides a CPFR capability assessment. It offers evaluation criteria and definitions for collaborative processes, integrated planning and fore-casting, replenishment, and supply chain management, and is based directly on the Global ECR Scorecard metrics developed in 1999. The assessment pro-cess allows buyers and sellers to initiate appropriate collaborative connections and set goals that can be achieved and leveraged to grow joint value chain capacity. At the same time, the Global Commerce Initiative (GCI) provides the scorecard for establishing the level of supply chain relationships. This enables firms to begin working in process areas at the correct level of engagement. It also provides a means of connecting with related key performance indicators (PKI's) to establish quantifiable collaborative goals and monitor performance.

Moreover, achieving the scalability of collaborative commerce relationships is directly dependent on the availability of open, neutral standards that can be used by firms of all sizes on a global basis. These standards enable trading part-ners to replicate new shared supply chain processes throughout the Supply Web Enterprise, spanning internal systems, processes, and inter-company transactions. The shared restructuring of supply chain processes involves the synchronization of data and a clearly defined execution of the collaborative trading partnership.

Successful supply chain management requires a focus on processes that will ultimately benefit the end user. However, this will only be realized by estab-lishing processes that replace older technology-based supplier agreements with collaborative partnerships that benefit all participants in a collaborative value chain.

3.1.2   Scaleable CPFR Requires Incremental Development

Moving beyond successful CPFR pilots to collaborative trading partner net-works requires a slow, methodical approach.

The transition to a process infrastructure that will enable and support the increased transaction volume and interactive complexity of extensive CPFR trading partner relationships calls for measured steps that build on the VICS CPFR initiative. The nine-step CPFR process model of this initiative necessi-tates scaleable technology to support exception-based decision management.

It also requires feasible processes to control the complexity of relationships in a trading partner network.

The objective of CPFR pilots is to develop mutually effective processes. In the same manner, the first steps in implementing CPFR trading partner networks call for the development of process links between trading partners at an appropriate level of collaboration.

In initial collaborative process development, technology has not been the primary focus. Recent CPFR pilots, for example, demonstrated that the largest retail and wholesale firms of the global supply chain first used spreadsheets to transmit CPFR data rather than use their extensive technical resources. Scaleable collaborative implementations, however, require more technological support, thereby allowing exception-based decision management to focus on process development and execution between trading partners, as opposed to the administrative issues of transaction management.

The next step in developing scaleable collaborative processes involves homogenous groups of trading partners implementing those processes . This can be aided by the VICS CPFR capability assessment worksheet, which provides a clear and objective means of segmenting trading partners within a supply chain network. By outfitting a cluster of trading partners with similar CPFR capabilities, organizations can achieve a common collaborative resolution of CPFR process improvement.

A further incremental process method would entail setting demand planning levels at the warehouse or distribution center by SKU before increasing volume and complexity at stores. In addition, firms initiating the construction of a CPFR network would simplify the complexity of process development among multiple trading partners by segmenting the product mix to focus more on stable and less on promotional or seasonal categories.

The preceding approaches provide a gradual rate of implementation, thus allowing trading partners time to mutually assess both collective progress and the capability of individual firms for managing supply chain processes and relationships. The move from a CPFR pilot of two partners to a network of fifty or more does not occur in a single step, and adds significant complexity to the

CPFR management process. Clusters of trading partner relationships will exist for each partner based on product mix, distribution model, promotional strategy, and systems. Limiting initial trading partner combinations will control the escalating complexity and size of the CPFR installation. This new level should be appropriate to the level of trading partner collaboration established in the initial CPFR front-end agreement process.

Future requirements for commercial implementations however will necessitate a scaleable technology to support the gradual development of CPFR relationships. Recent announcements of the creation of an XML-based directory service standard and of application service provider (ASP) solutions by major software vendors signal opportunities for successful CPFR implementations on a large scale.

IBM, Microsoft, Novell, Oracle, Sun Microsystems, and Netscape Communications expressed support for the XML-based directory services markup language (DSML) in 1999. In addition, Logility, Oracle, Manugistics, and i2 Technologies report ASP functionality for their customers and trading partners. In particular, Logility's i-Commerce, a Web-based ASP network compliant with the VICS CPFR initiative, shows particular promise for scaleable CPFR installations. These new developments will enable supply chain firms to access and manage the volume of transactions generated by multiple relationships efficiently and effectively.

In addition, the development of VICS CPFR requires that both sides learn, understand, and effectively use collaborative supply chain processes on an incremental basis. Otherwise, a rapid one-sided deployment of CPFR technology will simply become another supply chain initiative instead of a foundation for developing supply chain value.

The promise of this technology requires a disciplined gradual development of CPFR processes between trading partners. In response to this concern, the VICS CPFR committee has focused its recommendations on process first and technology second. The committee believes that the gradual maturation of each relationship is the core factor for success in building long-term commercial viability. Moreover, a premature implementation of full-scale CPFR networks can derail the initial proof-of-concept validation established by CPFR pilots.

Continued investment in incremental collaborative process development will enable high levels of cooperation, thus driving improvement in operating efficiencies for retailer and supplier.

3.1.3 The Power of One

The Voluntary Interindustry Commerce Standards Association has assumed many important initiatives of the defunct Joint Industry Project on Efficient Consumer Response (ECR) in the United States. As they began focusing on the demand side of the supply chain, these two major retail business-to-business organizations found they were becoming increasingly alike. With a sharper focus on consumer satisfaction, members of these two groups are now addressing ways in which they can enable the retail industry to leverage raw point-of-sale data and to do more refined forecasting.

Both standards organizations were deeply engaged in collaborative planning, replenishment and forecasting processes. In fact, both list the development of CPFR as having been one of their highest priorities for several years. Moreover, through its stewardship of CPFR committee meetings, VICS realized that its most active committee members were long-time participants in the ECR movement under the VICS banner.

In addition, as both supermarket and general merchandise industries grew closer over time, similarities increased. They now began to resemble each other in product lines and practices, buying from many of the same consumer product companies, such as Procter & Gamble, Johnson & Johnson, and Nabisco. Consequently, it was quite common for members of both organizations to struggle to explain the differences between them. Historically, the differences are more obvious. On the one hand, VICS was founded in the mid-1980s by a group of general merchandise retailers and suppliers, including the world's largest retailer, Wal-Mart. This group pioneered the development of inter-industry communications standards, such as bar codes, shipping container marking, and electronic data interchange (EDI), that are specific to the apparel portion of the general merchandise industry. This effort was named Quick Response.

ECR, on the other hand, was founded in the mid-1990s by the supermarket industry. Member stores were worried that they would not be able to compete with general merchandise companies, such as Wal-Mart, Target, and Kmart, as they launched supermarkets within the superstore format. These general merchandise companies had also successfully automated their warehouses and other supply-side aspects of the business. In response, therefore, the supermarket industry created an organization with consumer product companies that focused on optimizing logistics and product flow. It also developed innovative supply chain processes, including activity based costing (ABC) and scan-based trading.

At present, both industries are creating inefficiencies in standards and process development by not working together in a formal capacity. In addition, with recent consolidations in the retail industry, it is more than likely that neither organization will have enough participants or volunteers to meet its current goals domestically or globally. This same period has also seen increasing numbers of similar supply chain initiatives competing for resources available to ECR and VICS members.

Moreover, with the advent of the Internet as a platform for inter-industry commerce, it is possible that many current practices will quickly become outdated. New commerce opportunities such as Internet trading exchanges, built around industry hubs like UCCnet, will enable individual retailers to build either online trading communities or cooperative trading communities with like-minded retail partners. Although this evolution will occur during the next decade, these communities will decide who will have the best relationships with suppliers, the most cost-efficient trading practices, and, ultimately, products for the consumer.

In response to the potential of Internet trading communities and other new technology-driven commerce practices, *Supply Chain Alert* editors successfully encouraged VICS and ECR to contemplate more than an informal sharing of expertise and knowledge. The general merchandise and supermarket industries have now eliminated redundancy, or better still, by evolving into a common group they have established a specific mode of communication between business-to-business retail supply chain partners.

3.1.4   CPFR Optimization Requires Order Forecasts

CPFR relationships without order forecasts do not remove uncertainty from time-phased supply chain management for suppliers. The Collaborative Planning, Forecasting and Replenishment process model includes a single shared forecast of consumer demand at the point of sale. This forecast is the basis for the integration of trading partner supply chain processes. Such a sales forecast alone will enable improved coordination of value-chain process activities.

However, this is not enough to reduce significant constraints on supply chain effectiveness and efficiency. Shared demand forecasts alone will not optimize manufacturing flexibility or enable a make-to-order manufacturing process. Neither will they enable dynamic inter-enterprise scheduling to streamline asset utilization throughout the product flow from manufacturing through transportation and on to distribution centers. Therefore, order forecasts are necessary to extend the value of the CPFR process model through delivery execution. However, certain process barriers exist which make it more difficult to provide order forecasts than to provide shared demand forecasts.

One such barrier is the time horizon. Over time, the unit difference between demand forecasts of consumer demand at the point of sale and order forecasts diminishes. The long-term difference consists mainly of inventory required to fill store shelves and displays, as well as product shortage. The accuracy of demand forecasts improves when considered long term — it follows the law of big numbers. Conversely, the accuracy of order forecasts improves with its temporal proximity to actual delivery. A delivery forecast for tomorrow will be more accurate than one for next month. Manufacturing flexibility and the streamlined flow of product throughout the supply chain require closer monitoring to optimize scheduling of equipment and people.

The barrier for retailers in providing order forecasts to trading partners, after they have collaborated on shared demand, is that the temporal requirements for accuracy in demand and order forecasts are binary opposites. If the order forecast process is based on the same timeframe as that used for demand forecasting, the order forecast will be unusable and inaccurate as well.

Another barrier is the process workflow in transportation management between trading partners. The industry practice of using retailer routing guides for directing suppliers to ship via collect freight creates friction in the flow of product from supplier to retailer. This is a barrier to consistent and accurate order forecasting.

In 1995, AutoZone and J.B. Hunt Logistics designed and implemented a new supply chain infrastructure that converted 77 percent of supplier inbound product from prepaid to collect freight. This change in the process workflow of inbound transportation reduced the transit time from seven days to less than two days and created a high degree of control, accuracy, and visibility in AutoZone's pipeline.

In 1997, Best Buy Co., Inc. and Sharp Electronics initiated a similar collaborative transportation management (CTM) partnership that was integrated with CPFR in 1998. That initiative enabled the trading partners to reduce the sales forecast time frame from a rolling six months to a rolling 13 weeks. Additionally, order and shipment forecasting accuracy improved, so that orders were able to be frozen eight weeks in advance of delivery.

In order to provide usable order forecasts, retailers should use their shortest-term, netted order forecasts available as a starting point. This can begin at the time an order is transmitted from the retailer's purchase order management system to the supplier. A review of the accuracy, metrics, and synchronization of orders with the supplier will identify inconsistencies and errors that cause friction and limit the effectiveness of any order forecast. From this starting point, an extension of the order forecast time horizon will raise issues such as promotion inventory build-ups, new store openings, and seasonal inventory shifts. Selecting exception criteria values, researching exceptions, and analyzing exceptions collaboratively through the use of electronic messaging, phone or videoconferencing, or face-to-face meetings will enable resolution of order forecast inaccuracy.

In some cases, logistics requirements such as trailer loads, minimum order requirements, and case packs can be solved by leveraging the systems and process knowledge of supplier trading partners. This iterative process is no different from that of developing a shared demand forecast. It simply originates from an different time frame. The lessons learned in developing short-term order forecasts will enable reasonable accuracy in the long-term order forecasts used for production and capacity planning by suppliers.

If collaborative order forecasting is not part of a CPFR trading partner relationship, the shared risk that is at the heart of an effective CPFR relationship does not exist. It also limits the ability of suppliers to engage in dynamic inter-enterprise scheduling, or a make-to-order manufacturing process. By removing order forecasting from the CPFR process, retailers force suppliers to minimize uncertainty in order fulfillment by maintaining excess safety stocks in trade.

3.1.5   Collaborative Efforts Drive B2B Exchanges

The future success of B2B supply Web exchanges (SWE's) requires collaborative development.

B2B exchanges enable trading partners to interact in a multi-user environment using standard transactions. The long-term viability of an exchange is dependent on developing and maintaining an attractive assortment of participating firms that will satisfy the commercial needs of buyers and sellers. Many and varied related buyers and sellers enable industry segments to find common solutions to vertical issues, as well as to integrate horizontal applications with their transactions. This, in turn, fuels an iterative workflow process development cycle that will result in a new level of supply Web efficiency.

In the B2B community, buyers and sellers are targeting fewer and more defined segments of trading partners, with customer accounts ranging in the thousands. For example, the affiliated B2B trading exchange being created by the Big Three automotive manufacturers–General Motors, Daimler/Chrysler, and Ford–will comprise a trading community numbering over 10,000 firms, whereas traditional B2C automotive exchanges target more than several hundred million consumers. As e-commerce is extended up the supply chain, there is generally a consolidation of both the number of trading partners involved and the value of the relationships.

Purchasing decisions in B2B exchanges are generally based on strategic factors, with purchase costs being just one of several elements in the value equation. Trust, quality, reliability, product specifications, warranties, capacity, delivery, flexibility, and availability generally outweigh pure price considerations in SWE trading partner decision-making. The nature of SWE relationships is essentially on a variable sum basis, as trading partners collaboratively improve the efficiency, speed, and quality of their business decisions and transactions.

Moreover, both buyer and seller make an investment in each other when they decide to conduct business. This can range from the time and expense of configuring Web catalogues to incorporating the seller's product specifications and characteristics into the buyer's internal systems and processes. In a B2B environment, changing trading partners can be costly to both sides.

In addition, collaborative B2B communities provide valuable information that was formerly unavailable in traditional supply chain relationships focusing on specific segments within the demand chain. The information exchanged is generally valuable in reengineering business processes or enhancing products and services. Collaborative transactions are integrated into transaction systems of each trading partner, enabling internal efficiencies that a one-sided relationship cannot offer. These Internet trading exchanges enable the existence of many-to-many collaborative relationships using the same standards, communication links, systems, and metrics.

For these reasons, B2B exchanges supply value for members, not only by enabling greater efficiency in processing and managing transactions, but also by providing stability and growth in the availability of relevant buyers and sellers. The presence of targeted customers, and even direct competitors, will prove to be the main initial attraction for joining a specific trading exchange.

The future development of SWE communities will be driven by the nature of the transactions supported. The initial development of trading exchanges focused on spot purchases such as maintenance, repair, and operating services, as well as shared services and commodities. Services included the provision of online vendor product catalogue aggregation, procurement, bidder qualification, and financial transactions.

Internet trading exchanges are now expanding upon this initial functionality to include horizontal processes such as group buys, requests for quotation, delivery, design/build contracts, multiple vendor sourcing, and financing. Future horizontal development will focus on adding replenishment, promotion planning, new product introduction, demand forecasting, and load management to develop full trading life-cycle process support.

In addition, SWE's can add value horizontally by providing best-of-breed systems support for their members in an application service provider role. Independent B2B exchanges can use superior best-of-breed functionality to compete for members with affiliated supply Web exchanges. However, horizontal feature value will not be enough to retain members and optimize community value.

It is therefore necessary to provide non-transferable value for targeted member segments through vertical applications and functionality. Vertical features developed through community management will create benefits that are unique to the industries served by an exchange, foster member loyalty, and attract additional generated content and outreach efforts.

Vertical applications and functionality are the means by which an SWE provides non-transferable value for its targeted member segments. By adding vertical value to an SWE, the cost of moving to another trading venue is greatly increased, as the functionality is not directly transferable due to proprietary development and the smaller market for vertical applications.

Internet trading exchanges promise users significant long-term benefits. For example, they allow users to operate in a multi-user environment to exchange critical buying and selling information, as well as the ability to bid for different supplier contracts. The advantages of these exchanges are dependent, however, on establishing a wide assortment of participating firms that will satisfy the needs of all users. Although the existence of targeted users, and their competitors, will provide a significant short-term attraction for joining an Internet trading exchange, future growth of specific communities will only come from the nature of transactions supported.

3.1.6 Case Study: Wal-Mart Initiates CPFR With Sara Lee

The $118 billion retailer and $20 billion manufacturer developed collaborative sales forecasting processes.

To improve the performance of product lines between their companies, Wal-Mart Stores, Inc. and Sara-Lee, Inc. recently implemented two of the nine Collaborative, Planning, Forecasting, and Replenishment (CPFR) steps.

This collaborative effort builds on a successful long-term replenishment relationship, the improvement of which required an end-to-end process that leveraged the capabilities of all firms. In addition, the process required an industry model adaptable in a standard, yet flexible mode by the majority of each company's trading partners without requiring complex technology.

Wal-Mart and Sara Lee therefore decided to focus initially on developing a set of standard, baseline processes, and readily available technology enablers for the new collaborative sales forecasting process. Both retailer and manufacturer have taken steps to validate the CPFR industry model as the basis for further expansion of a collaborative standard within other supply chain relationships.

The retailer and manufacturer implemented the forecast collaboration process as follows:

▶ **Q1 1998.** As part of the CPFR pilot, Wal-Mart and Sara Lee focused on two of nine steps of the VICS CPFR business model. These involved creating a sales forecast and resolving and collaborating on exception items. At this time, the firms defined the pilot's scope, requirements, design, and metrics. Items selected for the pilot included 23 Hanes men's underwear styles from Sara Lee's extensive product mix. The metrics defined to measure success consisted of forecasted weeks on hand, store service level, and forecast accuracy.

▶ **Q2 1998.** Initial transmission of information began via a Web-based collaboration site, using secure email from Wal-Mart to Sara Lee. The format used for sending forecasts and revisions incorporated the EDI 830 transaction set. On a per-item basis, the supplier validated the forecast, using a pre-established special event calendar, as well as its product knowledge, marketing programs, and promotional input from the sales and marketing department. During this period, the firms mutually calibrated the lift effects of causal factors on retail sales, such as price reduction. In addition, exception criteria, such as store in-stock service levels and sales trends, were further refined.

▶ **Q3 1998.** Both companies automated the collaborative process of identifying and reconciling exceptions to the shared forecast. They also developed a weekly exception-analysis reporting format that enabled further refinement of defined item tolerances.

▶ **Q4 1998.** Wal-Mart and Sara Lee calculated initial pilot results through the first 41 weeks. This included a GMROI increase, as well as a sales increase with a comp store lift. In addition, inventory turnover improved, retail inventory weeks-on-hand dropped, and product market share rose. With these initial results, the companies discerned an increase in productivity derived from increased value to the consumer as the inventory level grew. Moreover, while the established continuous replenishment partnership eliminated excess inventory from the pipeline, the CPFR partnership developed an improved ability to deliver customer value on the selling floor.

▶ **Q1 1999.** The companies rolled out formal collaborative processes to include other Sara Lee branded apparel products and divisions within Wal-Mart.

The new venture has clarified an understanding of consumer demand, including how to stimulate and forecast demand, as well as how to leverage individual company expertise. Sara Lee, for example, has gained a deeper understanding of forecasting dynamics for store mix within distribution center service clusters. In addition, the consistency and credibility of a single shared forecast has enabled Wal-Mart to drive the forecast deeper into its internal demand requirements planning processes.

3.1.7 Case Study: Schering-Plough Reinforces Collaborative Trading Practices

Consumer products division of $9.8 billion Schering-Plough Health Care establishes CPFR relationships with retail trading partners.

According to the New Jersey-based health care products firm, its consumer products division has established a collaborative planning, forecasting and replenishment relationship with key retailers, including Walgreens, Kmart, and Target. In 1999 the company had enhanced retail replenishment processes with drugstore-chain The Eckerd Corporation. Since then, the firm has continued its effort to establish a consumer-based, bottom-up forecasting data program that gathers, models, and organizes data from both the company and its trading partners, to establish a single, shared source of information.

Previously, Schering-Plough's relationships with retail clients had resulted in certain logistical problems due to lack of shared product visibility. This included short and late product shipments, sub-optimal product forecasting, and a lack of consumer buying-pattern research. At the same time, several unknown demand variables, such as new stores, retailer promotions, retailer stock status, and item transformation/assortment changes put additional pressure on Schering-Plough.

To further enable collaborative promotion and execution among its trading partners, the manufacturer has begun to align data from retail clients into a single data source, thus allowing collaborative promotional planning and execution from one location. In addition, it has also begun to simplify supply chain management by improving in-stock positions and service levels, and optimizing replenishment strategies with joint ownership.

Beginning with a decision in 1997 to establish a customer-centric forecasting program, Schering-Plough has taken the following steps to improve its data-sharing relationship with customers.

▶ **Q4 1998.** With the help of the E3 Corporation (now JDA Software) E3TRIM software suite, Schering-Plough executed a majority of its retail replenishment processes with Eckerd. The company reported several benefits from the project, including a 52 percent reduction in overstocks, a 33 percent drop in inventory, and a 24 percent decrease in returns.

▶ **Q3 1999.** Based on its success with the Eckerd project, Schering-Plough met with Illinois-based Walgreens Corporation to address the inadequate amount of sales data exchange between the two companies. The supplier and retailer agreed to work together to improve forecasting and other sales data in a single, collaborative format.

▶ **Q1 2000.** Schering-Plough and Walgreens employed a collaborative software suite from Syncra Systems to engage in a CPFR pilot. The two companies began with a list of selected SKU's for forecasting data exchange. Walgreens sent inventory information to Schering-Plough for review on a weekly basis, and promotional and sales information was added.

▶ **Q2 2000.** Following the nine steps of the CPFR model, Schering-Plough and Walgreens increased the amount of SKU's involved in the project. Demand information, stock locations, and promotional and sales information were also included.
At the same time, Schering-Plough approached Kmart about a similar situation regarding inaccurate and inadequate promotional information exchanged between the two companies. After several meetings, they decided to initiate a CPFR pilot with the help of the Syncra Systems solution. A pilot was initiated using a select number of SKU's.

▶ **Q3 2000.** After a brief realignment of staff involved in the CPFR project, Schering-Plough and Kmart increased the number of participating SKUs. Also included in this process were demand information, stock locations, and promotional and sales information.

▶ **Q4 2000.** Following the success of the Walgreens and K-mart CPFR efforts, Schering-Plough met with the Target Corporation and established preliminary plans to initiate a CPFR pilot involving select SKUs.

Although Schering-Plough has yet to formulate quantitative results from the CPFR relationships, it has noted several qualitative benefits. In addition to a rapid implementation time, reliable production forecasting for manufacturing operations has been identified, as well as an improved order and item fill rate.

This, in turn, has helped the manufacturer identify and eradicate significant inconsistencies.

For Schering-Plough partners, high in-stock positions have resulted in increased sales, and customer demand and promotional forecasting fluctuations are now appropriately addressed by all parties involved in the transaction.

3.2 Consumer Centric CPFR

Lawrence E. Fennell, Wal-Mart Stores

3.2.1 Current Retail Environment and Looking Forward Five Years

Before discussing the strategic necessity of moving to the platform of CPFR I believe it important to manifest the current state of retail that exists on the global stage. There are events taking place that are and will continue to have profound impact on retailers and suppliers. One thing will be certain over the next five years; it will be more difficult to meet the expectations of shareholders and consumers in the global retail marketplace. What are the events and issues that will be driving these challenges? Here are some of the known facts:

Fact 1: The Pie is not going to get bigger
For the last several years, "one company's gain has been another one's loss". This can certainly be seen in the head to head battles between Wal-Mart and K-mart, Kohl's and Penny's, Best Buy and Sears or Service Merchandise, Walgreen's and Rite-Aide. The growth retailers in the industry have made public their store opening schedules for the New Year. The numbers seem to defy the current economic slowdown unless you measure them against the impact they will have on respective competitors. Please see exhibit below for the planning on new stores of major American retailers.

Retailer	Number of new stores in 2002 (planned)
Autozone	100
Bed Bath & Beyond	88
Best Buy	155
Costco	35
Dollar Tree	250
Home Depot	200
Kohl's	70
Lowe's	123
Staples	100
Target	100
Wal-Mart	430
Walgreens	475

Exhibit 3.1 Number Of New Stores Of Major American Retailers.
Source: DSN Retailing Today issue of January 7, 2002

These aggressive store opening plans of the growth companies will be offset by the consolidation and liquidation of those retailers not prepared to compete in the competitive global retail environment.

Fact 2: Prices are going down, not up

Any holiday shopper this season could verify that there were many opportunities to buy his DVD player and movie disc from a variety of retailers, including online at prices far below last year's. Not only were the prices lower, the supply was plentiful for those aggressive retailers who went after the business. From TV's to VCR's, from power tools to bath towels, from coffee makers to microwave ovens, the prices have been coming down and will continue to do so. With China joining the WTO and import quotas being dismenteled, the capacity for production will increase. This will be most noticeable in the textile industry; at the same time, advances in technologies will advance the deflation on pricing of hard goods

Fact 3: Margins are going down, not up

The Kroger Co., the largest food retailer in the U.S. market, recently did an about face from its earlier financial briefings when it stated that Wal-mart Supercenters were not affecting their top line growth. To quote an article by Scott Meyer in *MMR Mass Market Retailers*, dated December 17, 2001, he reports; "Kroger Co., most frustrated by its lack of topline gains, has reacted with plans to consolidate its operation and cut 1500 jobs. The cost reductions are intended to allow Kroger to cut prices as a way of driving sales. Albertson's Inc. and Safeway Inc. have also announced that boosting sales is a priority, and they are expected to make do with lower margins as a result. Analysts suggest that Kroger's move will spark further price cutting in response." As more traditional non-food retailers move to capture the customer in the mass food industry, prices and margin will fall; you can plan on that.

Fact 4: Operations costs are going up, not down

When you have a full time cashier at the front register who scans a TV or DVD player that sells for ten to fifteen percent less than it did three to six months ago, your productivity cost was negatively impacted for that transaction. High employee turnover and the rising cost of health care are increasing expense structures to retailers nationwide. Increases recently experienced in public utility costs, environmental impact costs for new construction, increases in transportation and warehouse storage costs, will continue to affect operating expenses and profit. Oftentimes the drive and passion to lower expense structures has been substituted for a weak effort to maintain current expense ratios.

Fact 5: Demographics and the collapsing birth rate

In most companies, it is standard practice to make exhaustive demographic studies before the approval process for retail site selection. This is an essential practice and very positive for early sales results if combined with the efforts of the marketing, merchandising and operational functions. The problem faced by many retailers is that they fail to keep abreast of constantly changing demographics. In his book *Management Challenges for the 21st Century* Peter Drucker states on page forty-four the following: "the most important single new certainty-if only because there is no precedent for it in all of history – is the *collapsing birthrate in the developed world*. In Western and Central Europe and in Japan, the birthrate has already dropped well below the rate needed to reproduce the population." He further declares on the same page, "In Japan and in Southern Europe, population is already peaking as it is in Germany. In the United States it will still grow for another twenty to twenty-five years, though the entire growth after the year 2015 will be in people fifty-five years and older." In conclusion on page fifty he observes, "The birthrate collapse has tremendous political and social implications that we cannot even guess at today. But it surely will also have tremendous economic and business implications-and some of those can already be explored, some of them can already be tested. Above all, any strategy, that is, any commitment of present resources to future expectations-and this, to repeat, is what a strategy means-has to start out with demographics and, above all, with the collapsing birthrate in the developed world. Of all developments, it is the most spectacular, the most unexpected and one that has no precedent whatsoever."

Fact 6: High/Low, or Everyday Low Price?

In an effort to increase sales against the likes of Wal-Mart/Sam's or Costco, many marketing/merchandising thinktank committees are grappling with whether or not they should, or should not, move into the everyday low price arena. There are examples of companies who continued to sit on the fence, or who have dived into everyday low price strategy, only to see their market share and customer loyalty plummet. Certainly K-mart is a current casualty of moving into the minefield of everyday low price with eyes blindfolded and having it blow up in their face. In the recent industry publication of *FORUM* of the GMA (Grocery Manufactures of America) a very alarming article by Gary E. Singer, Associate Partner, Accenture continues to raise serious questions regarding industry-wide trade promotions. The article is titled, "*The Daunting Dilemma, Redux*". It begins with a look back and states, "Four years ago Accenture (then known as Andersen Consulting) released *The Daunting Dilemma of Trade Promotions,* a comprehensive consumer packaged goods (CPG) industry study on trade promotion. In the study, we concluded that CPG manufacturers are seriously undercutting shareholder value through poor trade promotions practices."

In updating the industry the new analysis are stated as follows, "The top line statistics were – and still are – staggering. CPG manufactures spend $25 billion per year to generate incremental revenues of only $2to $4 billion."

To again quote from this article, "The dilemma is that the *concept* of trade promotion can make economic sense. *Theoretically,* manufacturers can increase short-term volume, and hence profit, by offering their trading partners financial incentives to enhance product presentation to consumers. However, the failure to realize the potential benefits of trade promotions is hardly a secret. According to AC Nielsen's 2000 survey, 98 per-cent of manufacturers and 95 percent of retailers ranked promotion efficiency/effectiveness as a critical issue." The debate on this topic will continue to be intense.

Fact 7: It's not win-win, it's I win, you lose
In the very competitive retail arena, many retailers turn to their suppliers to give financial support to offset the losses they are trying to divert from their Income Statement. These offerings come under many guises, but they do not and will not promote a healthy relationship between supplier and retailer. Furthermore, the consumer loses in the long run. In a very candid and frank editorial by a long-term industry advocate, David Pinto states in *Mass Market Retailer*, of Nov.12th, 2001, the following: "The breakdown in retailer-supplier relations has taken the fun, creativity and excitement out of both retailing and consumer goods marketing. It has retailers increasingly turning to the supplier community, rather than the consumer, to keep them viable. It's forced suppliers to focus more on funding the retailer's efforts and less on turning out innovative new products, products which, in any event, may never gain the support at retail to see the light of a retailer's shelf". These are very strong words for someone who has been so closely connected with this business for so many years. His concerns should be taken very seriously.

Fact 8: We are still demand forecasting using the rearview mirror
Those of us in the merchandise demand forecasting business remain concerned over the lack of understanding and adoption of new technologies that can add great benefit to forecasting merchandise trends and improve the demand planning process. There are investment market research firms employing the companies like *Planalytics* to gauge the sales potential of key elements of the retail sector based on forecasted weather patterns for an upcoming season. These predictions are being validated with a high level of success. However, the retail community has embraced this new technology slowly. Where it is being employed, too seldom is there any thought of working it back against unit plans or allocation of product based on regional weather deviation from the previous years' record.

In an article "Your Crystal Ball" by Robert L. Mitchell in the December 17th, 2001, issue of *Computerworld*, he observes: "Although the technology has been around for several years, many suppliers still don't use it. Market leader i2 Technologies Inc. (www.i2.com) in Dallas says that in 50% of new installations, no automated demand planning system is in place". The article goes on, "Microsoft [Excel] is the most widely deployed demand planning tool in the world," so Karen Peterson, an analyst at Stamford, CT based Gartner Inc. http://www.gartner.com "but it lacks sophisticated forecasting algorithms, can't track multiple inputs, and can't slice and dice the data for different audiences."

It certainly will be difficult for capital expenditure planning committees who have experienced slow growth these last five years to divert dwindling resources for infrastructure development versus the pressure to build, buy or expand current top line operations. To continue non-funding of infrastructure development is just "building a house on a sandbar on the Platte River in Nebraska", it will soon come crumbling down when the river shifts.

This concludes my review of the current and future state of the retail environment. Certainly there are other issues that are current. Those listed in this paper appear to be grabbing the most headlines as slow growth and non-growth companies try to exhibit out to compete and survive in the current and future environment.

3.2.2   It's Time to Crack the Books

The history books will record that the years of 1992 through mid 2000 will be noted as the greatest economic expansion in history. It certainly has been for the largest economic engine of this expansion, the United States. It is very important to understand the significance of this expansion for those companies who failed to participate. A must-read for the board members and all officers of a non-growth retailer/supplier during this unprecedented economic expansion is: "Good to Great: Why Some Companies Make the Leap... And Others Don't", by Jim Collins. In the book he goes into great detail the Greek parable to illustrate "The fox knows many things, the hedgehog knows one big thing". "The essential strategic difference between the good-to-great and comparison companies lay in the two fundamental distinctions," he writes. He develops his theory through research on eleven very successful companies, such as Walgreen's. The two fundamental distinctions are:

▶ "First, the good-to-great companies founded their strategies on a deep understanding of three key dimensions.

  ▶ What do they do best in the world
  ▶ What drives their economic engine
  ▶ What they are deeply passionate about"

▶ "Second, the good-to great companies translate that understanding into a simple, crystalline concept that guides all of their efforts."

In the early 1990's the company with which I spent nearly twenty-four years (Wal-Mart Stores, Inc.) went through a period of lackluster financial performance and execution, culminating in the first down quarter in company history. At a critical time during these very stressful days, David Glass, then CEO, asked a very insightful question at a management meeting where all division heads and corporate officers were present. His question was "What are the ten things Wal-Mart Stores, Inc. stands for?" We were all encouraged to write our responses down along with those who reported to us out of the home office and to forward them to his office. When the several thousand replies came back, the responses showed that eighty percent of respondents had the same eight out of ten points on their list. After a review of the responses, the point was then made by David that, while he had confidence we understood the message and the concept of Wal-Mart, we were failing to execute them.

In what now seems like a few short months since that exercise, a top leadership change was made and two key executives, Lee Scott (now current CEO of Wal-Mart Stores. Inc) and Tom Coughlin (now current CEO of Wal-Mart Stores and Supercenters) were put in charge. *They focused on execution.* To validate what Jim Collins was saying, "crystalline concept that guides all their efforts" was clearly demonstrated in the shareholders meeting in June of 1997. One must understand that a Wal-Mart shareholder meeting is like no other in the corporate world. Fifteen thousand associates from all over the world are brought in for what some characterize as a "revival" that starts at 7:00am and goes to about 11:30am. It was a very special moment, a moment like a Garth Brooks concert when the audience takes over and sings his song. Tom Coughlin started to cover the five operational execution points, which had been presented to store management teams at a year beginning meeting in January. As he started to cover the first objective, the fifteen thousand associates, without props or visuals, shouted out in unison the five points in proper order. Tom was somewhat speechless as he tried to convince investment bankers, the media and shareholders in attendance that this was a spontaneous event. He wanted to make clear that this demonstrated the passion and commitment throughout the entire organization to execute the direction that would gain market share and customer loyalty. Certainly, the financial performance over the next five years would give testimony to that event and the clarity of that direction.

Before I move into the third phase of this article, I think it critically important to make sure that all persons involved with the enterprise of selling to the consumer understand the concept of the "Hedgehog or the Fox". Without clarity, passion and determination, it will be very difficult to institute the objectives and strategies of CPFR.

3.2.3 Defining CPFR

Over the last several months, the definition of CPFR has undergone several revisions. My latest, and the one I feel represents it best, is, *"A business strategy between trading partners to collaborate on a single shared vision of forecasted consumer demand at POS (point of sale) level."* Let's take this definition apart for further analysis:

▶ "Business strategy": Because it is a strategy, it is measurable against performance and expectation standards.

▶ "Between trading Partners": The metrics for performance are agreed upon by those involved, not made in isolation and dictated terms.

▶ "To collaborate": The heart of CPFR is to share critical information in real time so all parties can see and have access to decision making responses.

- ▶ "Single shared vision": The measurements that will be applied to judge success must have the same basis. They cannot, for example, be independently derived forecasts from the buyer, sales/marketing, and replenishment teams. This measurement, the forecast, is a look into future events.

- ▶ "Forecasted consumer demand": Based on seasonal profiles in the automated replenishment system and events that stimulate consumer demand, the effort is to collaborate on the anticipated outcome and then measure the effects on actual demand.

- ▶ "At the POS level": The focus is the consumer, not the distributor/warehouse or sales people, not some static spread sheet-predicted outcome. It's the consumer response validated by actual POS sales and then everything rolled up starting from that point of contact.

What it is not, and what is it:

- ▶ **It is not about technology.** It is about a business strategy to collaborate on planning, forecasting, and replenishment so as to stimulate consumer demand and meet or exceed agreed upon, mutually owned business objectives.

- ▶ **It is not a paradigm shift.** It is an evolving, cultural change within each organization based on trust and open dialogue developed over time.

- ▶ **It is not about a new process or adding staff.** It is about re-analyzing current strategies and then repositioning the structure to match the strategy.

- ▶ **It is not about quarterly summit meetings, power point presentations, e-mail or video conferencing.** It is about Internet–based, real time communication, visibility, and feedback to all parties who can recommend changes.

- ▶ **It is not about multiple forecasts (buyer, POS/warehouse replenishment, sales marketing and production).** It is about a single shared, agreed upon forecast that will automatically update and advance itself on a timely, forward-looking schedule.

- ▶ **It is not about a strategy with a broad brush approach, or "rising tide lifts all boats" mentality.** It is about drill downs to discover the exceptions that are not meeting expectations and them collaborate to initiate a corrective course of action.

- ▶ **It is not about a targeted, specific outcome.** It is about interjecting strategies into a dynamic automated replenishment program at lower levels of settings that roll-up to the top line demand forecast.

- ▶ **It is not about a new "can do all" software package.** It is about enhancing and upgrading current planning, forecasting and replenishment systems with dedicated resources. In other words, "dance with the partner who brought you to the dance".

- ▶ **It is not a retailer to primary supplier collaboration.** It starts with the consumer at the POS level, and then flows out to collaborative alliances made up of retailer, supplier, raw material producer, packaging and transportation providers.

3.2.4 How do you get started?

How do you get started, or maybe you have already started?

- ▶ Have you have been involved in supply chain activities and strategies such as?

  - ▶ Just in time
  - ▶ VMI(Vendor managed inventory) at store or warehouse level
  - ▶ DSD (direct store delivery)
  - ▶ Co-management at warehouse level
  - ▶ Internet third party provider

  If the answer is yes, then you have already started.

- ▶ If your have scheduled warehouse, point of sale and seasonal forecast update meeting with your key trading partners, then you have already started.

- ▶ If the business theory (culture) of your company is to engage in a win-win environment with your trading partners, then you have already started.

- If your company looks like and resembles the "hedgehog", then you have already started. If your are more like the "fox", then you might have some work to do in defining yourself.

What are the Obstacles?

Consumer Centric CPFR is moving away from the command and control atmosphere prevalent in most retailer/supplier relationships where the retailer directs the response desired. The Co-managed warehouse inventory program at Wal-Mart is a great testimony to the move away from command and control. It was designed to build relationships of high expectations and execution through Internet-based real time information. The Co-manage program started in 1996 with four charter suppliers. It was built around some very basic, common sense understandings.

- Wal-Mart, through its Information System core structure, had and still has a very highly regarded warehouse replenishment system.

- The suppliers know more about their individual items stocked in the warehouses than the Wal-Mart replenishment managers that were reordering the merchandise for the warehouse.

- If we could arrange to give access to our systems via Internet (Retail Link), wouldn't the suppliers dedicated teams be better at ordering the merchandise, if they accommodated the guidelines and expectations they agreed upon when they entered the program?

The answer to this question has been a huge B2B success for all parties involved. It has demonstrated a move away from command and control, and towards trust building and knowledge sharing between the trading partners. It is also the platform that will move Wal-Mart and its key suppliers to the new Consumer Centric CPFR platform.

- Another obstacle is the "silo mentality" between divisions of a multi division corporation. One separate division of a supplier may enter into a CPFR look-a-like endeavor with a single buying division at a multi-division retailer, only to have its efforts stifled by a bureaucracies on both sides not involved in the collaborative effort. In the book, *Sam Walton. Made in America*, there is a great case study starting on Wal-Mart and Procter & Gamble, describing how these two companies set out to break down the obstacles between them so as to give greater service and value to the customer.

▶ Waiting for the "One size fits all" software solution, instead of improvising and enhancing what already exists. You then surround this effort with a well-trained, dedicated and motivated team.

▶ Must remove the inherent resistance to abandon in an organized manner the policies and procedures, reports and traditions that do not add value and support the strategic direction.

3.2.5 Where do you go from here?

▶ Start with a pilot project. Pull a team together from both retailer and supplier. Go over the big picture, and then line up strategies, objectives and metrics. Make sure all parties understand their responsibility to collaborate and share real time information.

▶ Set up a cross-functional steering team on both sides. Encourage openness on how these changes will affect multiple layers of participants.

▶ Listen to the users. Upgrade, reconfigure, prioritize enhancements, but keep moving forward, do not let it stall.

▶ Seek out, document and publish success stories. Make heroes out of those who show dedication and results in spite of the obstacles.

▶ Do not become fixated on monitoring and correcting a single issue. Remember, it is about in-stock, over-stock, out of stocks, planning, collaboration, flow of merchandise, replenishment and forecast accuracy.

▶ When you have recorded and validated a win-win scenario, share your results in an executive review presentation. Gather support, listen for instructive feedback and seek their leadership to promote the continued implementation of CPFR.

In conclusion, please allow me to quote once more from Peter Drucker's book, (page 122), *Management Challenges for the 21st Century.* "Inside an organization there are only cost centers. The only profit center is a customer whose check has not bounced".

3.3 CPFR – Views and Experiences at Safeway

Christopher A. Brady, Safeway

3.3.1 CPFR is about Communication

At Safeway, CPFR means Communication. CPFR is a process - it is not a software application. It is not a cure-all for a company's supply chain difficulties. Basically, it is better communication between two parties (in this case a supplier and a retailer). There have been many published reports stating the "CPFR Value Proposition." Analysts have thrown out savings estimates that are in the billions of dollars annually. In the end, it may just be a better way of doing business. Any time you make the supply chain more efficient, hence lowering the cost of delivering goods to your customers, you have added value to the enterprise.

With Safeway's size and the number of suppliers from whom we purchase product, the use of a process that improves order and/or sales forecasts could be effective in reducing costs. The impact could be seen not only on our "supplier to customer" supply chain costs, but our "manufacturing plant to customer" supply chain costs as well (Safeway operates 41 manufacturing and processing facilities in North America). Safeway has been sharing information with its suppliers and plants for quite sometime. Most of the time however, this transfer has been unilateral. Safeway provided information about future promotions but there was no collaboration as to the forecast quantities.

3.3.2 The Application of CPFR at Safeway

First attempts at CPFR involved trading spreadsheets detailing planned promotions with selected suppliers. The scope of these pilots was not large and the amount of data shared was limited. Recent collaborations have involved sharing additional data as well as increasing scope. The information is sent to a private exchange where the CPFR application is hosted. It is then accessed via a website by both our supplier(s) and us.

CPFR can be used to eliminate one of the biggest costs in the supply chain: the cost of last minute changes. In a competitive environment, changes are made at the last minute that can cause increased costs to both retailer and supplier. For the supplier, these changes cause problems as they have to shift product from other customers; make last minute changes to their production schedules (creating overtime and increased costs for procuring raw materials) or just the reverse, having to sit on significant amounts of inventory because of a canceled promotion. For the retailer, a last minute change could result in a higher procurement cost or increased carrying cost for product already on hand.

Of course the retailer is where the "rubber meets the road." This is where the ultimate goal occurs: the sale. In order to manage this, the retailer does not want constraints placed on him that will impact his ability to manage the business. If he decides to cancel a promotion because a better deal comes along, there should be no restrictions to the execution of the new plan. Some may consider this shortsighted.

Limiting last minute changes is mostly a by-product of business process change. A comprehensive analysis detailing the actual cost to the enterprise would likely result in a process change as costs incurred by suppliers are typically passed right back to retailers in the form of higher costs or limited (or restricted) promotional dollars.

A drawback to the process is the sharing of promotional data. For years, the retail industry has been very competitive. Sharing information such as when and where a product will be promoted, the type of promotion and the price point has been taboo. If this knowledge were shared with a competitor, it would be very easy to essentially negate a promotion. To mitigate these risks, secure transmission and hosting of data is critical. In addition, non-disclosure agreements (NDA) are necessary as well. In order for a CPFR relationship to work, there must be benefits for both the retailer and supplier that can be quantified. This allows management to make a decision to sponsor the project or not. Without executive sponsorship, the collaboration will not be successful.

In most cases, the CPFR relationship will initially be more beneficial to the supplier than the retailer. Once critical mass is reached, the suppliers will be able to realize a reduction in production costs, as they become more efficient in their production planning and raw material and packaging inventory. The retailer may see a benefit coming from increased on-shelf percentage and lower inventory carrying costs, but he would typically not see a lower product cost from the supplier until the supplier has realized a sustained material gain from lowered supply costs.

The biggest benefit is going to come from promotion planning. Obviously, items that are not aggressively promoted have average movement with very little variance. The benefit of better promotion planning comes from having a better in-stock percentage and not having leftover inventory after a promotion. The carrying cost of this inventory could negate some of the gains from the promotion. In addition, the decision could also be made to return the product to the supplier, which is costly as well.

3.3.3 Implementation Issues

Currently, Safeway is conducting its CPFR pilot(s) through a private exchange. It has taken on the responsibility for the technical aspects of the CPFR setup at the exchange and for providing a "road map" for both retailer and supplier to assist in starting and maintaining the collaboration.

Some of the issues we encountered included:

▶ How many IT resources do we want to commit to the CPFR pilot? Since we had no verified financial benefit, we decided on an IT allocation that would be sufficient for the pilot, but that would also build a framework that could be either easily expanded or abandoned in the future. If abandoned, the resulting loss from set up costs would not be significant.

Given these constraints, IT was able to develop a method to extract the necessary data from our proprietary systems and transmit that data to the exchange with little or no manual intervention. This was essential, as we did not want to add any additional labor costs to the model.

▶ Timing issues: Initially, issues arose due to differences in timing. Safeway does its forecasts on a week (Sun. through Sat.) to week basis. In our first pilot, the supplier was using a monthly forecast. The supplier made a process change so that they could provide a weekly forecast as well.

▶ Item maintenance: In the retail grocery business, items are discontinued, re-packaged or newly introduced on a weekly basis. A good CPFR tool must have the functionality to be able to easily maintain items. We ran into issues early on with discontinued items as some of the items on the initial collaboration list were discontinued. Instead of going through the process of having the items removed from the CPFR tool, we made the decision (along with our supplier partner) to just ignore the items and remove them from any post-pilot analysis.

▶ Business process: The CPFR process needs to be minimally invasive to current processes. This is true for both the retailer and the supplier. Within that framework, the data needs to be sent automatically and the supplier partner needs to review and resolve forecast exceptions prior to the retailer reviewing the remaining exceptions.

3.3.4 Suppliers Change their Existing Processes

What Safeway found with some suppliers was that they were not generating a forecast. They would use Safeway's forecast. This limited their liability if the forecast was short. So **creating a forecast was new to some suppliers**. In some cases, the business unit tasked with the CPFR pilot was completely separate from the customer service personnel who had the responsibility for creating orders and in some cases, managing inventory (Vendor Managed Inventory – VMI).

The supplier resolved these issues by making changes to his existing processes. In order for a collaboration to be successful, the supplier needs to change the process from receiving and fulfilling orders to a process of forecasting, collaborating, and filling orders. At times, system performance has varied. The main symptom of this is slow page loading in the Internet tool. The solution for that was to make the route to the desired page as efficient as possible. This was accomplished by using hyperlinks and custom bookmarks provided in the CPFR application.

Investment buys (purchases made because of extremely favorable terms offered by suppliers) will "muddy the water" as far as measuring the benefits of CPFR. Not only is the physical inventory increased, but also the on-shelf percentage is skewed, as there is less of chance of a stockout.

Safeway has seen some benefit in establishing collaborative relationships with suppliers. CPFR is one option for managing these relationships. We will continue to review supply chain costs and look for ways to reduce them or eliminate them altogether. CPFR will play a strategic role in the future but the format has yet to be determined.

4 CPFR in Europe

4.1 CPFR: Ready to take off in Europe

Dr. Dirk Seifert, Harvard Business School

4.1.1 Major Differences between the US and Europe

CPFR was originally developed by VICS and was thereby characterized by the conditions of the American consumer goods market. The **specific characteristics of European industry were not originally considered in the VICS prototype**. The European market is not homogenous, but rather is comparable to a conglomerate of country specific business structures. The independently developed structures and cultural preferences vary considerably in the planning and forecasting process.

One of the essential differences between the US and Europe is a higher degree of promotional activity. In Europe, the planning of promotions stands out in the relationship between manufacturers and retailers. According to industry benchmarks, the average number of promotional activities is about 25 to 150 per year. The high frequency of promotions in Europe demands a regular, detailed coordination of business activities, which must happen in a small space of time. The CPFR prototype only considers this to a limited extent. The European organization **ECR Europe** has set as its goal the adaptation of CPFR to the European market. The above mentioned higher frequency in Europe is considered in the recommendations made by ECR Europe in its detailed description of an additional step called 'Planning of Promotions'. In the nine-step model, this is inserted between steps two and three. The additional step describes the necessary activities, such as the creation of a promotions plan, the identification of exceptions and the cooperative handling of deviations from the plan. Depending on the original situation, coordination can occur monthly, daily, or weekly. For situations with intensive promotional activities, a rolling weekly cycle is recommended.

4.1.2   ECR Europe as a CPFR Pacemaker in Europe

One of the pacemakers in the European implementation and development of ECR and CPFR is ECR Europe. ECR Europe is a joint trade and industry body, launched in 1994 to make the grocery sector as a whole more responsive to consumer demand and promote the removal of unnecessary costs from the supply chain. With its headquarters in Brussels, the organization works in close cooperation with national ECR initiatives in most European countries *(ECR Austria, ECR Belgium, ECR Czech Republic, ECR Denmark, ECR Finland, ECR France, ECR Germany/CCG, ECR Italy, ECR Hellas, ECR Ireland, ECR Italy, ECR Nederland, ECR Spain, ECR Sweden, ECR Switzerland and ECR UK)*. Participation in projects at European and national levels is open to large and small companies in the grocery and fast-moving consumer goods sectors – including retailers, wholesalers, manufacturers, suppliers, brokers and third-party service providers such as logistics operators.

The vision of *ECR Europe* is "Working together to fulfill consumer wishes better, faster and at less cost". The ECR Europe Executive Board has equal representation from retailers and manufacturers from various European nations. The initiative is supported by four industry organizations: *EAN International, Eurocommerce, CIES-The Food Business Forum und AIM-European Brands Association*. Various consulting firms like *Accenture, A.T. Kearney, Roland Berger & Partner, Pricewaterhouse Coopers* et al support the studies of ECR Europe.

ECR Europe supports the use and development of CPFR in the European consumer goods economy with numerous publications and forums. Since 1996 *ECR Europe* has organized an annual ECR conference where retailers and manufacturers present current thinking on best practices on the topics of ECR and CPFR. To date, **ECR-Conferences** have taken place in Geneva (1996), Amsterdam (1997), Hamburg (1998), Paris (1999), Turin (2000), Glasgow (2001) and Barcelona (2002). A further prominent initiative is the ECR Academic Partnership, strengthened by the ECR academic network under the leadership of Daniel Corsten of the University of St. Gallen, Switzerland.

4.1.3 CPFR gets rolling in Europe

Since the beginning of 2001 CPFR has picked up the tempo in its implementation in the European market. A number of companies have initiated collaborations and begun CPFR projects. Other large European companies are about to begin pilot projects. The following list shows selected CPFR projects currently operated or planned in Europe. Next to the respective partners, the relevant e-Marketplace and the software application are noted.

CPFR-Collaboration Partner	Involved B2B-exchanges
Ahold/Procter&Gamble	WWRE
Boots/Johnson&Johnson	Unknown
Carrefour/Henkel	GNX
Carrefour/Kimberley Clark	Unknown
Condis/Henkel/Cartisa	Unknown
Dansk Supermarked/Procter&Gamble	None
Delhaize/Masterfoods	WWRE
Delhaize/Vandermoortele	WWRE
DM-Drogeriemarkt/Henkel	Unknown
dm-Drogeriemarkt/Unilever (planned)	Unknown
Eroski/Henkel	None
Globus/Unilever (planned)	Unknown
KarstadtQuelle	GNX
Londis/Sechszehn Lieferanten	None
Marks & Spencer	WWRE
Marks & Spencer/Gunstones	Unknown
Marks & Spencer/Telfer Foods	Unknown
Metro/Henkel	GNX
Metro/Kimberly-Clark	GNX
Metro/Procter&Gamble	GNX
Metro/SCA	GNX
Sainsbury·s/Johnson&Johnson	GNX
Sainsbury·s/Kimberley Clark	GNX
Sainsbury·s/Kraft Foods	GNX
Sainsbury·s/Unilever	GNX
Sch ler/Europa Carton	None
Superdrug/Johnson&Johnson	Unknown
Systeme U/Lesieur	None
Tesco	WWRE

Exhibit 4.1 Selected CPFR-Projects in Europe.
Source: Accenture, Seifert 2002

Important European retailers like Carrefour in France, Metro in Germany, and Tesco in the UK understood early on the significance of CPFR and are consistently working toward the exploitation of potential improvements in efficiency. The prominent position of retailers in their respective home markets gives encouragement to the hope that the system will take root on a broader basis. The suppliers to these companies will increasingly have to ask themselves: "Will I still be in a position in three to five years to supply my primary trade partner if my business systems are not CPFR compatible?" Many consumer goods manufacturers have already answered this question for themselves and are currently developing, alone or with the help of outside consultants, their own CPFR strategies.

4.2 CPFR in Germany, Austria and Switzerland

Saskia Treeck, Centrale für Coorganisation (CCG)
Michael Seishoff, Centrale für Coorganisation (CCG)

4.2.1 ECR D-A-C-H – the Platform for CPFR in German speaking Countries

Since the mid-nineties ECR initiatives have existed in Germany, Austria and Switzerland. For a long time, the three countries worked independently on ECR recommendations at a national level. A close collaboration between Germany and Austria came into existence in 1997, and the logical extension of that was to expand it to include Switzerland. ECR GERMANY-AUSTRIA-SWITZERLAND was grounded in July 2000 in order to organize ECR projects more efficiently and to obtain synergy effects, particularly in view of the demands of new technologies. This platform uses the long years of experience in dealing with over 100 million consumers. Additionally, the already established ECR network was used for development and realization.

At present, many different international and national initiatives on the further development of CPFR business model are being pursued. There is the Gloobal Commerece Initiative (GCI) working closely with the Voluntary Interindustry Commerce Standards committee and ECR Europe which is coordinating global

CPFR activities. Beyond that, the work of realizing CPFR pilot projects at ECR Europe continues. The inclusion of the requirements of the German-speaking market in the CPFR business model are being realized through the ECR GERMANY-AUSTRIA-SWITZERLAND initiative.

It is important however that all initiatives do not operate independently, but instead that they work in a continual process of coordination in order to secure reciprocal knowledge transfer.

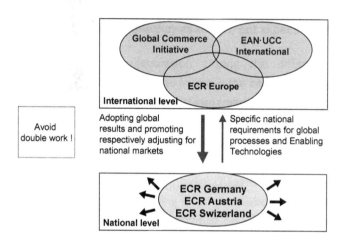

Exhibit 4.2 Collaboration in the global network. Source: Centrale für Coorganisation (2001)

With the CPFR business model as well as the ECR concept, the objective is to fulfill the consumer's wishes efficiently and reliably. The realization of this objective can be achieved through an inter-organizational collaboration on strategies and processes.

In keeping with that, one cannot wonder that economy would like to deal with CPFR at the national or international level.

4.2.2 The Necessity of a CPFR Management Paper in the German-Speaking Market

As a consequence of the differing market conditions a differentiated approach to the implementation of the nine-step CPFR business model is critically needed. The publications on CPFR to date reflect primarily the conditions in North America and Europe. The differences between the US market and the European are considerable, there are also essential differences within Europe with respect to sales strategy and consumer behavior.

While the sales policy in the US is determined by the every-day-low-price (EDLP) policy, in Europe a higher percentage of sales is determined by retailers' and manufacturers' promotions. There are also differences in the execution of promotions in individual European regions. As an example, in Germany promotion activities are very important. The regional and national peculiarities lead to different approaches to corporate strategies through the CPFR business model and thereby a different approach to planning forecasting and replenishment processes, differentiated according to standard or promotional sales. A sufficient consideration of these connections is not a part of the VICS CPFR-Guidelines.

In addition to the high significance of promotional activities, there are further important differences between the North American market, Europe and German-speaking economic markets. The following points speak for a differentiated implementation of the CPFR business model:

▶ **Different standards of living in the industrial nations**: Within Europe, wages and living standards vary greatly, precipitating different degrees of purchasing power.

▶ **Consumer behavior**: While in some European countries consumers have become very quality conscious, in others consumer behavior is dominated by price.

▶ **Business strategies**: Recently, many retailers have promoted in-house brands, leading to independence from established brand name manufacturers and a positive effect in the marketplace. Other companies tried to obtain advantages through negotiations with their trading partners.

▶ **Internal corporate culture of collaboration**: The willingness to collaborate with trade partners depends on the corporate culture inculcated by senior management. In particular, the preparedness to share data and risks is noteworthy.

- ▶ **The extent of ECR implementation**: The acceptance and implementation of ECR in Europe is less than in the North American market. Retailers and manufacturers in North America have understood how to overcome conflict and implement ECR in that they have concentrated on common goals and improved business bilaterally.

- ▶ **Logistical conditions**: Many European companies have entirely different distribution systems compared to the US. Compared to the American market where distribution over long distances is handled through cross-docking, in Europe companies prefer direct delivery to retail outlets, or through a central warehouse. There, cross-docking and VMI are also used. The high number of different replenishment techniques in Europe must be considered in the realization of CPFR.

Despite the individuality of the market, the CPFR concept can be adapted for Europe, and thereby for German-speaking economic regions. The particulars of the market must be accommodated however. It has been clearly recognized that the efficiency enhancing aspects of CPFR in the supply chain will work independently of the distribution models found in North America or Europe. It is clear today that CPFR will support the integration of different ECR solutions and thereby contribute to a higher prevalence in the European market.

4.2.3   ECR Concept – CPFR Business Model

CPFR distinguishes itself through the fact that experience and information gained are systematically drawn into the control of the processes (feedback loop).

This simplified diagram Exhibit 4.3 on the following page reduces the complexity of the VICS nine-step workflow and shows the cyclic character of planning, forecasting, and replenishment.

While in the last few years there have been many recommendations made with respect to planning and replenishment processes, the creation of joint forecasts remains wanting. For the planning of business processes, the eight-step category management process is worth mentioning. For the realization of efficient replenishment techniques like vendor managed inventory and cross-docking, and optimization strategies for distribution are being developed.

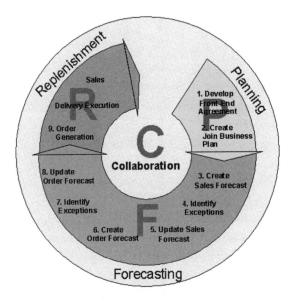

Exhibit 4.3 The CPFR Process model according to the CCG.
Source: Centrale fuer Coorganisation (2001)

As an integrative step, recommendations for POS data management and sales forecasting are being developed. From the perspective of German-speaking economic regions, joint forecasting is an especially critical element in the improvement of product availability. Available publications on this topic are listed below.

4.2.4 Sales Forecast

It was already apparent in early 2000 that the CPFR business model developed by VICS contained new stimuli for the optimization of business processes for German-speaking economic regions. Building on the CPFR business model, an implementation-oriented guide for the realization of joint forecasting by retailing and manufacturing was developed. It takes into account concrete recommendations from the guide published under the title *Joint Forecasting*.

The objective was the establishment of best practices for the creation of higher quality sales forecasts, which would secure significantly better product availability and optimized levels of inventory along the supply chain. The objective documents the consistent implementation of the pull principle including joint forecasts. The realization should be achieved through an inter-organizational data exchange. Step 3 of the CPFR business model was handled in sufficient detail. These recommendations do not contradict the VICS CPFR guideline, rather they should be understood as supplemental to them.

The joint forecast is used as an instrument of control over product availability. To implement the forecast, reference amounts (capacities, locations and product changes, logistics concepts) from the company's strategic planning are cross referenced with criteria from actual business (sales behavior, inventory trends).

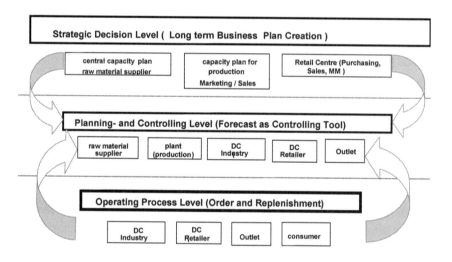

Exhibit 4.4 Levels of collaboration. Source: Centrale fuer Coorganisation (2002)

In the context of a status quo survey, it became clear that both retailers and manufacturers currently make forecasts, but with different objectives in mind. While in retail this is often used for automated ordering, in industry the criterion of highest priority is the planning and control of production capacity. A joint estimation of the expected demand through the exchange of forecasts is not yet being done. As a consequence, out-of-stock situations occur, in particular during promotions, whether they be run by the retailer or manufacturer. As a result, all parties require security in the form of safety stock.

The Value of Joint Forecasting

Consumers
Through joint forecasting, a higher degree of planning security for product replenishment is assured. This means that the consumer will actually find the product on the shelf when he goes to look for it. In particular when a product becomes more attractive through a time-limited offer, the consumer expects it to be there through the end of the promotion. The value for the customer is also clear when new products and product variations are available in sufficient number. Furthermore, the reduction of safety stock accelerates product through the supply chain so that the customer receives fresher, more current goods.

Retailers
Through the consumer's increased benefit, the retailer profits through stronger customer retention, as the consumer repeatedly visits the retail outlet. The improved image represents something of qualitative utility for the retailer.

Through joint forecasting, out-of-stocks can become the exception to the rule. Consequently, the cost of shortages through lost revenue and the undesired sales in alternative categories is avoided. Thus, the connection between distortions in the sales of a given product can be eliminated. Additionally, unused shelf space is avoided, a positive development for the image at the image at the point of sale (POS).

Through the reduction of out-of-stocks, manually placed special orders are eliminated which must always be placed when products are no longer available. Consequently, the additional costs for special orders in terms of ordering, receipt of goods, warehousing, and transportation are eliminated. Additionally, safety stocks are reduced in the central warehouse. In case an out-of-stock situation cannot be avoided by the manufacturer, he can inform the retailer in time to allow alternative measures to be taken.

Manufacturers
Finally, the manufacturer profits as well from the added benefit to the con-

sumer. If the customer finds the product on the shelf, the likelihood of him choosing an alternative brand is reduced. Hence a connection to the manufacturer's respective is created.

Rush orders by retailers lead to problems for the manufacturer, in particular when large amounts are ordered. If the amount ordered cannot be covered by inventory on hand, the planned production agenda must be quickly changed, as well as machinery taken offline, refitted and put back into production. This can mean that shifts must be added to meet deadlines. The result is additional costs for production, warehousing, transport, and administration. In particular, the following factors should be noted: material waste through machinery breakdown and set up, the need for technicians, idle time of the production line and personnel, changes in product program, the organization of additional workers, transportation, etc.

Unexpected orders can lead to orders not being able to be delivered, when production lines are not capable of reacting to additional demand. Precisely then, manufacturers too suffer from lost revenues.

Through joint forecasting of anticipated demand, existing production capacity can be used more efficiently provided, critical mass among the participants is reached. The additional costs described can be drastically reduced and lead to lower per unit costs.

Additionally, safety stocks of raw materials and completed goods can be reduced along with the risk of unsalable leftovers, which is high for items produced especially for time-limited offers.

The Significance of Relevant Data Sources

Today there is a great deal of information at all levels of the supply chain, which is not however used for the creation of a joint forecast. It is often the case that the technical means to obtain and process this data are not in place. To the extent the data exists, appropriate tools must be delivered which are able to interpret and draw conclusions for future demand development. Next to the technical question, there must be a willingness on the part of the partners to exchange data in order to improve the process bilaterally.

To this must be added the problem of internal communication between departments which are responsible that data flows into a forecast. The reasons can often be found in the organizational structure in so far as different departments are directed by different areas of responsibility. In the framework of process recommendations the various data sources of manufacturing and retailing are analyzed in order to make clear which data are necessary for the creation of a forecast.

Influences on the Creation of a Sales Forecast

The determination of demand consists of a complex relationship of logistics optimization and market-oriented measures. The many influences on the forecast throughout the supply chain characterize long-term the development of sales. A component of the process recommendation is a detailed schematic of the most important influences at each stage of the supply chain.

The consideration of all amount-relevant influences is really a theoretical illusion. A factor like the weather is nearly impossible to predict. Decisive is the selection of factors which have a significant influence and the creation of systems solutions that translate these factors into the demand forecast.

Detailed Creation of the Demand Forecast

Basis
For all participants in the supply chain to achieve a unified definition, it is necessary to define the basis of the demand forecast. In the context of a best practices implementation, the determination should be made based on the EAN of a trade unit. The trade unit is understood here as an amount agreed on by the trade partners which the retailer can order from the manufacturer.

The following are the advantages of this approach:

▶ From the number of trade units, the number of consumer units can be derived.

▶ For planning and control of production capacity the number of trade units to be produced is necessary.

▶ The creation of an order forecast is made easier

Time line

While the control of production and replenishment systems often require considerable advance notice, order forecasts should cover a time frame of 13 weeks.

In line with this recommendation, a realistic timeline can be defined which is usable for most product mixes. This is not true for all products, obviously. Perishable goods require a considerably shorter space of time as production and delivery systems have quicker reaction times, as determined by the nature of the product.

Amounts

In the forecast, all amounts should generally be oriented to weekly net demand. In keeping with the treatment of the time-frame, it can also make sense to orient to a daily basis when the planning parameters dictate.

Considering the fact that in German-speaking economic regions a large portion of sales runs over promotions, the sales forecast must be accommodating. Therefore, amounts for promotions and normal sales should be represented independently.

Through this differentiation, the expecting posture of the consumer, which comes with promotions, should become more transparent not only during a promotion, but before and after the volume effect in the supply chain is apparent. The differing data sources from which amounts are determined also speak for separate representations. The following table shows the most significant differences.

Forecast for every-day Business	Forecast for Promotion Activities
Use of historical data (time span analysis)	Little historical data, which are seldom comparable
Future sales development can be well determined	Estimation of sales development difficult
Use of system based forecasting possible	Unknown influences on promotion: ▶ Consumer behavior ▶ Reaction of competitors ▶ Success of advertising

Rolling Actualization

For high accuracy, the demand forecast cannot be static, it must reflect current market conditions. Here is where fluctuations between forecast and market should be shown. Through this approach, step four of the CPFR business model (Recognition of exceptions) is realized. Where possible, tracking of fluctuations should be automatic so that upon recognition a manual amendment to the forecast can be made.

For the reduction of exceptions, it is necessary that the trade partners define a tolerance in their joint business plan (CPFR step 2) where no manual action is necessary. Only when the threshold is crossed does a revision of the forecast become necessary.

Promotion Activities

Promotions at the POS have a significant influence on the demand forecast and should be included in the forecast process. Noteworthy are:

▶ Short-term price reductions of more than 5% relative to the previous week: While price is a deciding factor on anticipated demand, price information should be considered as an indicator of demand in the forecast. Especially during the promotion, high product availability at the POS is decisive for success of the promotion.

▶ Product specific advertising in leaflets and daily newspapers
Giving information about the advertising medium used allows one to draw conclusions about the size of the promotion.

▶ Secondary placement
The placement of displays increases the degree of contact with the product at the POS, through which sales are increased.

These and other measures are usually done in combination with one another.

Transmission of the Forecast

Where possible, the forecast should be automatically transmitted to business partners (EDI) so that the forecast can be used without manual effort and in the in-house system. For this purpose EDIFACT Subset EANCOM® are available. For the transmission of forecasts, the EANCOM® sales forecast report is used.

The forecast can also be exchanged through web-based procedures. At present however, there are no general rules, which assure a standardized exchange. The necessity of Internet communication standards is, in view of e-marketplaces, a current challenge.

The management paper developed for Germany, Austria and Switzerland as economic regions should provide a conceptual basis for creating forecasts. Access to data and the willingness of partners to change are also required.

In addition to safeguarding the results in Germany, Austria, and Switzerland, the process recommendation, Joint Forecasting is integrated into the work of European project groups under the auspices of ECR Europe. Beyond that, the experiences of GCI are drawn upon, which has the project documentation available on its homepage.

Conclusion

Building on the initial experiences of CPFR, pilot projects in Germany/Austria/ Switzerland, the CCG developed a CPFR management paper. This document gives a general overview of the structure and operation of the CPFR business model and integrates the solutions already pioneered in ECR. Additionally, there are concrete steps for the internal and external use of the CPFR philosophy. Parallel to the detailed instructions on the creation of an order forecast, the guide also contains a concrete description of an order forecast and the significance of the POS data (sales and inventory at the retail outlet level) in the CPFR business model. In describing these substantive details, the demands of the target market were considered in the guide.

To foster a better understanding, a model case for the implementation of CPFR was developed which is a component of the guide. This is especially intended for firms which do not yet have any experience with CPFR. Based on a concrete project by two fictional business partners, the implementation of a CPFR should be made transparent.

Numerous pilots in the German-speaking market show that CPFR is not only a theory but well on the way to broad use. The road from pilot to standard practice in Germany, Austria and Switzerland is becoming shorter. Beyond that,

ECR Germany-Austria-Switzerland will continue to serve as a platform for the exchange of experience and to support CPFR through events.

4.3 CPFR-Implementation at dm-drogerie markt and Henkel in Germany

Gunter Baumgart, Henkel
Dr. Birgit Ester, dm-drogerie markt
Christian Schick, dm-drogerie markt

4.3.1 Development of the Collaboration between Henkel and dm-drogerie markt

The Companies: Henkel and dm-drogerie markt

Henkel consists of 340 firms in 70 countries, which produce more than 10,000 products and employes 61,000 people worldwide. In Germany, *Henkel* is among the largest producers of consumer goods

dm-drogerie markt (thereafter dm) consists of more than 1,300 outlets with 8000 employees and is the second largest drugstore chain in Germany. The entire product line includes 13,000 products.

For several years, Henkel and dm have been cooperating closely at the operational level. The beginning came in the middle of the nineties with the implementation of electronic information exchange between the two companies. Initially, baseline information was exchanged through SINFOS. Thereafter, electronic ordering was done through EANCOM-Format Orders, the electronic invoicing via Sedas, in Germany standard, and EANCOM-Format Salesreport was used for the transmission of sales data. Finally, in 1998 Continuous Replenishment/Vendor Managed Inventories was begun based on EANCOM-Format's Inventory Report. After Henkel took over inventory control of dm's distribution center in Weilerswist, the availability of Henkel product there rose to 99.5%. At the same time, inventory in reserve was reduced by a value of between 1.5 and 2.5 days. (Compare to exhibits 4.5 and 4.6.) Deliveries by full trucks were made on an almost daily basis.

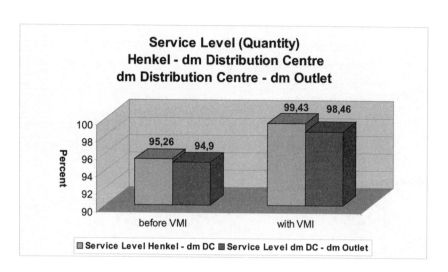

Exhibit 4.5 Development of delivery service from Henkel to the dm distribution center and from there to dm outlets before and after the introduction of CRP/VMI.
Source: dm-drogerie markt

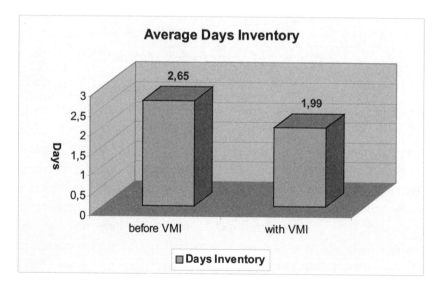

Exhibit 4.6 Change in the stock-on-hand of Henkel products at the dm distribution center before and after the introduction of CRP/VMI. Source: dm-drogerie markt

The interpretation of the individual results should be considered in light of the complexity and fragmentation of the entire replenishment process. Exhibit 4.7 shows the stages and participants in the value chain using the product Persil (laundry detergent).

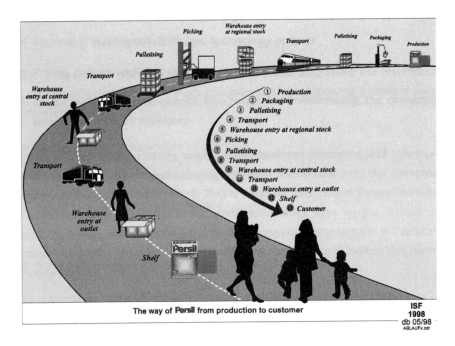

Exhibit 4.7 Complexity of the value chain. Source: Baumgart/Bieber (2000), S. G 6.

In category management, there is also a high level of cooperation between Henkel and dm. For working out assortment strategies, not only innovative placement concepts, but also the newest technology is being employed. In the year 2000, dm developed, with the support of several of its suppliers, the dm extranet. Through this system, staff at Henkel now have access to daily updated information on sales, deliveries and inventory from dm as well as promotion planning and listing status of individual sku's. The dm extranet makes all relevant information immediately available for the joint business process, leading to greater transparency.

VertiKo

The basis for the joint introduction of CPFR at Henkel and dm was, among other things, the collaboration on the research project VertiKo (vertical collaboration in the channel of distribution). At the end of 2000 both companies had begun work on this project sponsored by the Germany's Federal Ministry of Education and Research. VertiKo has the objective of discerning the critical success factors for the creation of a successful cooperation between manufacturer and retailer, thus countering tendencies to the contrary. The results are supposed to be transferable to value-adding partnerships for their improvement. Contents of the project are all relevant complete product-, data-, and cash-flows as well as the relationship management between the companies.

One of the first steps in the project was the completion of a jointly run SWOT analysis.[1] Everyone working at the interchange between the two companies met for a one-day workshop and paired off for doing SWOT analyses. At the conclusion, both viewpoints were brought together and the evaluations' similarities and differences compared.

An up to now unsolved problem in the collaboration is the control of the process of product introductions and sales promotions. For parts of Henkel and dm a large information deficit and hence uncertainty were diagnosed. Both companies agreed with the recommendation that the entire process should be made considerably more transparent. An additional criticism on both sides was that of frequent delays in the process. A solution was suggested in which a common system controlled the entire process. This would include everything from order generation through promotions and the introduction of new products to performance reviews based on jointly defined indices. Such a comprehensive workflow would constantly reflect the status of the process and identify sticking points. Based on the good experience acquired with dm extranet, the Internet was chosen for use in the pilot project.

In parallel, Henkel was jointly developing a system with other suppliers in an e-market. The system was developed using experience that Sainsbury had been accumulating at Nestlé in the UK. The central idea of this system is that

---

1   Strengths, Weaknesses, Opportunities and Threats

events can best be controlled through a tool to which the manufacturer as well as his trading partners have access.

Henkel worked together with Nestlé and Danone on a prototype for an Internet based workflow, which represents the information flow between the creation of a bid all the way through to the evaluation of a promotion. The system had to be tested for practicability and utility in the cooperative agreements through two pilot projects. Encouraged by the experience with dm, Henkel decided to conduct such tests. The test procedures and results are elucidated in the next chapter.

Both companies relied on the experience of their work in the CCG work groups Joint Forecasting and CPFR. Through these two forums, important foundations for a European version of CPFR were established.

The use of scanner data takes on particular significance in allowing so-called online-tracking during an actual promotion. Scanner data is compared with the forecast while a promotion or introduction is running in order to see if shortages or surpluses are to be expected. In addition to this short-term feedback loop, there is the opportunity to use the information strategically long-term. This is accomplished in part through an event database where information on completed events is stored.

4.3.2   CPFR as a Further Step in the Joint Business Process

CPFR is a comprehensive model which optimizes the relationship between business partners through cooperative planning which is responsive to customers, combined with joint forecasting and improved information exchange along the supply chain. Based on a readiness to cooperate, planning, forecasting and inventory control have been integrated into a nine-step plan.

Improvements in these areas are necessary, as they remain inefficient due to appreciable uncertainty. Up to now, firms in the supply chain have tried to optimize their processes individually. This approach however leads to the following problems:

- ▶ insufficient internal and external communication

- ▶ different focuses in planning

- ▶ large safety stocks resulting from missing information

CPFR is an attempt to find a complete solution. Thus corporate boundaries are lowered to the extent that retail and manufacturing are put in the position of pursuing common objectives. Building on better relations and improvements in forecasting and planning, product availability can be increased and simultaneously inventory throughout the supply chain reduced. The benefits include increasing sales by virtue of higher customer satisfaction and cost reductions for both partners.

The 'C' in CPFR, the collaboration, is the predicate for all further steps. The more pronounced the collaboration is, and the higher the quality will be, the better it will be for Planning, Forecasting and Replenishment as well. Control of the collaboration is no less important for processes inside a company than for those with external partners.

In the past, it was a common mistake to optimize single units and not the whole process or company. Today, many companies are restructuring their organizations to make collaboration easier in order to correct this problem. Through multifunctional process-oriented teams, collaboration in the future will become demonstrably simpler.

4.3.3 The Pilot Project

Fundamental Agreements
At the beginning of the project, it was decided who would provide which information and which common goals would be pursued. The type of information and its flow are shown in exhibit 4.8.

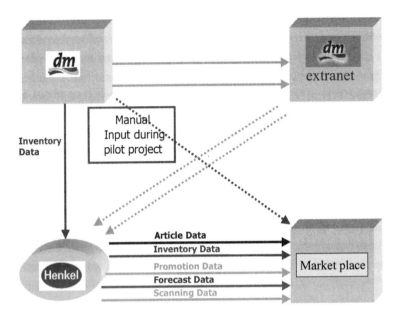

Exhibit 4.8 Dataflow in the CPFR Pilot Project. Source: dm-drogerie markt

It was decided in the pilot project to send most of the data directly from Henkel to the marketplace because there was already a large, up-to-date database there, and a direct connection to the dm system or dm extranet would have led to serious delays. Besides raising revenues through increases in product availability and the reduction of surplus at the conclusion of promotions, there were other measures to be tested.

▶ The synchronization of forecasting and replenishment processes

▶ The integration of supply and demand side

▶ The streamlining and standardization of communication

▶ The acceleration of the development of promotions

▶ The simplification of communication between suppliers and retailers

4.3.4 The CPFR Workflow in a Marketplace

The system tested in the pilot project is an Internet supported workflow application with clearly defined phases and responsibilities, as shown in the exhibit below.

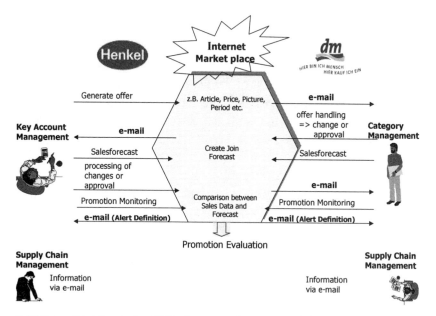

Exhibit 4.9 Workflow in the CPFR pilot project between Henkel and dm.
Source: dm-drogerie markt/Henkel

Process step	Responsibility
Offer Generation	Key Account Management Henkel
Offer handling	Category Management dm
Sales forecast	Key Account Management Henkel/Category Management dm
Order forecast	automated
Promotion monitoring	Key Account Management Henkel/Category Management dm
Promotion evaluation	Key Account Management Henkel/Category Management dm

Offer generation

The entire event process is put in motion when the Key Account Manager enters an offer for a product introduction or promotion into the system. He defines the timeframe for the event, chooses the appropriate products from a catalogue in the system and has the opportunity to state his preferences on presentation in the outlets as well as the cost price for the retailer. It is also possible to attach supplementary information to the bid, like a picture of the product, price calculation, or a product folder. As before, initial estimates of possible sales during the event can be entered. In this step it is determined whether the further development of the bid occurs at the corporate level or through individual distribution centers. The initiator of a step can finalize it by handing it off to the next person in the workflow, canceling it, or saving it for further editing later.

Offer handling

In the next step, the Category Manager at dm receives an e-mail stating that Henkel has prepared an offer for him on the system. Through a link in the e-mail, the manager has direct access to the bid after inputting his username and password. He can then examine the offer, add comments and finalize the step by accepting the offer, rejecting it or requesting additional information.

Sales Forecasting

When both partners have agreed to run an event, the concrete planning begins. Both companies make an estimate of how much they think can be sold in which outlets. Which partner does this first is irrelevant. The step is completed when both partners agree to a forecast amount which is then translated into a percentage for each day of the week by established values already in the system.

Order Forecasting

The creation of an order forecast is a purely mathematical procedure. Based on the jointly agreed sales forecast, the size of the order is determined. The process considers existing inventories of the retailer as well as pending orders. The manufacturer then checks this value to see if he has sufficient stock or must start production to cover the demand. The earlier and more exact the forecast which the manufacturer receives, the better he is able to control his internal processes.

Promotion Monitoring

During a sales promotion, retail sales are compared with the forecast daily. Only in this way can product availability throughout the promotion be assured. To utilize the recognition of an impending shortage or surplus at the end of a promotion, it is necessary that the supply chain be flexible enough to accommodate those fluctuations.

Promotion Evaluation

After the conclusion of a promotional event, efficiency and success are evaluated based on jointly defined indices. Important is that what has been learned is preserved for application in future events. Only in this way can long-term optimization in the promotional event process be achieved.

4.3.5 Experiences from the Pilot Project and a Perspective on CPFR

The pilot project was completed at the end of October 2001. The concept and its execution have shown that the process as described, is functional. It also showed that it was sensible to begin with a small scope to reduce the complexity to the lowest possible level. Likewise, it became clear that, in promotions, the discrepancies between forecasts used for production planning and actual sales could be very significant. In the end, there is much room for improvement in their implementation

The speed of the internet based system was identified as a critical factor. In comparison to intranets, the delays nullify the advantages of a workflow-based process. The participating staff agreed that the difficulties were acceptable for a test application, but that for full-scale implementation the system should be a time saver, not a time waster.

Through CPFR, and with or without the support of a workflow tool, the network between retailing and manufacturing is growing. Beyond that, CPFR implies a closer collaboration between logistics and key account management on the manufacturing side, and assortment management on the retailing side. Through the merged planning and treatment of sales, inventory and delivery service data, the connections of this magnitude for the overall success of an article will become apparent. Thereby, a mutual understanding of the different participants in the supply chain grows, and closer coordination is the result. To that end, CPFR can be seen as a new element in the structure of ECR which is to be understood as a link between the demand side and the supply side.

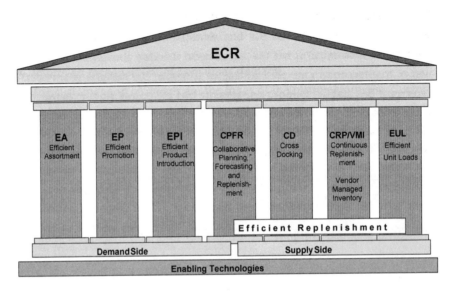

Exhibit 4.10 CPFR as a Link between the Demand Side and the Supply Side. Source: dm-drogerie markt/Henkel

Decicive factors in the attainment of this goal are the willingness and the determination of all participants in the supply chain, in good times and bad, to work cooperatively towards collaborative solutions.

4.4 CPFR Implementation at Henkel Spain

Esteban Garriga, Henkel Spain
Sergio Duque, Henkel Spain
Hans Teuscher, Accenture Spain

Henkel has had a very close relationship with supply chain initiatives during the last few years. Henkel has become deeply involved in different ECR work groups in order to share experiences and knowledge. CPFR has been one of these initiatives. CPFR, a cross-industry initiative designed to improve the supplier/manufacturer/retailer relationship, works through co-managed planning processes and shared information and builds on the concepts of ECR and Demand Planning through a structured approach to closer collaboration among value chain partners.

The implementation of CPFR processes at Henkel, Spain has gone through different stages recently. It started with the implementation of a new demand planning system, a CPFR pilot initiative (Henkel-Eroski) thereafter, and the evaluation of the results of this initiative in a business case in order to consider implementation with other partners of Henkel. The experience was then used in another pilot implementation (Henkel-Condis), which incorporates upstream processes. In the meantime, some internal procedures have already experienced the impact of the collaborative approach.

The collaboration allows the companies to redefine the planning processes in order to broaden their horizons. The global process to integrate all the actors of the supply chain is structured as follows:

▶ Forecast generation: To generate an accurate forecast collaboration is a key factor.

▶ This collaboration allows the manufacturer to integrate the knowledge of the distributor and in addition to fostering the consistency in promotional communication, it allows the companies to achieve higher accuracy in their forecasts.

▶ A broader horizon of production planning is achieved through collaboration and this provides the manufacturer with the opportunity to collaborate with suppliers, especially with the suppliers of the critical materials.

The exhibit below highlights the different processes addressed in this last initiative that integrate all the actors in the supply chain.

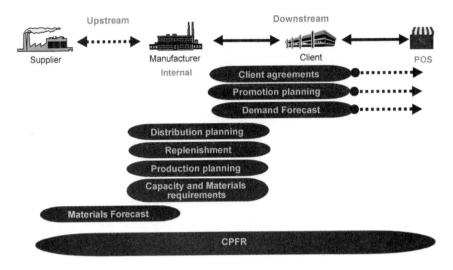

Exhibit 4.11 Global Process Map. Source: Henkel Spain/Accenture

So far the experience has been entirely positive and the organization has experienced both the benefits and the initial difficulties of implementing CPFR.

4.4.1 New Demand Planning System

The first stage was the implementation and the integration of a **new demand planning system**. Recognizing that the basis for successful CPFR is a high-quality internal forecast of the trading partners, Henkel decided to focus first internally before setting out to collaborate externally on demand planning.

The demand planning system is of particular importance, because the uncertainty in future demand is translated into inefficiencies in:

▶ production (higher costs)

▶ high level of inventory

▶ out-of-stocks, which consequently generate dissatisfaction among retailers and consumers

▶ inefficiencies in logistics

The first step in implementing this new demand planning system was to assess the initial situation, the current inefficiencies and their consequences: The main features of the initial situation were:

▶ Lack of a (Technical) system in order to support Demand Forecasting

▶ No integration of a Continuous Replenishment Program (CRP) in the forecast

▶ Increased Henkel assortment complexity

▶ No communication of events and knowledge of factors which influence the forecast

The consequences of that situation were:

▶ Costs associated with high inventories and a high number of changes in production planning.

▶ Low service level, which generated the dissatisfaction of retailer/consumers and a high number of out-of-stocks.

Project Objectives and Implementation Plan

Considering the issues mentioned above, several project objectives were established:

▶ Improve service level to retailer & consumer:
  ▶ Avoid internal inefficiencies: out of stocks, invoicing complaints, delivery mistakes, etc.
  ▶ Reduce the Point-of-Sale (POS) out-of-stocks and lost sales
  ▶ Improve Henkel's service to CRP/VMI retailers
▶ Eliminate / Reduce inefficiencies in the supply chain.
  ▶ Increase the demand forecasting accuracy
  ▶ Synchronize forecasting with production
  ▶ Integration of the supply chain: Purchasing and distribution

- ▶ Support Henkel's Management & enhance retailers' loyalty:

  - ▶ Provide useful information from "demand management tool" to other areas like sales, marketing, etc.
  - ▶ Identify activities which offer advantages to retailers (CPFR)

In pursuit of the objectives defined, Henkel developed an implementation plan that was composed of:

- ▶ Implementation of a Demand Planning Tool based on statistical models which allows Henkel to obtain more accurate demand forecasts.

- ▶ Develop adequate internal information flows in order to obtain more accurate forecasts.

- ▶ Integrate the efforts and establish information flows between sales, marketing, production and distribution.

- ▶ Integrate the CRP management in the demand forecasting process.

The project focused on two areas for improvement: the integration of a new demand planning system and the reengineering of business processes.

Another important issue that the company analyzed was the complexity of the business. On the one hand, as the number of SKU's at Henkel increases the volume per reference decreases. This leads to a significant increase in complexity in the management of the supply chain. On the other hand, the retailer structure becomes ever more complex.

As part of the implementation of the Demand Planning System, the demand planning processes were redefined as highlighted in exhibit 4.12. At each stage of the process, the involved actors were identified, their roles and responsibilities and the Key Performance Indicators (KPI) defined.

This involved both modules, the Demand Planning Extended Edition (DPEE) and the Distribution Requirement Planning (DRP), in other words the whole process, in which the forecast is the key input.

The main KPI's defined were related to the Forecast Accuracy and to the Promotion Planning. Henkel developed a fulfillment analysis tool that took into account:

▶ The planning and modification horizon

▶ The promotional volume within planning and modification

▶ Follow-up of Henkel's internal process of comunication

Henkel defined an Event-Plan with the objective that all of those in a position of responsibility from the different parts/areas/departments/etc. of the supply chain collaborate and plan jointly the scheduling of events like retailer or product promotions

Due to the structure and complexity of Henkel's activities, assortment, and the market, there are many different events which affect sales. However, only a few of these events are crucial for the performance of the business. Henkel also defined the DRP processes where the forecast is the main input, to the Demand Forecast Unit (DFU) to Stock Keeping Unit (SKU) process (CRP). These efforts led to a considerable improvement of the forecast accuracy within Henkel, Spain.

Demand Planning Process

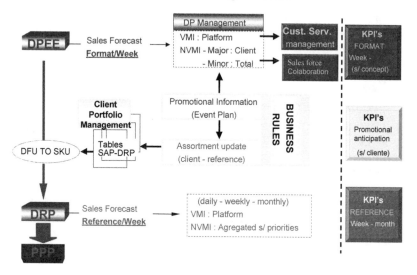

Exhibit 4.12 Demand Planning Process. Source: Henkel Spain/Accenture

The Demand Planning tool implemented provides 95% of the total forecast at Henkel, as shown in exhibit 4.13, with the different inputs such as the latest information from marketing and sales and on assortments. Controlling, adjusting and reviewing are the last steps in the Demand Planning Process.

In order to implement this new demand planning system, Henkel analyzed information flows, procedures, organizational models, the involved resources, tasks and departments. The information flows among the different departments were defined and established in order to avoid inefficiencies and problems of communication.

The procedures and responsibilities of demand planning were defined at different levels:

▶ **Annual procedures**:

  ▷ Forecast the demand of the following year
  ▷ Produce forecasts for the Marketing Plan
  ▷ Produce forecasts for the Sales Plan

▶ **Monthly procedures**:

  ▷ Elaborate the demand forecasts for the next four months
  ▷ Input on Sales: Sales forecast for each large customer. Sales forecast for each VMI customer Ad-hoc activities for each customer: i.e. dates, products, volume and delivery dates.
  ▷ Output: Monthly forecasts at product/format/SKU level. Detachment per week in the current month. Detachment per month in months n+1/n+2. Reporting to: Top Management, Marketing, Sales, Production, Trade Marketing

▶ **Weekly procedures**:

  ▷ Check the forecast of the month. See if it fits the monthly forecasts, correct if necessary
  ▷ Analysis of deviations, specific promotions, problems (production, purchases, distribution)
  ▷ Output: Modification of the monthly forecast and detachment per week.

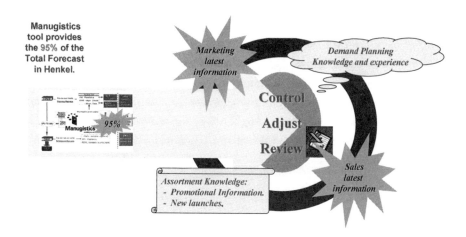

Exhibit 4.13 The last step in the Demand Planning Process. Source: Henkel Spain/Accenture

Demand Forecasting Model

The company continued to generate a demand forecasting model. The steps were:

▶ Design "Demand Forecasting Model" based on:

  ▶ Henkel's activities & requirements

  ▶ Specifications/functions of Software available Manugistics)

▶ Identification, gathering and loading of data into the software

  ▶ Definition of data based on the model (sales, stocks, etc. from specific retailers, Henkel)

  ▶ Validation and cleansing of data (history)

  ▶ Designing automated interfaces to introduce data from existing IT systems (CRP, SAP, etc) into the software

▶ Define 'crucial information' for the demand planning model designed

  ▶ Identify qualitative and quantitative inputs to inform, retailer promotions, new product introductions, etc.

  ▶ Reengineering of the Business Process and workflow communications.

The differences and benefits obtained with the new demand forecasting model were very important:

▶ In the past, the forecast was generated at monthly and reference levels. After the new demand forecasting model implementation, it was generated at different levels, yearly, monthly and weekly and always per reference. The amount of information used to generate the forecast was larger and different inputs were provided from all departments involved.

▶ Henkel went from a bi-monthly revision of the forecast to a weekly revision with daily adjustments.

▶ The method of calculation went from lineal to one that is based on the Lewandosky and Winters Series.

▶ The amount of data processed increased considerably, from 12.000 data to 30.000.000 data.

▶ Previously staff spent 60% of their time processing data and 40% analyzing and managing. This distribution of time changed considerably with 80% of their time now invested in analysis and management and 20% on data processing.

Henkel decided to implement the Manugistics demand planning tool within the organization. This decision support tool provided the required elements for planning supply, manufacturing, distribution and sales, and the integration of the supply chain. A demand planning road map for the implementation of the tool was developed consisting of the following elements:

▶ Definition of the structure of the information

▶ Loading of the information from the last 2 years

▶ Selection and preparation of historical information

▶ Definition of the statistical model

▶ Incorporation of the future events into the model

▶ Demand forecast

Furthermore, a Continuous Replenishment Process implementation plan was developed covering the following:

▶ Training of a Customer Service team responsible for the Forecast module (DPEE), the Replenishment modules (Distribution Requirement Planning) and the interfaces and value-added tools implemented.

▶ Communication to retailers about the objectives, potential benefits, tasks, roles and responsibilities and critical processes.

▶ Generation of first orders and change of IT interfaces

▶ Ensure process performance

▶ Review and analysis of the objectives

Job Descriptions and Responsibilities

Henkel developed job descriptions for the staff involved in the processes including their profiles, their competencies and their requirements. The different players involved and their responsibilities were:

Demand manager

▶ Responsibilities: This person is the owner of the process of integrated planning. He guarantees the process and the procedures defined for the demand planning, and is responsible for the definition and collection of the information defined from the different areas involved. He elaborates the forecasts at area / format / SKU levels, follows up on the events and the impact per event, communicates the forecasts and their review to Production Planning, develops the definition and the control of the KPI's of the demand planning and checks the parameters of security stocks, service level, costs..

▶ Competencies and requirements:

  ▶ Human Resources management
  ▶ Analytical thinking
  ▶ Team work and cooperation oriented

- ▶ Knowledge of Manugistics tool
- ▶ Excellent knowledge of SBU's & SKU's

Customer Services

▶ Responsibilities: Elaborates the monthly forecast per retailer / group level with Manugistics. (VMI, Major VMI and total Minor), is responsible for the establishment of the CRP process and of order generation by retailer. He assures system performance and defines CRP retailer replenishment.

▶ Competencies and requirements:

- ▶ Retailer orientation
- ▶ People Management
- ▶ Excellent knowledge of SBU's – SKU's and retailer
- ▶ Knowledge of Manugistics tool
- ▶ Familiar with management and control tools in processes related to the retailer

Production Planner

▶ Responsibilities: Elaborates the weekly manufacturing plan and the programs of the factories, coordinates the plan with the factory and the suppliers, and reviews the exceptions. He is the representative of and link with the factory, and he communicates the availability of products.

▶ Competencies and requirements:

- ▶ Results oriented, team worker, and flexible
- ▶ Excellent knowledge of SBU's & SKU's
- ▶ Excellent knowledge of Henkel factories
- ▶ Capacity to coordinate internal manufacturers

Henkel developed a matrix of responsibilities of the different processes, with different roles such as executor, consultant and informer.

4.4.2 CPFR-Pilot Henkel and Eroski

Despite the complexity of the Demand Planning system, the accuracy of the forecast was not sufficient. We realized that some final demand information had been lost. The manufacturers' drivers of the forecast are not the same as those of the retailers' (please see exhibit 4.14).

The first initiative after the implementation of this new demand planning system was to develop a CPFR pilot with one of the most important retailers for Henkel Spain, Eroski, a Spanish retailer. This case study was one of the first European pilots to follow the CPFR process. The special aspect of the CPFR program developed by Henkel and Eroski lies in the willingness of both companies to harmonize their procedures of cooperation.

Eroski is a food-retail industry leader in Spain. The company was founded in 1969 and comprises an integrated net of 47 hypermarkets, 800 supermarkets and 2000 mini-markets. Their main domain is in the Basque Country, but they are also present in France with 3 hypermarkets and 17 supermarkets. The group employs 23,300 people and achieves a turnover of 4,208 million euros.

MANUFACTURER FORECAST DRIVERS	RETAILER FORECAST DRIVERS
Shipments	Consumer demand visibility
Order lead time	Instock position
Capacity	Shipments variance
Product availability	Promotional activity
Promotions	Growth Plans
Raw materials supply	Distributor structure

Exhibit 4.14 Forecast Drivers. Source: Henkel Spain/Accenture

Out-of-stocks in the hypermarkets revealed major shortcomings. Out-of-stocks were frequent for a number of articles (90% promotional). Customer service was also unsatisfactory at the central warehouse of Eroski, where products were not always delivered on time due to lack of visibility. The two companies decided to unify their attempts in order to improve their sales forecasts. The acquisition of the Demand Planning (DP) module (Manugistics) by Henkel and the change of integrated planning processes in the supply chain were the first steps to put CPFR into place at Henkel and Eroski.

Therefore, **Henkel and Eroski started a CPFR pilot**. All phases of the CPFR process were put into place according to a scenario in which Henkel bore the sole responsibility of providing the forecast, calculating demand and creating orders.

Objectives of the pilot

The objectives of the pilot, through harmonization and improvement of the procedures of cooperation, were:

▶ To improve customer service

▶ To reduce lost sales

▶ To increase stock turnover

▶ To improve punctuality of deliveries

▶ To reduce time required for the order cycle

Scope

All Henkel detergent category products at Eroski were part of the project between the central warehouse of both Henkel and Eroski. The data exchanged were:

▶ Outgoing stock (once per day)

▶ Stock figures (once per day)

▶ Events calendar (once every 4 months)

▶ Sales forecasts (every 15 days)

▶ Order forecasts (once per week)

▶ Orders (calculated once per day)

Technology used

The data exchange is based on EANCOM standards for all messages, INVRPT, ORDERS and INVOICES. No standard was established to transmit sales forecasts and order forecasts.

Performance Indicators

Some KPI's were defined by Henkel and Eroski such as customer service at the central warehouse, number of out-of-stocks, number of promotions, stock rotation, full truck, full pallet, number of urgent orders and so on.

Resources

The multifunctional project team consisted of five employees at Henkel, one project leader, one person responsible for ECR, the Key Account Managers of Eroski, one Demand Planning expert and one consultant from Manugistics. Four people were involved at Eroski, one project leader, one forecaster, one supplier and one logistician.

In addition, the project relied on the external support of Accenture. As in all CPFR initiatives at Henkel Spain, Accenture helped to define the scope and the strategy for the future expansion of CPFR (roll-out).

Methodology

One of the challenges of implementing CPFR was the integration of Customer Service representatives in the process of sales forecasting generation due to their extensive knowledge of the retailer, especially his products and promotions.

After the implementation of the Demand Planning and DRP modules from Manugistics, the project started with the central warehouse of Eroski

The experience gained during the pilot implementation allowed Henkel to improve forecast accuracy and order generation (DRP). There were also changes to the promotion planning process such as new information flows, and changes in the forecasting processes such as involving customer services in the forecasting process.

The experience with this pilot revealed the relevance of CPFR concept for the collaboration of commercial and operational planning. Controlled by both partners, the process helps to achieve the objective of increased sales forecast accuracy, improved customer service levels, reduced stock levels and increased sales.

Each company tried to improve its demand reliability in order to improve internal processes and relationships with its retailers. CPFR formalizes this approach and shows how important it is to enter good quality data into systems. The internal collaboration of the sales force is also a crucial element of success.

CPFR will reach the next phase through the integration of points of sale in the future. At first, the data was gathered at the central warehouse of Eroski. Currently, the parties are working to directly include the data from the points of sale, reflecting the real demand of consumers.

4.4.3 Development of a CPFR Business Case

Once this new system was integrated and Henkel gained experience with its first pilot, the next step was to analyze the CPFR environment, its characteristics, requirements, current situation and, potential benefits that would allow Henkel to take a decision regarding the initiation of other pilots with different partners. For this reason, Henkel, Spain developed a Business Case that includes:

Analysis of the Background

The CPFR Concept (Collaborative Planning Forecasting and Replenishment). CPFR means the cooperation of inter-company and intra-company retailers in the following processes:

▶ Collaboration in planning promotions and special events.

▶ Collaboration in sales forecast values

▶ Collaboration in proposed orders

It must be borne in mind that the implementation of CPFR requires an important technological step forward.

The major objectives of implementing CPFR were:

▶ Increased sales

  ▶ Reduction of out-of-stocks
  ▶ Increased promotional activity

▶ Increased profitability

  ▶ Reduction of coverage levels

▶ Reduction of supply chain costs

  ▶ Optimization of Promotion planning
  ▶ Integration of Point of Sale Information

▶ Process alignment

  ▶ Single joint forecast
  ▶ Process improvement and automation

Henkel analyzed the Value and the Difficulty of CPFR compared to other major initiatives (please see exhibit below).

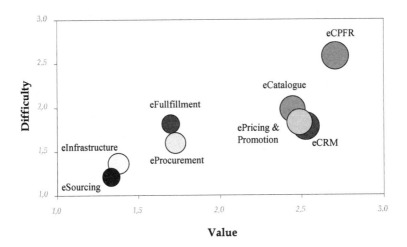

Exhibit 4.15 CPFR compared to other major initiatives. Source: AECOC/Henkel Spain/ Accenture

Objectives of the CPFR-Business Case

The major objectives of the Business Case were to:

▶ Define alternative CPFR models in alignment with retailers' characteristics and their potential for collaboration.

  ▶ Basic CPFR : e.g. just with the Sales Force

  ▶ Medium CPFR: e.g. internally and with retailers on sales and inventory reports

  ▶ Advanced CPFR : e.g. automation of forecasts and retailer orders

  ▶ Very Advanced CPFR:e.g. promotion information and planning at point of sale level

▶ Segment retailers in alignment with their CPFR cooperation potential

▶ Define the CPFR processes based on the nine step model

▶ Evaluate technological solutions in the short term and integrate them with existing HIBSA systems (e.g. SAP, Manugistics DPEE, Infoservice)

▶ Evaluate CPFR costs and benefits in view of their impact on the Henkel value chain with retailers, depending on the models. Seek not only quantitative benefits but also qualitative.

▶ Define the approach priority (retailers, CPFR models and solutions)

▶ Analyze the current situation of CPFR in Spain and Europe

▶ Propose an action plan taking into account short and medium term solutions

▶ Roll-out in the rest of Europe

Definition of the CPFR Models

In order to classify the Henkel retailers in groups depending on their collaborative features, different CPFR models were defined according to the type of retailer, the potential of collaboration and the technological and information level.

Major components in CPFR models

The CPFR model proposed includes:

▶ Promotion planning through EVENT PLAN

  ▶ Retailer promotions
  ▶ Chain promotions
  ▶ Product promotions

▶ Generation of forecasts in the Manugistics DP from

  ▶ Henkel output
  ▶ Platform output
  ▶ Consolidated POS output

▶ Introduction of event effects and their description in DP

▶ Orders generation in Manugistics DRP from

  ▶ DPEE Forecasts

- ▶ Platform Stocks
- ▶ Consolidated POS stocks

▶ Capacity for retailers to make and send forecasts, shipments and inventory data

▶ Collaboration on, and validation of the forecasts in the collaboration tool

- ▶ Sales, Demand Manager, CS
- ▶ Retailers

▶ The establishment of the anticipation of collaboration is a basic point in the agreements.

The classification of the CPFR models as basic, medium, advanced and very advanced was done according to:

▶ Type of retailer: Classification of retailers according to their replenishment mode with Henkel, CRP Pull, CRP Push, NO CRP Pull, NO CRP Push.

▶ Scope of collaboration in the processes, the interlocutor in each process

▶ Technological levelof the retailer:

- ▶ Capacity of the retailer to send computerized shipments and inventories
- ▶ Capacity of the retailer to make and send computerized forecasts

▶ Information level: The level at which the retailer provides information

▶ Platform level

▶ POS level

Henkel classified the retailers into four models:

▶ **Basic**: The retailers included in this model are those with whom no collaboration exists and who do not send any information on shipments or inventory levels. Collaboration is done internally. (Customer Services (CS), Sales, Demand Planning)

▶ **Medium**: Retailers who provide information on shipments and inventory at platform level. Either they collaborate manually with forecast values or collaboration only exists within Henkel's internal departments.

▶ **Advanced**: Those retailers who collaborate and who are sufficiently well developed technologically to be able to generate forecasts and send them automatically.

▶ **Very Advanced**: Includes those retailers who, in addition to collaborating and sending forecasts, provide information on POS sales and inventories.

A preliminary assignment of retailers to the models was made. The objective was to segment retailers according to their potential for providing information on shipments, forecasts and orders and their potential for changing their replenishment method. From this first analysis, we identified the retailers best positioned to implement CPFR: Carrefour, Eroski and Condis.

An exhaustive definition of the processes related to the nine step model was developed for each of the different models.

Potential Benefits

The potential quantitative and qualitative benefits of applying the different CPFR models were evaluated, especially Basic CPFR and the More Advanced CPFR, for four of our retailers, which represented approximately 30% of total sales.

These potential qualitative benefits were:

▶ Increase in sales volume through:
  ▶ Reduction in out-of-stocks in stores
  ▶ Improvement of service
  ▶ Reduction of inventory on platform
▶ Reduction of distribution costs
  ▶ Improvement in production planning
  ▶ Improvement in transport resource planning and utilization

- Reduction in material purchasing costs

  - Anticipation in material purchase planning

- Reduction of marketing costs

- Better knowledge of market behavior (end consumers)

- Improvements of company image in the market

Technological Solutions

With regard to the technological solutions to implement CPFR, Henkel Spain analyzed the possible tools, taking into account the requirements needed and the level of collaboration that we would be able to achieve. For instance, we evaluated the tools data inputs and outputs, their collaborative components, the exception alerts, the exception resolution, the graphs and their costs.

The conclusion was that the tools studied were either oriented towards promotion planning or collaboration in the demand forecast values. None covered both processes simultaneously. Different marketplaces started offering CPFR functionality and requirements, Henkel as a direct member of one these marketplaces made the decision to test two tools. In the meantime, it was decided to develop internal workflow tools for the implementation of the pilots.

The decision was to implement an internal tool which:

- Covers collaboration in promotion planning (Event Plan) and collaboration in demand forecast values and potentially orders and stocks.

- Creates a workflow, inserting the tasks to be performed on the desktop of the persons involved in said task.

- Uses standard protocols and development tools in the Internet environment.

- Allows easy incorporation of the tool in a marketplace whether it be the Spanish Commercial Codification Association (AECOC) or a Henkel supported marketplace at the European level

CPFR in Europe

Furthermore, in April 2000 Henkel analyzed, with the support of Accenture, the situation of CPFR in Spain and Europe highlighted in the exhibit below (as part of a larger study regarding the situation of B2B practices in Europe).

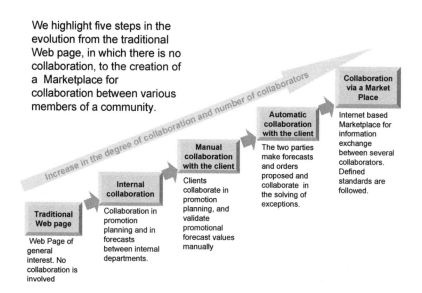

We highlight five steps in the evolution from the traditional Web page, in which there is no collaboration, to the creation of a Marketplace for collaboration between various members of a community.

Increase in the degree of collaboration and number of collaborators

Traditional Web page

Web Page of general interest. No collaboration is involved

Internal collaboration

Collaboration in promotion planning and in forecasts between internal departments.

Manual collaboration with the client

Clients collaborate in promotion planning, and validate promotional forecast values manually

Automatic collaboration with the client

The two parties make forecasts and orders proposed and collaborate in the solving of exceptions.

Collaboration via a Market Place

Internet based Marketplace for information exchange between several collaborators. Defined standards are followed.

Exhibit 4.16 Levels of CPFR-Development. Source: Henkel Spain/Accenture

The most suitable levels of the potential application of CPFR varied depending on the countries studied. This was due to the differing number of retailers, the coverage level, the amount of promotional activity and so on.

The conclusion was that the best options for applying CPFR in Spain were Basic or Medium depending on the retailers selected in view of the market environment.

Another important conclusion of the business case was that the implementation should be in phases, starting with the collaboration with internal retailers and continuing with the adaptation of the implementation of processes to each retailer in accordance with its technology and capacity for providing information.

Three phases were defined for implementation:

▶ **Phase 0**: Collaboration with the retailer in bringing forward processes and agreements. The retailer provides all the necessary information and plans promotions sooner. Henkel makes forecasts and orders, giving the retailer access to this data.

▶ **Phase 1**: Collaboration with the retailer in bringing forward processes, on agreements and in forecast values. The retailer also makes the forecasts, thus collaborating in their values and in solving the exceptions. Henkel fills orders based on the agreed upon forecast and gives the retailer visibility.

▶ **Phase 2**: Collaboration in all processes. Orders proposed by both parties are compared and a unique joint order is generated.

Basic Requirements

The basic requirements identified in the business case for applying CPFR were:

▶ Functional requirements. Collaboration in the following processes with a minimum horizon of 4 weeks.

▶ Promotion Planning

▶ Forecast value

▶ Alignment of assortment

▶ Technical requirements.

▶ Retailer's capacity to send information

  ▹ Inventory and Sales Report. Must be capable of automatically sending outputs and inventories and/or points of sales on a daily basis.

  ▹ Automatic creation and transmission of demand forecast values on a weekly basis.

  ▹ Standard coding. In order to automate processes between retailers and suppliers it is necessary to use standard coding.

Another conclusion of the business case was that the application of CPFR has great potential for improvement. The collaboration influences both internal processes and distributor processes.

CPFR is a key activity for Henkel. The development of CPFR must be aimed at including it in a marketplace, either Henkel's own at the European level or through its integration in the AECOC (Spanish commercial codification association) portal.

Therefore the next steps after the business case were developed were to:

▶ Put into operation the detailed internal action plan.

▶ Seek out retailers prepared to collaborate in CPFR concepts.

▶ Put into operation the general CPFR process with the retailers chosen.

4.4.4 CPFR-Pilot Henkel and Condis

The good results obtained through the pilot with Eroski and the business case helped Henkel decide to start another initiative with Condis, a Spanish regional retailer based in Catalonia. Established in 1961, Condis is the largest supermarket chain in Catalonia with 300 points of sale and the second in terms of sales volume. It operates under two brand names, Condis Supermarkets and Distop. The group employs 2900 people and achieves a turnover of 462 million euros (2000) with an increase of 17,5% in 1999 Currently the group is involved in an expansion, with plans to expand to other regions of Spain.

This **CPFR pilot Henkel – Condis** aims to identify all the benefits of involving all the actors of the supply chain, not only the relation between manufacturer and retailer but also with an upstream supplier. The objective is to integrate the entire supply chain, from one end to the other.

The pilot started in September 2000 and is planned to end in February 2002 with positive results for both partners, and we are prepared to be present it during the ECR Conference in Barcelona in April 2002.

The scope of the project, from the perspective of the relationship with the retailer, is focused on the detergent category, with a particular emphasis on promotional SKU's.

Within Henkel, the internal forecast, replenishment, purchasing, promotion planning and production planning processes will be adapted to processes that are more suitable for collaboration.

Pilot Objectives

The pilot objectives defined were focused on proving the CPFR concept and validating the model. An additional objective was to generate stable delivery plans which would move the pilot toward more quantifiable objectives such as the reduction of out of stocks at the point of sale, increased sales growth, improved forecast accuracy, reduction of inventories and a broadened promotional plan horizon.

In the pilot, no specialized tool is used. The collaboration data is shared, using specially defined spreadsheets for each of the processes, and collaboration will be conducted through e-mail messages and phone calls. Currently, Henkel is running several pilots in Europe, testing their own tools and retailer exchanges' tools. These will be used to develop, via the Internet, their business plans, common promotional plans, comparisons of sales forecasts of each partner, exceptions, shared sales forecasts and order forecasts, and to obtain diverse other information derived from different workflows.

Current Status of the Pilot

The current status of the pilot is as follows:

▶ Downstream collaboration with Condis is completely established

   ▷ Collaboration on promotional planning
   ▷ Shared forecasts
   ▷ Replenishment of two warehouses according to the forecast
   ▷ Collaboration on solving problems directly at the POS

The Key Performance Indicators defined by Henkel & Condis were:

▶ Forecast Accuracy, measures of the forecast deviation

▶ Promotional Planning, the number of days between accepted promotion plan and the day when the promotion starts.

▶ Promotional Plan changes, the number of unplanned changes in the promotional plan during the frozen period.

▶ Service level, in terms of time, quantity, and out-of-stocks.

▶ Inventory level, measures the number of days demand could be satisfied based on the current stockholding and previous demand.

▶ Rush orders, full pallet, full truck.

Results

The first results showed a 15% improvement in forecast accuracy and an improvement in the joint planning of the promotional activity.

As for results, Exhibit 4.17 highlights the improving quality of sales forecasts over a period of seven months (January – July 20001). The figure represents the evolution of the sales forecast generated collaboratively by Henkel and Condis.

▶ The 'good' segment symbolizes the percentage of references with a forecast deviation of less than 20%, that is, references where the difference between the sales forecast and real sales is less than 20%.

▶ The 'bad' segment represents the percentage of references where this deviation is more than 50%. The graph shows the positive development of the 'good' segment (increasing) over the 'bad' segment (decreasing) over the past seven months.

In addition, first results indicated significant improvements in a variety of areas. Sales forecast accuracy increased and this, in turn, led to a customer service level of 99% which was sustained without increasing inventory levels, even during promotions that traditionally experienced high out-of-stocks. Furthermore, the companies reduced supply chain costs through a 6% decrease in rush orders, and increased the truck fill and pallet fill rates to 99%. Additionally, expanding the forecasting horizon to five weeks allowed Henkel and

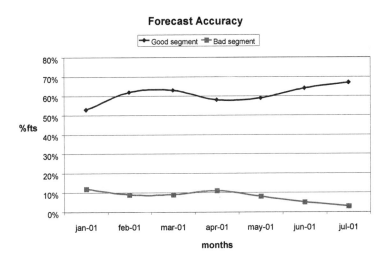

Forecast Accuracy

Exhibit 4.17 Sales Forecast between Condis and Henkel. Source: Henkel Spain/Condis

Challenges

The results convinced the companies involved to extend the CPFR initiative in order to quickly gain critical mass and harvest additional benefits. Henkel is currently evaluating various options, including adding trading partners and applying the best practices established to other customers in order to achieve critical mass. We are increasing the level of detail of the exchanged data, expanding the geographic reach, automating data exchange through the implementation of a CPFR IT solution and including further product categories.

These new partners involved will help Henkel to achieve a critical mass that will allow the company to focus its efforts and the processes on the critical products overall in promotional periods.

Currently, Henkel can improve the inefficiencies in the production of these critical products due to

▶ Changes in the Production Planning of these formats

▶ Lack of packaging

▶ Costs of storage

▶ High number of obsoletes due to sales forecast deviations

▶ Unusual costs

Therefore, if the collaboration among the different partners involved increases, and they are able to improve the collaborative processes of promotional planning and sales forecast generation of these critical products (please see exhibit 4.18), this will produce benefits for our suppliers through:

▶ Higher consistency with the lots ordered

▶ Improvement of their production cycles

▶ Reduction of their delivery costs

▶ Improvements in transportation planning

▶ Due to new internal processes of promotional communication in Henkel, suppliers will receive the information earlier so they will have more time for planning their production and distribution.

Another important issue, on which both companies are collaborating, is the out-of-stocks at the point of sale. Condis noted that even though service levels were improved, product availability on the shelves was significantly lower than in the stores' warehouses. Condis and Henkel have begun to analyze in-store operations with the objective of further improving product availability to the customer.

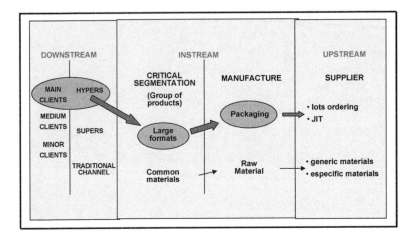

Exhibit 4.18 Stream-Management of Henkel Spain and Retailers. Source Henkel Spain/ Accenture

Impact on the Organization

▶ New roles and responsibilities were defined.

▶ New demand planning process were established and measured within the organization.

▶ Availability of the promotional information with enough horizon to allow the company plan in the middle and long term.

▶ Willingness to collaborate with retailers in order to develop collaborative processes in forecasting and replenishment.

Conclusions

Willingness to collaborate is the most critical factor for success. Companies' lack of awareness of this necessity is the most obstructive barrier to effective CPFR implementation and to achieving the potential benefits of CPFR. Another issue that requires clarification is the differences between countries, especially for multi-national companies. In order to foster that awareness, the GCI (Global Commerce Initiative) is developing standards for CPFR, taking into account the knowledge and experiences of American businesses, VICS (Voluntary Interindustry Commerce Standards) and ECR (Efficient Consumer Response).

4.5 CPFR – Views and Experiences at Procter & Gamble

Peter Hambuch, Procter & Gamble

CPFR is an idea which is not simply being discussed currently by retailers and manufacturers worldwide, but also one which the early movers are beginning to implement. This means CPFR has become an internationally recognized and supported concept. In plain language, one can describe CPFR as follows:

▶ Based on commonly formulated business plans, a forecast is jointly defined, which

▶ in particular adjusts production and warehousing in response to collaboratively determined demand,

▶ and governs the constituent flow of goods between individual participants in the supply chain.

▶ The consumer is central to these cooperative efforts.

In addition to explaining the CPFR concept in general and the presentation of actual cases, this article should serve to eliminate a confusion on terminology. That is to say that, an attempt is being made to locate the terms category management, efficient consumer response, CPFR and e-Commerce in their proper place with respect to one another.

4.5.1 CPFR as an inter-industry initiative

CPFR is an inter-industry attempt to improve the relations between business partners in the supply chain through cooperative planning and information exchange. The following diagram (please see exhibit below) shows in simplified form the interplay between participants in the process. The term 'Customer CPFR' denotes the collaboration between customer teams (CBD stands for customer business development), and retailers. The flow of information upstream continues via the collaboration of CBD with demand planning, which we call internal CPFR, ending in production planning and manufacture.

Supplier CPFR stands for the collaboration between manufacturing and its suppliers. An improved information flow (customer demand) upstream allows a synchronized flow of raw materials, packaging and end products downstream, resulting in the efficient fulfillment of consumer demand.

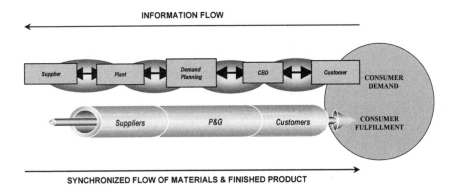

Exhibit 4.19 The flow of information and finished products in the supply chain.
Source: Procter&Gamble

The improvement of the relationships between partners is sought, because in the contemporary supply chain, the individual participants operate in relative isolation from one another.

▶ Communication is insufficient and discontinuous.

▶ Planning is not coordinated.

▶ The planning process of retailing is primarily focused on revenues at the POS.

▶ The planning process of manufacturers is primarily focused on the size of deliveries made to the retailer's central depot.

▶ Planning is based on assumptions

▶ Supporting systems do not exist

▶ Because of uncertainty, the supply chain is burdened by large safety stocks, a consequence of insufficient knowledge on the expected demand of all other participants.

The results of a study by Benchmarking Partners in the US makes this clear. In the year 2000, retailers achieved revenues of 3.2 trillion USD. But in parallel 1.1 trillion dollars worth of goods were held as stocks over the whole supply chain. This corresponds to an equivalent of a 4.1 month supply.

Let us look more closely at the unsatisfying and costly inventory situation on both sides of the equation. The reasons why the so-called safety stock is maintained at unnecessarily high levels are uncertainty and process inefficiencies.

▶ Uncertainty about consumer demand

▶ Uncertainty about the supply process relative to production and logistics

▶ Inefficiency in the process between the participants

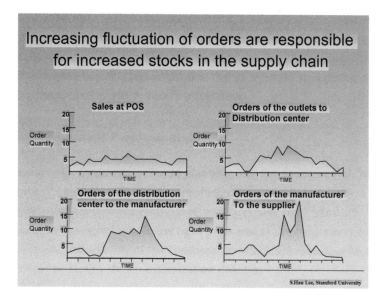

Exhibit 4.20 Reasons for increased stocks in the supply chain.
Source: Lee, Stanford University/VICS (1998)

The diagram above illustrates the consequences of the above mentioned problems. Although consumer demand in this example is relatively stable (graphic upper left), uncertainty and inefficiency causes observable swings in the flow of goods between

- warehouses and retail outlets (graphic upper right);

- the central depots of retailers and manufacturing (graphic bottom left);

- and on the production side between manufacturers and suppliers of raw materials and packaging (graphic bottom right)

Manufacturers and retailers pursue the same goals.

- Both see potential for the reduction of inventories in outlets, warehouses, and at their suppliers.

- Both want to increase the availability of product throughout the supply chain

- Both want to increase revenues and reduce costs.

Nonetheless, we find a number of inefficiencies in the supply chain

- Overstock throughout the chain

- Unsatisfactory delivery service from manufacturer to retail, but also from the retailer's central depots to the POS

- Lost revenues through unavailability of product on the shelf, or during promotional activity

- Deficient communication between participants

- Frequent and cost intensive 'firefighting' in the form of rush orders or short-term changes in production planning

All of the information necessary to attain these common objectives is already in existence, but is scattered and not available in the required measure for all of the business partners. This is hindered by closed systems on both sides and in particular through the attitude of the business partners and their corporate culture.

This is where CPFR is instrumental in eliminating the absolute boundaries, so that a complete solution for the common goals can be sought. Through CPFR and supporting technologies, it is possible that

- ▶ the relationships between business partners improve;

- ▶ the projections for future sales and orders become more precise, thereby reducing inventories, improving delivery service and avoiding shortages;

- ▶ and transparency is achieved through standards of measurement which allow the monitoring of progress towards the goals which have been set.

Udo Scharr of Procter & Gamble and Rita Marzian from Metro AG coined a very appropriate phrase on the occasion of the ECR Days of ECR DACH in Bonn, Germany, in September 2001. They said, "We, P&G and Metro, want to reach the C-Level in our cooperation."

It is also important to know what CPFR is not. The concept is not only usable by large but also by mid-size and small companies. CPFR is not a software solution that is simply installed on the computer. Even when technology plays a significant role in the exchange of information, this is only one aspect of what makes CPFR possible. It is by no means a replacement for efficient consumer response. The concept lives through the commitment of participating retailers and manufacturers and the engagement of all employees affected.

How does CPFR relates to ECR? To that question a quotation of Zygmunt Mierdorf, member of the board of the Metro AG: "The basic idea behind CPFR is ECR. And the basic idea of ECR is the improvement of business processes between business partners." Metro is seeing CPFR not as a replacement for current or future ECR activities. Moreover CPFR is a linking element for ECR activities, what could be visualized by a picture (see Exhibit 4.21).

The Centrale für Coorganisation, Germany refers to the following figure as the ECR house. Up until now, the ECR house has been a duplex. In both halves, different measures were used in order to meet the objectives of ECR in order to offer the consumer more value.

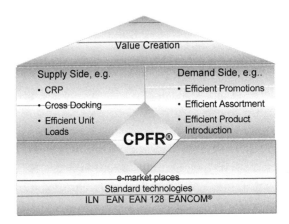

Exhibit 4.21 CPFR and the the ECR-House. Source: Centrale für Coorganisation, Germany

One side concentrates on the supply side and increasing the efficiency in the supply chain by logistical concepts and supporting technology like Electronic Data Interchange. In this area Supply Chain Manager and IT-experts are working together

The other side concentrates on the demand side, ergo the consumer and for that purpose uses the Category Management concept. Here people from departments like Purchase, Operations, Sales and Marketing are working together.

The two sides work relatively separately from one another. CPFR integrates existing, but isolated considered, ECR solutions of the supply and demand side into a comprehensive approach. The core of a CPFR implementation is the willingness of the business partners to jointly control the planning, forecasting and ordering processes. This means coordinating and linking strategic, tactical and operative planning in pursuit of common goals.

In the lower region of the ECR house are found the so-called enabling technologies. Like those for product identification (EAN), the EANCOM standards for data exchange via EDI or the offers becoming available in e-marketplaces. E-marketplaces have the advantage of not requiring that every participant have implemented his own complete in-house CPFR solution, but rather can obtain information through the Internet. Thereby, e-marketplaces will act as pacemakers for the implementation of CPFR.

The essential elements of CPFR potential for both manufacturer and retailer are seen as

▶ Increased revenues through better planning and thereby reduced inventory problems at the POS

▶ Improved cash flows through long-term inventory reduction

▶ Better coordinated organizational processes

▶ Reduced administrative and operational costs

In addition to the potential susceptible to measurable differences, the element of "better coordinated organizational processes" has a particular meaning.

▶ The collaboration between companies and functions is process driven.

▶ Responsibility is shared by business partners

▶ The information exchange within and between companies is better coordinated.

▶ Both partners work with the same information

▶ Decisions are made jointly

CPFR – a Learning Process

CPFR is a learning process, which means that lessons learned and information gathered flow continuously into the further process controlling. That includes gap analysis of the joint business plan, an analysis of the precision of the forecasts, or analyses of completed promotions and the flow of those insights into future forecasts.

In particular, the collaborative evaluation of the results of completed promotions vs. forecasts offers important understanding and enables the comparison and use of historical data for future planning. That includes the effects on the targeted sales influenced by

▶ the price;

▶ the type and quality of promotional support;

▶ or the season and the weather

CPFR as a learning process is reflected in the collaboration with our customers in North America. The following example (please see exhibit below) shows in a simplified illustration the CPFR workplan that a Procter & Gamble Customer Team developed together with a customer and followed since more than a year.

▶ temporal frequency of the individual steps (yearly, quarterly, weekly)

▶ expected results of the individual steps (business planning, target performance comparison)

▶ responsibilities (from senior management to analysts)

Frequency	Expected Outcomes	Responsible
Annually		
Renew Team Charter	Corporate Objectives / Expectations	Customer / P&G Senior Mgt.

Review / Renew Joint Business Plan	A) Joint Category Goals:
	  - Role of Category
	  - Pricing Plans
	  - Merchandising Plans
	  - New Item Introduction Plans
	B) Joint Results Tracking & Review Process:
	  - Develop Score Card to Track results
	  - Confirm gaps between goal and target
	  - Exception Resolution process
	  - Schedule Quarterly Reviews
	C) Joint Alignment Process:
	  - Verify Goals/Results will deliver
	    Corporate Objectives Charter
		Account Manager &
		Buyer: Lead Process

Quarterly		

Joint Business Plan & Gap Analysis	- Review Score Card / Gap Analysis
	- Review Merchandising Results from Previous
	  Quarter /Gap Analysis Plan
	- Develop / Revise Merchandizing Plans
	  Volume Forecast and Calendar for Next Quarter
	- Review Base Volume Results from Previous Quarter
	  and Gap Analysis
	- Develop / Revise Base Volume Forecast for next Quarter
	- Develop Plans to resolve Volume Gaps
	- Review and Revise Exception Criteria
	- Document CPFR Wins
		Account Manager &
		Buyer: Lead Process

Weekly		
Exception Management / Review Actuals	- Resolve critical Exceptions - Revised POS and Shipment Forecast	Data Analyst

Exhibit 4.22 CPFR workplan used by Procter & Gamble. Source: Procter & Gamble

Taken collectively, the CPFR business model can be broken down into the three following base processes.

▶ The business planning between manufacturer and retailer

▶ The forecast of expected sales and deliveries

▶ Inventory control from production and distribution through to POS.

Collaboration – the Core of the Concept

CPFR is a business model, which breaks with behaviors and processes which have been superseded, offers a comprehensive solution, draws the consumer into its considerations and connects the demand side with the supply side. The core of the concept is the 'C'. The relevant business processes involved are coordinated and synchronized across company lines. The prerequisite for this is the willingness of the business partners to guide collectively the planning, forecasting and supply process. The 'C' for collaboration is a necessary condition for integration. Business processes which were previously isolated are being bound together through CPFR. The quality of 'C' becomes apparent through the fair handling of exceptional situations, when for example the development of business does not follow as expected and solutions must be jointly sought. The more strongly 'C' is present, the higher the quality that will be achieved in the dimensions of 'P', 'F', and 'R'.

The 'C' fosters a cooperative culture, builds trust, aims for communication and information exchange, and creates win-win relationships between business partners. It is proactive, and not reactive.

The development of joint business plans and the measurement of results throughout the supply chain is based on a cooperative process. Cooperative processes support continual improvement.

Cooperation enables the necessary changes in organizational structures toward multi-functional teams, whereby the necessary training and the selection of appropriate criteria for measurement supports the formation of efficient team structures.

Technology which supports cooperation is being implemented and thereby supports the entire CPFR process. Integrated systems will close the gap between processes and technology.

CPFR leads to tangible and intangible advantages, which have been evaluated through pilot projects between manufacturers and retailers (Source: Transora, VICS):

▶ Improvement of forecasting accuracy 10 – 40%

▶ Inventory reduction in the supply chain 10 – 15%

▶ Improvement in service 0.5 – 2.0%

▶ Growth in revenues 2 – 25% (through reduced out-of-stocks on shelf and during promotions)

▶ Reduced warehousing and transport costs 3 – 10%

▶ Improved relations between business partners

▶ Better internal communication/planning

Around the globe a tremendous effort is being made to prepare for the implementation of CPFR. Manufacturers and retailers are at the same time busy validating the advantages within pilot projects. These projects also seek to play a formative role in defining the CPFR service functions of the electronic marketplace (GNX, WWRE, CPG, Transora). Based on input from the real world, the tools are being improved and enhanced further in collaboration with their respective software developers. In the same way, the respective organizations (GCI, VICS, EAN/UCC) are working on the standards which will be necessary to support data exchange over the Internet.

4.5.2 Collaboration through the entire Supply Chain at Procter & Gamble

As we are speaking about the entire supply chain, the topic of CPFR is not complete with a collaboration between P&G and our trading partners. The collaboration continues internally, in order to ensure the information flow between company departments concerned. Essentially, this means the collaboration between the Customer Teams and demand planning on forecasting and product availability. The constantly updated forecast from demand planning is the basis for production planning in the factories. Logically, the CPFR concept is useful in the collaboration between the plants and the suppliers of raw materials and packaging.

Procter & Gamble has begun projects across the entire supply chain in order to bring CPFR to realization.

▶ Between Customer Teams and retail companies

▶ Internally, between Customer Teams and demand planning

▶ Between factories and their suppliers

4.5.3 CPFR with Retail Organizations

A whole array of projects are underway with our partners in retail, primarily in North America and in Europe. The goal is to evaluate the potential of CPFR and to jointly test and improve the necessary tools in the field and to bring us in a position to implement CPFR on a large scale. As has been presented at many conferences, in Europe we are cooperating with Metro AG in Germany, Albert Heijn in Holland, and with Dansk Supermarked in Denmark. Further cooperations are in progress. With reference to the technology, we use Syncra software and the tools of the e-marketplaces GNX and WWRE. We also have pilot projects which are serving the development of tools for extranet of retailers. In Europe, the focus of CPFR cooperation is on the optimization of business processes linked to promotions. This begins with joint planning (product, week, advertising support, etc.), and continues with the forecasting up to sales tracking and inventory monitoring during the promotion in the outlets. The success of the common work is then measured by the ontime availability of the required volumes at various stages along the supply chain and the avoidance of out-of-stocks. Short-term firefighting in the form of costly rush orders should also be avoided. Concrete results from the cooperation with Dansk are shown below.

- ▶ Forecast accuracy for promotional revenues. Improved 83 – 98.5%

- ▶ Inventory reduction in Dansk's central depot. Reduced from 2.1 to 1.9 weeks reserve

- ▶ Product availability in Dansk outlets. Improved from 98.36 to 99.38%

- ▶ Rush orders. Reduced 20%

The pilot project with Metro AG in Germany also addressed the insufficient planning of promotions. Through collaboration, the following problems were identified:

- ▶ Inadequate communication in planning

- ▶ Insufficiently defined business processes

- ▶ Responsibilities not clearly defined

- ▶ Differing evaluation criteria (units of measure)

- ▶ Information which was insufficient, inexact or outdated

In response to the problems identified the objectives were identified.

- ▶ Increase sales through a reduction in out-of-stocks

- ▶ Cost reduction along the supply chain through, among other things, inventory optimization including promotions left-overs

- ▶ Learn, test, develop further

Within the cooperative agreement the focus was placed on the following individual elements. The work process was supported through a work flow tool.

- ▶ Planning the promotion

- ▶ Forecast the promotion volume

- ▶ Control of outlet orders and inventory

- ▶ Monitoring the promotion sales

- ▶ Evaluation of the promotion after its conclusion

There have not yet been any results made public. The teams on both sides have expressed their joint views about their work.

▶ We do promotion management with our partner, Internet supported with common systems, data and processes

▶ Through cooperation with our partner we are able to achieve more

▶ We have an improved promotions process

▶ We are convinced we can increase sales and reduce inventory

▶ It is doable

▶ CPFR begins with small steps. Start small and simple, be patient and expand

4.5.4 CPFR internally

It is the responsibility of our Customer Teams to pass on the customer specific forecasts based on the business plans they have developed jointly with the retailers to demand planning where the customer specific forecast is incorporated into a total forecast. In particular in Germany, information on planned promotions plays an essential role, as enormous peaks in the forecast, production and delivery to the retailers and on to its outlets will result. Exhibit 4.23 on the following page will serve to clarify.

The chart shows the course of the delivery forecast, the P&G deliveries, and the sales in the outlets at the weekly level. The sales peak in July is readily apparent along with the accompanying peak in deliveries, which was accurately anticipated eight weeks before shipment along with the development of inventory in the preceding two weeks. In the week of the promotion, sales with an index of 500 points over the normal volume were recorded. In order to ensure availability along the entire supply chain with such severe changes in demand, very good planning and communication are necessary on the part of all involved.

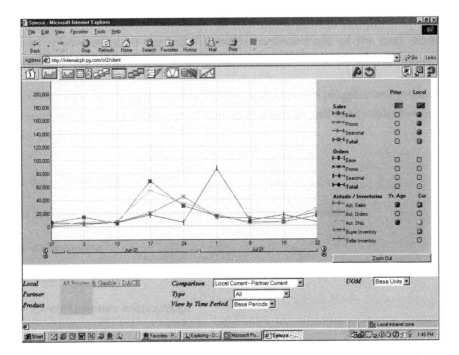

Exhibit 4.23 Forecast-Management of Procter&Gamble. Source: Syncra/Procter&Gamble
Legend:
I Line: Sales of a retail chain (sale at POS according to scanner data)
- Line: P&G deliveries to the distribution center of a retailer
■ Line: Delivery forecast for deliveries from P&G to the distribution center
x Line: Average weekly inventory in the distribution center of the retailer

In order to support the Customer Teams with the planning and to improve P&G's internal communication, we began a pilot project in the first half of 2001 and began to test a tool named Syncra. Syncra was developed by Syncra Systems of Cambridge, MA. The system is designed to support CPFR. It is based on e-commerce standards and supports the communication between cooperating partners. Procter & Gamble chose Syncra as its CPFR software as well as the e-marketplace Transora. In principle, Customer Teams have a large amount of data available to them, which they can use for forecasting. Depending on availability, this information is composed of items like delivery amounts form P&G to its customers, POS scanner data from its customers, details of the customer's warehouse movements and inventories, access to the customer's extranet, or historical information on offtake figures during promotions. These data come from different sources at P&G and the retail partner and are accessible through different systems.

Based on that it is not a minor effort for the Customer Teams to use all of this information in order to forecast for example promotional volumes with the expected accuracy. We have defined the following requirements in order to support the process of volume planning, We want **one** tool for planning, plan supervision, and communication.

▶ Volume planning ➔ Forecast

▶ Volume tracking ➔ Delivery vs. Forecast

▶ Communication ➔ Demand planning

The tool should make the data transparent which comes out of the systems at P&G and its customers.

▶ Begins at the lowest level (week, EAN)

▶ With aggregations over the customer structure and product hierarchy

▶ Planned promotional business

▶ Planned base business

▶ Customer's POS data

▶ Customer's inventory

▶ P&G deliveries

Syncra is a tool which meets these criteria, presenting the various pieces of information transparently in a tabular or graphic format. Working with the system is easy, and readily learned. Access to Syncra is via a web browser after inputting a user name and password.

With the exception of the planned promotional volumes, we load the above-mentioned information centrally into the system. For the calculation of forecasts for base business, we prefer to use offtake data from our customers distribution center or our weekly deliveries to his DC. It is the responsibility of the Account Managers to create the forecasts for promotional volumes in the system, and to keep them up to date. That can take place online directly or through a tool based on Excel that automatically transfers planning data into Syncra. The planning time frame shown is three months with weekly buckets.

The test with selected Customer Teams in Germany, Austria and Switzerland and the chosen product categories was successful. On the technical side, the flow of information met our expectations. More important however was that the forecast accuracy of our Customer Teams markedly improved. Currently we assume that six weeks before delivery, 80% of the delivery amount on EAN and at the weekly level can be estimated within plus or minus 25%. Similarly, the tools have proven themselves with respect to communication between Customer Teams and demand planning. Both parties use the same system and work with the same data. In addition, there is the potential to open the system to trade partners in order to support CPFR from the retail side. As appropriate to the success, the roll-out decision was made so that the system will be in production by beginning of 2002 for all Customer Teams and all product categories in Germany, Austria and Switzerland.

4.5.5 CPFR with Suppliers

The collaboration with factories and their suppliers is comparable to that between Customer Teams and their customers. Of course the information exchange doesn't have to do with the finished product, but rather with raw materials and packaging. After the production planning is based on the processes described, the production, storage and delivery of the suppliers is collaboratively determined with them. CPFR between all partners in the supply chain assures that information on the expected sale at the outlet flows through the entire chain and is translated into meaningful information at every stage. On a weekly (t) timeline, such a process appears as follows.

Activity	Week	Information basis
Execution of a promotion in outlets	t	EAN consumption units
Delivery to outlets	t-1	EAN shipment units
Delivery to retail central depot	t-2	EAN shipment units
Delivery to manufacturers central depot	t-3	EAN shipment units
Production	t-4	IAN internal article number
Delivery of raw material to plant	t-5	EAN, IAN
Production of raw materials	t-6	EAN, IAN

This example, which naturally does not apply to all manufacturers in all industries, nonetheless shows that forecasts, forecast accuracy and above all communication between all parties are the keys to success. Success is product availability at the right time at the right spot in the supply chain.

Procter & Gamble has begun several projects which, with the help of the Syncra System, are testing CPFR between factories and suppliers. Here we use Syncra to support vendor managed inventory (VMI) as well. This means that, based on the information in Syncra, our suppliers take over the responsibility for inventory control in our plants.

4.5.6   Experience at Procter & Gamble with Pilot Projects

The use of CPFR across the entire supply chain is realizable, even though there remain shortcomings on the systems side. Work is being done to rectify them. Interfaces between the systems are being developed and we are using this unique chance to create global standards for data exchange via the Global Commerce Initiative. The desire for collaboration between business partners must be present on both sides and documented in a contract between them. CPFR must be brought to life by team members on both sides. The joint business plan is the basis for collaborative work in forecasting. At the outset, a collaboration must set priorities. One should not begin with all nine steps of the CPFR model at one time. Focus allows a quick start, which also allows both sides to learn quickly. One priority for CPFR between manufacturers and retailers could be that, one begins with sales forecasts for promotions. Inventory build-up with new product introductions or the yet more complex task of product relaunches (inventory reduction with the old EAN, inventory build-up with the new EAN) are likewise appropriate for collaboration. At the beginning, partners should make jointly process analyses so that they learn from one another and jointly recognize inefficiencies in the current process. The technology is important, but at the beginning it need not be perfect. it is essential that the necessary information should flow. In the long-term we need to automate forecast creation and exchange. Otherwise the expansion of pilot projects is not scalable.

Afterword

The CPFR concept was developed in 1997–1998 by a number of manufacturers and retailers in the US. Now CPFR is being discussed around the world and as progressive accepted and supported. Its potential has been validated. The coming e-marketplaces will support CPFR with their service. The necessary standards for the required data exchange are in development. It is up to us, the participants in the supply chain, whether supplier, manufacturer, or retailer, to support the concept and to work towards the realization of its potential. No link in the chain can do it alone. It only works when we work together.

5 CPFR Perspectives and Roads to Implementation

5.1 From Pilot Stage towards Scaled Application: How scalable is your CPFR Solution?

Georg Engler, Accenture

5.1.1 The Consequences of Cooperation for the Supply Chain

Retailers and manufacturers are currently undergoing major changes within their supply chains. Increasing competition, complex distribution channels, shortening Product-Life-Cycles and changing consumer patterns are challenging the FMCG (Fast Moving Consumer Goods) industry. Therefore companies must ensure that they are both flexible and agile enough to adjust to changing conditions.

Increasing supply chain efficiency requires that companies eliminate inefficiencies, such as high inventory, out-of-stocks, poor service, limited information sharing, and replenishment strategies which are not demand-focused.

Designing a synchronized and flexible "breathing" Supply Chain is the basic requirement for gaining sustainable improvements and achieving competitive advantage.

The focus of Collaborative Planning, Forecasting and Replenishment (CPFR) is cooperation among the individual value adding steps within the supply chain and a synchronization of the supply chain processes:

▶ Collaborative promotion and event-management

▶ Collaborative sales and order forecasting

▶ Collaborative replenishment.

In various countries, pilot projects and first implementation projects have proven that CPFR can deliver benefits and added value. To take advantage of the potential benefits, the realization of CPFR has to be proactively addressed by both trading partners involved in the collaboration.

Currently, various CPFR Pilot Projects are demonstrating the following benefits[1]:

▶ **Improved management of consumer demand**
The customer and his needs are the focus of the planning process. Customers' needs can be forecast more accurately and through better use of disposal POS data a simultaneous response can be generated along the entire supply chain.

▶ **Increased forecast accuracy through the development of a single forecast between the trading partners**
The exchange of forecasting data between the collaboration partners and the development of a joint forecast by adjusting the planning process for the trading partners leads to increased forecast accuracy.

▶ **Sustainable Improvements in the collaboration relationship**
Open and trusting communication between trading partners increases the trust and understanding for the trading partner's individual situation.

▶ **Increased sales**
Reducing Out-of-Stock situations at the point of sale will lead to an increase in sales.

▶ **Inventory reduction**
By increasing the forecast accuracy and avoiding rush-orders, the planning horizon for both manufacturer and retailer is extended and therefore leads to decreased "buffers" for demand variations.

▶ **Reduction of Supply Chain Costs**
Increased planning reliability leads towards a better utilization of the production capacity. Reduction of rush-orders decreases the need for manual

---

[1] Results of various European Pilot Projects.

intervention in the production process and therefore significantly decreases set-up and production times.

▶ **Better use of production and supply chain resources**
Reliable planning data allows the development of a long-term plan for the use of available production and logistics resources.

▶ **Increase promotion effectiveness**
Increasing the transparency and agreed coordination leads toward an increase in Return on Investment.

To gain long-term benefits from CPFR, a successful pilot project needs to be scaled and integrated within the internal business processes of the trading partners. Within CPFR pilots, the data exchange is often handled on a manual basis (spreadsheet, fax, etc. may be sufficient for a pilot) instead of using a collaboration software tool. The quality of the data will be limited and, if put into the companies planning or production system, can lead to erroneous conclusions. For simulating the underlying business processes, manual data exchange is sufficient, however it is not an option for scaling CPFR throughout the company. The failed integration of business processes and collaboration software can even doom a promising CPFR pilot to failure. Starting from the euphoric pilot results, missing system support will lead to employee frustration and thus resistance towards the initiative.

Parallel to a CPFR pilot, management must consider in advance how they are going to implement the CPFR initiative within their IT strategy and the overall company strategy.

Within the ECR Europe CPFR-Project, Accenture and ECR Europe developed the "Guide to CPFR Implementation"[2], which describes in depth the different steps trading partners need to conduct to move from internal collaboration to pilot implementation and full-scale Implementation of CPFR.

---

2   ECR Europe "A Guide to CPFR Implementation, 2001

5.1.2 Supply Chain Collaboration – Are you ready?

Retailers and Manufacturers are currently successfully piloting CPFR, but full-scale CPFR implementations are not yet on the agenda. One explanation of the situation is that during CPFR pilot projects, companies get their first real impression of the complexity of full CPFR implementation into internal processes, organization and technology. Looking more closely, the complexity can be differentiated as IT-complexity and organizational complexity. To scale up the collaboration process companywide, and with all major trading partners, company specific IT solutions are required.

Organizational and cultural adjustments are even more challenging to implement than the IT solutions are to be managed. The organizational adjustments include structural adjustments, training of the changed functions and cultural adaptations to support the CPFR goals. Realization of cooperative benefits within the supply chain started in the early 1990's with the development of Efficient Consumer Response (ECR). All ECR methods are based on collaborative elements. Therefore the collaboration partners who have already implemented ECR methods (VMI, CRP, Category Management, etc.) are already familiar with collaboration and will have an additional advantage. The experience thus gained can be used as a starting point to spread CPFR-Collaboration through the whole supply chain.

So far, supply chain optimization or collaboration has been based on peer-to-peer relationships within the supply chain, but the up- or downstream aspects have been neglected. The transformation of the supply chain structure – from a company focus towards a supply chain focus – requires adaptation of processes, organization (structure, culture, qualification) and of the IT System within the company. Within these areas, paradigms and company values, which traditionally grow between and within the companies, will be replaced by collaboration. Rethinking and re-learning is the only possibility for the employees to adjust to the rapid changes.

Collaboration Levels

Collaboration can be differentiated by several criteria:

▶ **Information and data exchange**
The first level of collaboration is defined by the exchange of information and data without defining specific processes or following specific rules based on the idea that alone the exchange of information will have positive effects for the participants. The insights gained from information sharing can be used internally to adapt high-level processes towards the requirements of the trading partner, thereby simplifying day-to-day work.

▶ **Bilateral communication**
In bilateral communication, the data and information exchange is focused on specific subjects which are of interest to the trading partners. The aim is to define common goals within the trading relationship and set up a communication plan to reach those goals. For the exchange of the data, industry standards or pre-defined standards can be used if necessary. Bilateral communication supports the aims of aligning the business of the trading partners and enhancing the cooperation between the companies.

▶ **Integration of business processes**
The trading partner is involved in the strategic, tactical and operational planning and expects sustainable benefits from the partnership. Based on the exchange of information, the partners design collaborative business processes and agree on confidentiality. The benefit for the partners is the early exchange of information and therefore early involvement in significant trading relationship changes. Furthermore, the information can be used to internally align processes and procedures towards the requirements of the cooperation. The developed processes need to be integrated into day-to-day business.

Prerequisites for a Collaborative Agreement

A collaborative organization is created by strategically establishing partnerships across company borders. For the trading partners, collaborative organization requires open communication, process transparency, and identification with the collaborative ideas. One of the advantages for partners is the cultivation of flexiblity within an environment of constant change.

The following are the main characteristics of a collaborative agreement:

▶ It fosters knowledge exchange between partners

▶ It strengthens the collaborative culture

▶ It creates a proactive climate for problem resolution

▶ It establishes a collaborative incentive system

▶ It measures collaborative success

▶ It builds partnerships and win-win solutions

Knowledge Exchange between Partners

Collaborative organizations are defined by the exchange of knowledge. An understanding of behavior patterns or the knowledge of internal processes in partner organizations allows for better prediction and evaluation of events. The partners have to agree in advance on what kind of knowledge they want to exchange, the way the knowledge is exchanged and when the knowledge exchange will occur.

Knowledge Exchange is based on:

▶ **Data Exchange**
Collaborating companies agree on the scope, format and type of data which is necessary to achieve the goals of collaboration. Within a CPFR project, items like weekly sales inventory data from the regional distribution center or the planned demand of a promotional item are of interest to partners.

▶ **Employee Support**
Conducting collaborative projects requires support from several business and organizational units. The units contribute to the project team either as subject experts or by dedicating full time project support. The project team consists of team members from both companies.

▶ **Resource Sharing**

When implementing IT solutions, the exchange of specialists across company borders can support project efforts significantly. Especially smaller companies often do not have the required resources available or they are deployed in day-to-day business.

▶ **Strengthening of the Culture**

The close and intensive contact between companies during collaboration will result in companies' own cultures being influenced by the culture of their partners. The exchange of small ideas and suggestions in the long-term results in large scale changes to the culture. Traditionally, major cultural difference exist between retailers and manufacturers. Influenced by the culture of the collaborative partner, in-house culture will be critically reviewed and, if appropriate, the necessary adjustments made. The employees within a partner's organization should initiate adjustments within their own organization if possible and proclaim the advantages of a collaborative culture through their actions. The collaborative spirit will influence even employees who are not directly involved in the collaboration.

▶ **Problem recognition and solution**

Every innovation meets with difficulties and reservations within the company at its inception. Compared to other initiatives, CPFR requires not only that reservations within an organization be overcome but also those of its trading partners.

▶ **Employee Hesitation**

Planning a CPFR implementation always needs to confront the hesitation and concerns of employees. First of all the employees tend to want to keep business as usual instead of engaging the risks they perceive to be associated with collaboration. To overcome this hesitation it is necessary to establish open communications with all employees and to discuss the opportunities of CPFR for the whole organization. Employees have to live with the proposed collaboration in their day-to-day activities, and therefore it is important that they understand and support it. Within a pilot project or inter-company collaboration, the employees can get a feeling and understanding for the sort of collaboration being planned, and profit from their experiences later on in a full scale CPFR implementation.

▶ **Know-how**

Knowledge is required to set up the project's collaborative processes and to identify how IT can support collaboration. Management needs to prepare for the collaborative challenge by gaining the necessary competencies and knowledge.

▶ **Senior management support**

The involvement and support from senior management is required to secure necessary resources and to coordinate the collaboration with the overall business strategy.

▶ **Resources**

A collaborative project requires adequate resources in terms of project budget and team members. Senior management is responsible for ensuring that sufficient resources are available in terms of quality and quantity from the start.

Collaboration Partner Selection

The overall success of the collaboration depends on the selection of an appropriate partner. Next to the capabilities of the collaboration partner, the following questions should be considered:

▶ Can the relationship with the potential trading partner be characterized as open and trusting?

▶ Does the trading partner have strengths and weaknesses complementary to one's own organization?

▶ Does the trading partner have appropriate resources (personnel, IT, etc.) to make CPFR successful?

▶ Is the trading partner conducting other collaborative initiatives with one's company or with other organizations?

The complete questionnaire for a capability assessment of a potential collaboration partner can be found in the ECR Europe Publication "A Guide to CPFR®️ Implementation" , which was jointly developed by ECR Europe and Accenture.

Establishing a Collaborative Incentive System

Through their joint responsibility for the supply chain, partners have to consider installing incentive systems that are linked to the achievement of the collaborative goals. Traditionally, incentive systems such as the annual bonus have been linked to squeezing the highest possible benefit out of trading partners, neglecting the efficiency of the supply chain. Within retailer-manufacturer relationships, the goal of the retailer is to obtain products at the lowest possible price, whereas the manufacturer is targeting high sales volume. As a result, high inventory levels occur due to forward buying behavior. Incentives should be oriented towards improvements in efficiency, such as inventory reduction, lead-time reduction, or increased on-shelf-availability.

Measuring Collaborative Success

Continuous measurement of collaborative success based on agreed Key Performance Indicators (KPI) is required to ensure that:

▶ The actual developments and future plans are generating value for the collaboration partners.

▶ As supporters of the collaboration, senior management receives relevant feedback and overcomes any lingering skepticism. The generated information should be used to critically review the collaboration and to identify improvement areas.

When installing a system to measure collaborative success, it is important to involve the controlling department to analyze the consequences for future planning. A recalculation of prices, including savings realized by the collaboration, leads towards a repositioning in the competitive landscape. Selling the same product at lower prices will significantly improve total sales.

A Partnership Win-Win Solution

The collaborative partners expect higher sales and increased profits. The idea of win-win means a fair distribution of the efforts of the collaboration and the results. For the companies, win-win is the incentive to intensify the collaboration. Within the collaborative arrangement, the partners must agree on how to distribute the collaborative benefits. Nevertheless, in addition to the benefits, it is necessary to include in the arrangement provisions for the risks of the collaboration.

There are several types of collaboration which must be differentiated. For the purpose of simplification, we focus on downstream collaboration between retailers and manufacturers.

5.1.3 Guidelines for CPFR Implementation – From CPFR Pilot to Full-scale Implementation

What is important when implementing CPFR?

CPFR implementation is based on long-term and encompassing planning between collaborative partners. Implementations vary in scope and intensity, depending on the underlying technical solution and the organizational and cultural integration of the partners.

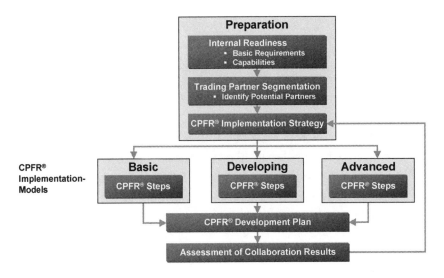

Exhibit 5.1 CPFR Implementation. **Source: ECR Europe**

Basic CPFR

The objective of Basic CPFR is to enhance collaboration within an organization. Basic CPFR provides an implementation framework for trading partners who are unwilling to collaborate, not ready to collaborate, or for whom collaboration with partners would offer limited potential but for whom collaboration within their own company may generate benefits. In some cases it may be used to prepare the company for future CPFR implementation with trading partners. It aims to foster collaboration between departments within one company. For example, Basic CPFR brings together the Sales, Demand Planning, Marketing, Production, Purchasing, Logistics and Customer Support departments. Basic CPFR can focus on a few or all areas for collaborative processes. The potential benefits are significant but limited, since no trading partners are involved.

Developing CPFR

The objective of Developing CPFR is to prove the CPFR concept and assist companies with an easily implemented CPFR initiative that will reap benefits. It also enables companies wishing to focus on supply chain integration to prepare the organization for an Advanced CPFR implementation. Developing CPFR implies generally limited collaboration with a trading partner. It is often restricted to a collaborative promotion plan and sales or order forecast collaboration, or to a reduced number of SKU's. It may also be used as 'easy-to-implement' CPFR that embraces all the CPFR processes and all the company SKU's and delivery points. There are however limited potential benefits, as it does not integrate the whole supply chain. Developing CPFR can also be seen as a key entry level with trading partners (e.g. pilot phase).

Advanced CPFR

The objective of Advanced CPFR is to roll-out CPFR, reach critical mass, and achieve full potential benefits. Advanced CPFR implies collaborating in promotion planning, sales, and order forecasting through the development and maintenance of a close relationship with trading partners. Complete integration of all processes may be effected gradually, beginning initially with a limited scope. The collaboration process is usually automated through an advanced IT solution which is integrated with the company's back-office systems (ERP, Production Planning, etc). Advanced CPFR includes the use of orders, POS, and inventory data. Advanced CPFR may also include collaboration through one or many exchanges.

From Pilot to CPFR Implementation

In the preparation phase, trading partners have to assess their own capacities for a CPFR implementation and in selecting a collaboration partner. The step from developing CPFR towards advanced CPFR is mainly determined by higher IT requirements and the deployment of adequate resources for implementation. The benefits collaboration partners can realize from pilot implementation are mainly a reduction in variable costs, depending on the scope of the pilot and the SKU's involved. Those cost savings are based on inventory reductions along the supply chain, reduction in rush orders, and administrative savings. Collaboration leads to a better balance of supply and demand and therefore gives an indication about savings which could be realized through full-scale implementation.

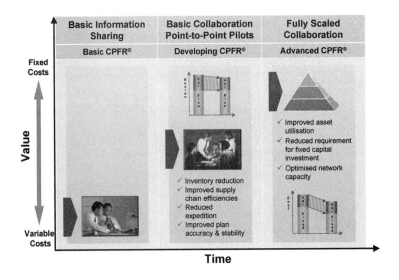

Exhibit 5.2 *Migration of CPFR implementation. Source: Accenture*

In most cases, a successful CPFR pilot is the baseline for rolling out CPFR and a full-scale implementation. Through pilot projects, companies can learn and acquire experience which they are able to apply later for quick implementation.

Within the pilot phase, all involved parties can learn step by step the meaning of collaboration and the necessary changes the companies have to undertake. By integrating the main collaboration processes to simulate an implementation, the necessary requirements in terms of strategy, IT, personnel, and process alignment become obvious.

After the pilot stage of CPFR, companies have either grown aware of the requirements for IT-collaboration tools, or if a specific tool was used during the pilot they can assess the its value directly. An additional advantage is that intra-company processes between departments are already established. Good preparation during the pilot stage delivers advantages in terms of shortening set-up times, when implementing CPFR.

Complexity of CPFR Implementations

The complexity of implementing CPFR is based on two major components.

▶ **Integration of collaborative processes between the collaboration partners**
All processes between collaborating companies need to be identified, regardless of whether they are already automated or partially automated. Depending on the collaboration goals, i.e. next to promotion and special event processes, regular sales / standard assortment processes require a detailed analysis. Detailed analysis allows one to optimize the processes in accordance with the collaborative partner's company. For all semi-automated processes this means an assessment of interface requirements.

▶ **Collaborative Process links to internal infrastructure**
A detailed analysis of the existing IT-Infrastructure is required before implementing CPFR. Given an increasing number of available systems, the system landscape in most companies is rather heterogeneous. Implementing a CPFR solution requires that an interface be named to link the systems peer-to-peer.

Enterprise Application Integration (EAI), is a technology for the structured integration of different IT-solutions into the existing IT-landscape.

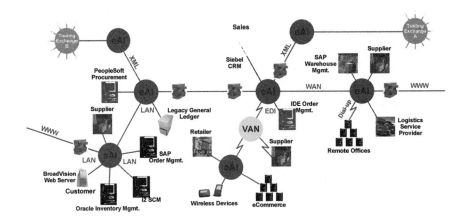

Exhibit 5.3 Structure of Enterprise Application Integration. Source: Accenture

EAI ensures that the company is able to react quickly and precisely when adding additional applications to the existing IT-infrastructure by:

▶ Analyzing the existing business processes and workflows

▶ Defining and managing interfaces of the various applications

▶ Transforming and formatting of data and information and simultaneously synchronizing the information on the different systems and within various data sources

▶ Serving as the data flow architecture between the linked systems.

All major B2B Exchanges are offering CPFR functionality. The Global Commerce Initiative is currently working on the definition of CPFR standards to ensure global applicability.

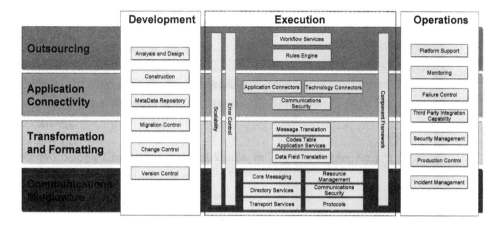

Exhibit 5.4 Major components of Enterprise Application Integration. Source: Accenture

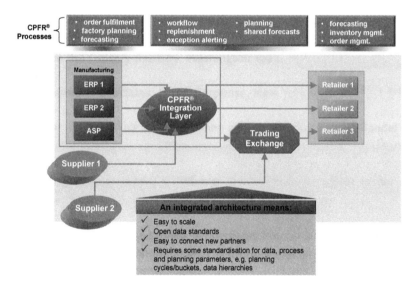

Exhibit 5.5 CPFR and Trading Exchanges. Source: Accenture

Technological Requirements for CPFR

A successful CPFR Implementation requires technical support to describe the collaborative processes and the data used. Many retailers and manufacturers are comfortable with the CPFR concept and have realized the benefits, however few companies have implemented a fully scaled CPFR and realized sustainable benefits.

The question is why?

Actually, the answer is very simple. The internal processes, the organizational status, and the current IT structure are not prepared for the collaborative challenge. In a first step, the internal requirements need to be aligned to start a full-scaled CPFR implementation. However, this investment can not fully account for the CPFR Initiative. Companies must always change some of their processes and systems to solve specific business issues, if for example, a company does not have a sufficient demand planning engine. To implement a solution will bring benefits which are not attributable to CPFR.

There are several areas which need to be addressed before starting collaboration; nevertheless the critical areas for success are:

▶ The collaborative forecast challenge

▶ Data management and workflow application

▶ Forecast adjustment and exception management

▶ Trusting relationships among trading partners

▶ Difficulty of intensified data exchange

The Collaborative Forecast Challenge

Adjusting the forecast detail for one or two trading partners is manageable, but for broader applications this can be a time-consuming process and an opportunity for error or misinterpretation. Manufacturers and retailers must address this issue and decide how willing they are to modify their current forecast formats.

For example, compressing a forecast from a weekly to a monthly time period or breaking down a national- or category-level forecast to a SKU/location-level forecast might be the only way to get to a true "apples to apples" comparison. This is necessary for meaningful collaboration in setting exception thresholds and taking exception resolution action on exceptions that will truly add value. The mechanics of this process can be aided if forecasting and collaborative tools are in place or outsourced. Another solution is for one trading partner to perform this build-up or break-down of forecast detail for another, provided the other partner trusts him with this task.

Data Management and Workflow Application

Business process definitions, resources, timing and adequate infrastructure are all prerequisites to ensure the flow of collaboration-relevant data. In the early stages of CPFR implementation a long-term strategy for the management of the data must be defined. Especially the question of which standards will be used for data management requires an early decision. Without a decision on one standard agreed upon by the partners, the collaboration cannot enter the next implementation step.

The automatic data Retrieval Process triggered by an exception appearance – by for example an e-mail of an automatic update of the forecast within the internal planning systems – will further spread and accelerate the usage of CPFR processes. Here there is an opportunity to use available, technically mature data management tools or a range of external service providers who also offer services.

Forecast Adjustment and Exception Management

Based on the agreed upon exception criteria, resolving exceptions has top-priority for partners. It seems simple, but priorities are not necessarily the same for retailer and manufacturer. Within the arrangement, it must be clearly defined what an exception is and how the trading partners will resolve it. The collaboration process requires that the partners agree on a specific format for data exchange.

A major part of the collaboration cycle is the "window of action" concept. The "window of action" is a period when the partners can address the final result within a pre-defined scope. Forecast changes can therefore be addressed within the "window of action" by each collaboration partner without the direct involvement of his counterpart. The idea is that the partners do not have to activate the collaboration process for small changes in the forecast.

Trusting Relationships with Trading Partners

Changes in the behavior of the trading partners are the major challenges to be overcome in implementing CPFR on a scaled basis. In implementing CPFR on a full scale basis one is confronted with a different mentality on the part of the trading partners from that of the short-term pilot project. Additionally, the timeline for a pilot differs from a long-term strategic CPFR implementation. As the duration of the pilot project is limited, both sides can easily cancel the pilot if the results are not as expected or a trading partner could not fulfill expectations.

Due to the shorter duration of a pilot, the cooperation of those involved is easier to assure than in a full-scale implementation. In the short term people can change their attitude because they might already have the end of the project in mind. A full-scale implementation is the start of collaboration and has no end in sight. Therefore, it is more difficult for people to adjust to the new rules, since doing so demands lasting change. Trust in the accuracy of collaboratively developed forecasts is especially limited because companies tend to use incompatible methods for forecasting. Depending on company structure, different departments are involved in the forecasting process which are not directly involved in the collaborative process and not able to assess the consequences of their actions.

Therefore not all information is shared with the partner, which impairs transparency along the supply chain. As a result, we must conclude that a forecast based on 'instincts' and experience not be exchanged. To avoid this situation, trading partners must adjust the roles and areas of responsibility for their decision makers and stakeholders in the changed environment. This is an especially difficult step for the retailer – manufacturer relationship, because both are focusing on the customer as the reason for acting. Historically this has not been the case.

A joint business plan, emphasizes the goal of customer centricity due to a common understanding of the partner's business processes and working patterns. The development of a joint business plan is only possible if the organization allows and supports those kinds of changes.

Difficulty of Intensified Data Exchange

So far the term data exchange has been viewed in a negative fashion, even though it is a part of our daily business. In speaking about collaboration, data exchange is seen from a different perspective.

Collaboration does not mean that there is free and uncontrolled data flow between companies. Collaboration regulates the data exchange and uses data in the best possible way to support management decisions. Therefore the collaborative partners have to decide on rules for the exchange of data, and who is to provide which data and of what quality. Experience have shown that within collaborations the stronger trading partner tries to force his ideas on partnering companies. In the supply chain, a possible effect might be that a retailer provides POS data to all following members in the supply chain.

Intensive data exchange should be established between all supply chain members, independent of their current position. At first sight, it might seem ridiculous to send POS data to a packaging supplier, but if the supplier has the knowledge and infrastructure to use the data, there is no reason to exclude him. Each collaborator must individually agree to the extent he is willing to share data and to what extent it makes sense to exchange data along the supply chain. It is necessary that partners are open to share data and overcome traditional boundaries for data exchange.

5.1.4 Collaboration – the Outlook

Supply chain collaboration is a logical step in optimizing the supply chain. Through collaboration, the trading partners will be able to fulfil the customer needs, such as flexible delivery, shorter lead-times and On-Shelf-Availability. Furthermore, collaboration will include transportation planning.

Cultural changes and the necessary process adjustments between the trading partners will be the main challenge for the implementation of a collaborative scenario.

New technologies will allow faster collaboration between companies by providing sophisticated tools to cover the interaction between the companies and improving data quality. The transactional Business-to-Business approach quickly leads to decreased costs. For large-scale supply chain optimization, companies must develop individual collaborative models which best represent their collaborative strategy.

5.2 Migration to Value Chain Collaboration through CPFR

Robert Bruce, President, VCC Associates, formerly Wal-Mart
Ron Ireland, Vice President, VCC Associates, formerly Wal-Mart

Leading retailers are on a migration path to Value Chain Collaboration that will allow them to surpass the competition in customer service and profitability for the shareholders. The road map consists of foundational, strategic and transformational journeys which guide the organization's projects, initiatives, priorities and goals. Collaborative Planning, Forecasting and Replenishment is the initial step in a multi-step process towards full "Value Chain Collaboration" and competitive Transformation. CPFR is the joint planning between retailers and major customers on the key elements of the demand and supply chain processes. CPFR is a **core transformational** strategy which takes business process, people and technology to a **higher level of performance** by promoting openness, information sharing, data exchange, visibility and joint decisions. This Value Chain Collaboration is an important segment of a business strategy and provides a foundation for solid best practices in business processes which include:

▶ Building business alliances focused on jointly-managed processes

▶ Development of a single, mutually-owned, consumer-driven forecast

▶ Higher level of accuracy than statistical measures

▶ Link consumer demand with supply planning and execution

▶ Improved value chain integration

Value Chain Collaboration vision begins with CPFR and migrates to collaborative account/merchandise development and collaborative transportation management. Early adoption is valuable to be competitive in the marketplace.

5.2.1 Key Attributes of Successful CPFR Management

The question is not whether to embrace collaboration and more specifically CPFR, but **how quickly retailers and Consumer Package Goods manufactures can implement this strategy**. Being early adopters is important from a competitive point of view. Taking a significant step in enhancing the value position to improve the profitability, sales and revenue on retailer's brands is a key to beating the competition in the market place. Embracing collaborative principles is more a cost of doing business and transforming the way business is done than taking a strict single project payback and return approach.

A key attribute is the joint linkage of all business units focused and aligned to the corporate vision and migration plan. Communication planning and executive ownership, sponsorship and visible leadership are also critical components to the success for implementation. The true ownership of execution relies heavily on change management to assure that associates embrace this new vision, own, participate and drive the execution. All need to be orchestrated to assure that the organization is breaking down old barriers and paradigms while laying the foundation for a cross-functional **collaborative** environment.

The organization needs to be assured that all members of management support the change and are able to "Walk the Talk" to actually become Customer Centric. Being Customer Centric means being focused on the customer, adding customer value and driving all decisions based upon customer demand. Assuring that everyone is working on satisfying the consumer can reinforce this customer centric direction. If they are not contributing value to the stores servicing the customer, then they are working on the wrong things. Leadership, competency and enabling technology are essential attributes in successful management teams that help promote and foster a collaborative atmosphere – leadership, competency and enabling technology.

Leadership

To be successful a company's leadership must preach the necessity for all employees to think in collaborative terms and act in more real time. The competitive landscape is forcing the traditional retail senior management to evaluate how collaboration will affect the future of their industry. More importantly, senior management must determine what course if any their company will take. Will retailers take this journey? That question depends totally on the state of the retailer's leadership. Although some retailers are beginning to develop and incorporate a collaborative strategy into their overall vision and business strategies, some traditional retailers have not created or communicated a collaborative culture or mindset throughout their organizations.

Organizations that have strong leadership have already developed and integrated their Internet initiatives within their overall business strategies. They have promoted risk-taking to stimulate a collaborative culture throughout the organization. For traditional retailers to develop the new culture in their companies, they must become more adept at breaking down the impediments that have prevented them from moving forward with collaborative initiatives. Senior management leadership must champion a collaborative culture by demonstrating commitment to Internet initiatives, encouraging internal and external collaboration, openness in trading partner relationships, risk-taking with Internet related projects, and fostering the development of stronger bonds between the IS. Some industry leaders in consumer products manufacturing and retailing have taken giant steps toward CPFR. They have management organizations committed to developing collaborative cultures and they have promoted their Internet focus internally and with the investment community, customers, and suppliers.

Competency

As retailers have organizational competency attributes, the retail industry has traditionally used these strengths in providing higher levels of customer service and in developing stronger relationships with supplier partners to effectively manage product delivery in the supply chain. Most retailers however have not discovered the ability to use the Internet to leverage their traditional strengths in customer care and supply chain management. Most traditional retailers have not utilized the Internet's potential to provide solutions for their business or operational issues.

Organizations with **strong collaborative competencies** have the ongoing ability to be very **responsive to customer needs, the capability to execute ruthlessly and move with incredible speed**. Retailers need to develop relationships with complementary collaborative players to leverage their brand or core competencies on the Internet. They must learn and understand how these initiatives could improve their own enterprise as well as the total value chain.

Technology

A key driver supporting this path to transformation resides in the arena of technology. For most traditional retailers, the industry's bottom line focus has positioned the retailer with an IT infrastructure that is unable to meet the needs of today's New World environment in the Internet. The traditional retailer has had limited exposure and experience in implementing collaborative solutions. Success requires an IT infrastructure to implement collaborative initiatives rapidly without taking time to justify the ROI for incremental improvements in the infrastructure. Technology is the vehicle for process scalability. To ensure success retailers and manufacturers must build and drive standards across the enterprise having the competencies in place to develop, scale, and support collaborative Internet initiatives rapidly with trading partners.

5.2.2 Trading Partner Relationship Management

This internal focus extends outward to the trading partner community beginning with a select group of core alliance vendors who are critical to success. A top-to-top meeting of key executives with the executive team at the retailer must occur to convince those involved that this is not the same old organization. Management needs to understand that it works for a company truly committed to addressing and resolving the ills of the past through specific action plans. **This is no longer a "We Win – You Figure Out How To Win" relationship.** It is now an opportunity to make a retail organization the "Preferred Retailer" for vendor collaborative relationships.

Formulating strong and scalable trading partner relationships takes a set of guiding principles that are continually reinforced. Within these principles a trading partner strategy can be defined, piloted, and implemented. The new evolution of these relationships focuses on a common set of goals and objectives, a high level of mutual trust, a willingness to openly share data and a desire to link all business elements concerning Win/Win results for manufacturer, retailer and customer.

Key steps in formulating strong alliance relationships are:

▶ Executive Education and Training

▶ Defining a Strategic Direction and Migration Path

▶ Aligning Executive Sponsorship, Ownership and Communication Planning

▶ Defining the Joint Team Mission, Core Objectives, Metrics, Rewards and Account Level Profit and Loss Statement

▶ Clarifying Supporting Cross-Functional Initiatives and Targeted Objectives

▶ Formulating Quarterly and Monthly Communication Plans, Performance Tracking and Accomplishment Reporting

▶ Planning Executive Visioning Retreats Semi-Annually or Annually

▶ Promoting an Internal and External Collaborative Environment

Setting a structure of strong relationships with trading partner vendors, carriers, and solution providers is paramount to support the migration to best practices. The migration may start with solidifying business operating fundamentals, but moves towards defining a dynamic and collaborative set of interrelationships internally and externally all focused and driven by the customer. This is where the real competitive strength and geometric results originate.

Leveraging the skills of others both internally and externally is a basis for collaboration cross functionally and with trading partners. Trading partners are often experts in their categories on consumer and market analysis. As part of building a collaborative relationship with trading partners opening retailer data to key suppliers to jointly analyze customer sales and market basket data is very important. This analysis can be focused on category/market analysis and assortment planning, as well as market and demographic analysis defining market potential, and share and gap analysis. These are important steps that will lay the foundational business processes and migration path for successful implementation to CPFR. Moving in a planned and incremental way towards Collaborative Planning, Forecasting and Replenishment (CPFR) will assure real business benefits. This process is dependent on communicating, educating and training associates and management on a set of building blocks and sequence of actions promoting internal and external collaboration across business units.

5.2.3 Four Foundational Strategies

The four pillars for success are foundational and organizational core competencies that enable best practice migration and implementation of key transformation strategies.

▶ Build Trading Partner Alliances Vertically and Horizontally

　▶ Sharing Consumer Data for Merchandising and Demand Planning
　▶ Joint Collaborative Decision Making
　▶ Vertical Account Profitability Analysis

▶ Consumer Driven Integrated Value Chains

　▶ Vertically Integrated and Optimized Value Chains
　▶ Demand and Supply Chain Linkage (From Shelf to Production)

▶ Internet Enabled Collaboration

　▶ Planning, Forecasting & Replenishment
　▶ Account Planning & Management
　▶ Merchandise Assortment Optimization
　▶ Transportation Management

▶ Full Value Chain Visibility & Information/Decision Management

   ▷ Information Visibility & Real/Near Real Time Accessibility

   ▷ Joint Decision Making

   ▷ Exception Management

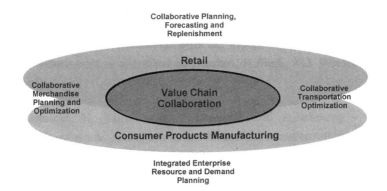

Exhibit 5.6 Collaborative Value Chains. Source: Bruce/Ireland, VCC Associates

A migration path laying key foundations and competencies must be in place to maximize execution, and determine the degree of success, return on investment and competitive positioning. These four pillars are the foundation to scalable implementation of CPFR over multiple trading partners as well as other collaborative and integrated value chain initiatives. The common thread tying these strategies together blends several attributes and characteristics of a company's culture, focus, capabilities and strategic vision.

Foundational

To lay out the road map to transformation, key steps must be followed to assure sustainable success. A basic foundation must be put in place to build upon. The focus is on the basic business processes, organization and behaviors that support all other initiatives. This is also the phase where quick hits are possible that fund further strategic initiatives giving momentum to the drive towards a transformational vision.

Strategic

Laying the cultural, basic operational, and tactical initiatives developed in the foundational stage, key strategies pull together a multifaceted approach to transformation. These strategies guide the migration path of the organization across key business units keeping the company focused and on path. This stage is where CPFR and furthering trading partner relationships reside.

Transformational

This is where the picture is painted for the organization, a picture which reflects the corporate vision that is a catapult into the market place, industry positioning and a new source of competitive advantage. A transformational vision aspires towards a fully integrated value chain linking demand and supply from shelf to supply in an optimized and visible collaborative environment

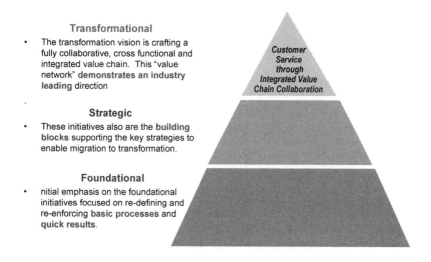

Transformational
- The transformation vision is crafting a fully collaborative, cross functional and integrated value chain. This "value network" demonstrates an industry leading direction

Strategic
- These initiatives also are the building blocks supporting the key strategies to enable migration to transformation.

Foundational
- nitial emphasis on the foundational initiatives focused on re-defining and re-enforcing basic processes and quick results.

Customer Service through Integrated Value Chain Collaboration

Exhibit 5.7 Migration path to collaboration. Source: Bruce/Ireland, VCC Associates

5.2.4   Starting the Journey with CPFR – Nine Critical Steps

Some of the same criteria suggested in the VICS/CPFR Guidelines and Road-map documents should be used during the CPFR pilot planning and partner selection process. Some key objectives that drive CPFR implementation help determine the selection, rate and speed of implementation to achieve short range, intermediate and long-range results. Success breeds success, as the saying goes, and is valid for helping to define which trading partners are selected for your graduated roll out program. The first trading partners selected must be those that are considered industry leaders, highly competent, not resource constrained, embracing best practices and having CPFR as a supporting corporate strategy.

Key rules for CPFR implementation are:

▶ **Do Your Homework** – Hit the calculator and determine the category and trading partners that will deliver the most impact

▶ **Remember the 80/20 Rule** – Define the top 10-20% trading partners that will give you critical mass, but don't forget about the other 80%

▶ **Fund Your Program with Results** – Compound the growth of results over time and communicate at every milestone

▶ **Walk Don't Run** – Start slow and remember it's 80% planning and 20% doing – well thought-out and orchestrated programs – that win

▶ **Success Breeds Success** – Competency check your trading partners – the good ones will set the pace for others, better guaranteeing results

▶ **Bring In the Big Guys** – Discuss and implement organizational, risk and change management issues with your executive champions

▶ **Go For the Gold** – Select items and categories that will deliver early business process wins and visible financial paybacks

▶ **The Book of Law** – Multi-tier project planning is critical in aligning business process, organizational/change and technology timelines

▶ **Inspect What You Expect** – Measure everything and translate it back to the key financial measurements your company uses

▶ **Pick Your Wins** – Then communicate and celebrate with a passion

CPFR is not rocket science and is not dependent on sophisticated technology to be accomplished. Like anything in business you must **first focus on business process before technology.** Furthermore, being a large corporation is not a pre-requisite and often CPFR can help level the playing field between the large industry leaders and more intermediate-sized companies. Success with CPFR is dependent upon a company's understanding, ownership, process and openness internally and externally. The biggest issues I have seen with failed programs or marginal results came from a lack of understanding of what CPFR is really all about, short changing implementation or sitting on the sidelines and doing things the same way as always, but expecting different results.

Taking CPFR to Scale

With a solid foundations in leadership, governance, competencies and technological architecture the question must be asked, is the organization in place to support the migration of collaborative processes? Piloting CPFR gives organizations the opportunity to learn, test and otherwise lay the foundation for the business process and technology changes that must be planned for scalable rollout as well as migrating to other collaborative applications. More specifically there are key issues that must be addressed, planned and staged to successfully implement a scalable rollout of CPFR.

Scalability Issues

▶ Visioning and Strategic Alignment

▶ Business Justification and Case for Action

▶ Executive Ownership & Sponsorship

▶ Migration Planning to Critical Mass

▶ Multi-Tier Project Planning & Management

▶ Current Process & Gap Analysis

▶ Roles & Responsibility Definition

▶ Organizational, Risk & Change Management

- ▶ Communication Planning and Project Management

- ▶ Technology Review & Architectural Assessment,

- ▶ Software Partner Selection & Implementation

- ▶ Trading Partner Implementation & Execution

Before undertaking this journey champions need to build internal corporate energy around a collaborative strategy, translate its support and alignment with the existing corporate strategies. Corporate impact must be defined financially and communicated over a clear time horizon while clarifying its organization implications and requirements. Most importantly, in some organizations executives need to be guided and coached through the process. Executive understanding, ownership, support and participation are critical in driving the speed and ultimately the success of implementation. Executive leadership can align the vision, issues, organization, resources and focus to radically move the organization. In other situations executive leadership can perpetuate skepticism, near term tactical thinking, sustain existing paradigms and otherwise limit the potential of the organization

The CPFR evangelists of the organization must align themselves internally with multi-tier champions to help drive the understanding and ownership at all levels. Additionally, selection of an executive champion is critical whether it is the President/Chairman, Executive or Senior Vice President. Otherwise the project will not be grounded within the company, organizational focus will be distracted and resource assignment questionable on a consistent basis. Through proper communication planning the organization will be in tune with the importance and role of CPFR and value chain collaboration as a key corporate transformational strategy. All too often I see companies whose **executive management team does not understand what CPFR is**, what it will do and how it lays the foundation supporting their corporate strategic vision to competitive advantage. Even more dangerous, they think they understand what CPFR is but **approach new thinking in an "old world" context**.

Business Process and Change Management Issues

Companies have mentioned that technology is the easy part of piloting and implementing CPFR, but the process is difficult. Laying down the core competencies and foundations are the first two steps on the roadmap to successful implementation. Technology is the enabler to scalability. It is the business process supported by the internal culture that makes CPFR successful. Defining and implementing the basic collaborative processes provides the structure needed to support the transition from piloting to scalable implementation. Many miss the importance of change management in support of the piloting and rollout process. Not addressing the organizational aspects of collaboration will limit or minimize the over-all success and bottom line financial results from CPFR.

The basic processes were redefined in the pilot stages of implementing CPFR. Existing processes need to be reinforced along with putting measures in place to make them permanent. Additional processes need to be changed to support linking the demand plan and forecasts to internal production systems for both trading partners. For the retailer forecast, quantities need to be tied through forecasting, replenishment and order management systems. For manufacturers, forecast quantities need to be part of their internal demand planning and the advanced planning and scheduling process as well.

A blueprint must be laid out representing the current (as is) business processes compared to the new (to be) business processes required to support full implementation. The most important aspect of planning the roll out plan for CPFR must be focused on business process change, associate development and organizational alignment. The internal CPFR champions and human relations associates must drive this change management plan. Staffing capabilities and capacity issues associated with the changes in business processes along with new roles and responsibilities will need to be managed. Process roles and responsibilities need to be defined at two to three levels of detail for each related position. Communication flows should be developed reflecting inputs, decisions and outputs prior to conducting one on one discussions and group training sessions with associates.

To offer **permanent solutions** that produce the desired results, performance metrics, measurements, incentives and rewards need to be in place to **re-enforce execution**. Organizational alignment and staffing issues will arise and also must be addressed as part of the change management process. Along with the multi-functional process ownership that has previously been put in place, communication planning must be a part of the change management process defining the key messages conveyed by executives to further building understanding and involvement at all levels of the organization.

It is advisable that a risk assessment be part of one's change management plan. The risk assessment, milestone and alert processes can help one keep on track, avoid pitfalls and otherwise make on-going adjustments in process, change management or technology project plans. The important issue is that the organization, governance teams and CPFR project manager need to have three project time lines sequencing activities and running in parallel.

▶ Project Plans and Timelines

▶ Business Process

▶ Risk and Change Management

▶ Technology

Technology vs. Process

Most technology in this space is robust enough to support scalable roll out of CPFR. Three issues exist, however, one being the question as to each company's systems architecture and its readiness to support existing and future requirements of Internet enabled collaboration, initially focused on CPFR. Second is the state of industry standards defining XML. Third are the business processes which need further definition and tailoring within each organization. Technology is the facilitator and enabler of rapid, scalable implementation and roll out. More than technology, basic process related issues need to be addressed – **do not make IT a scapegoat**.

Demand Aggregation

For manufacturers, sales force demand aggregation is a paramount issue in scaling CPFR. Building critical mass is the process and systems supporting collecting, processing, aggregating and then separating sales/demand forecasts by retail account or, conversely, supplier. Clearly defining the organizational alignment, sales team processes for collaboration on sales forecast, translation causal factors to a demand forecast and processing customer specific forecasts and feeding APS systems must be done. Within the sales forecast collaboration process tools must be provided to standardize and translate the promotional, event and pricing causal factors affecting the demand forecast

Conversely, this is also a challenge for retailers. A jointly agreed upon demand plan for a retailer must be fed back into internal systems, merchandising systems, replenishment, order management, inventory deployment, distribution, transportation and logistics forecasts. Middleware offers focused solutions to many connection issues, but does not address these process-related demands. When addressed it is important that the systems are part of the natural workflow processes to assure timely integration.

Replenishment Fundamentals

Bottom-up consumer demand planning has the fundamental focus on consumers' buying needs at the store shelf. Consumer demand drives "pull based" replenishment fundamentals that supports the right products in the right place, at the right time, at the right price and at the right profit margin for the business. The visibility of the consumer forecasted demand and actual demand drives the supply driven optimization process:

5.2.5 Moving towards Strategic Transformation

CPFR is not just a replacement for VMI, but is a first step in a migration path to transformation and industry leadership. If you are not stepping forward then you are falling behind. You cannot be successful in your business tactics if your tactics do not complement a **long-term set of strategies** and support a

transformational vision for your organization. It is not an issue of whether you should implement CPFR, but rather how quickly you can assess your readiness and how fast you can begin your program.

Moving from foundational to strategic initiatives requires an assessment of the organization that supports a "customer driven" store process and alignment of activities and decisions. Starting from the point of customer purchase, store level focus is on linking product on shelf with modular/planogram optimization and replenishment. Buyer and merchandising guidelines and disciplines are then re-defined and reinforced to assure accountability to supporting store performance. Further product channel development and channel strategies need to be defined and implemented to better optimize and support the stores with product flow to assure execution. These processes are oriented to linking the following:

▶ Store Level Ordering Processes

▶ Planogram Integration with Demand Planning and Replenishment

▶ Inventory Management and Flow Focus

▶ Replenishment Effectiveness

▶ Assortment Optimization and Order Planning ROI Maximization

▶ Process Integration and Internal Collaboration

▶ CPFR as a Gateway to Other Applications for Collaboration

▶ Channel Strategy Definition and Optimized Selection

This further lays the next steps supporting demand and supply visibility, process integration and optimal joint decision-making. If you do not properly implement these strategic initiatives you minimize the return and speed in implementing collaborative networks.

Collaborative Planning, Forecasting and Replenishment is the initial step in a multi-step process towards full **Value Chain Collaboration** and competitive Transformation.

5.3 The Foundation is in Place – it is Time to transform

Ralph W. Drayer, Supply Chain Insights, formerly Procter & Gamble

Savvy executives are seeing the opportunity to drive the use of the Internet and supply chain partnerships to transform their supply chains, delivering differentiated capability, value and competitive advantage in the process.

5.3.1 The Quiet Revolution

Much has been written about the subjects of Logistics, Supply Chain Management, Value Nets and e-Business but most companies have been slow to take advantage of what has become one of the most dramatic and dynamic changes to business in the last 100 years. Leveraging the Internet with the best supply chain management techniques creates not only greater efficiencies but, more importantly, differentiated value and customer loyalty through the creation of entirely new business models. Witness the success of the early transformers, companies like Dell and Cisco.

When viewed in the context of today's consumer driven marketplace – extremely rapid changes in consumer preferences, behaviors and shopping options –, the need for, and opportunity of advantages through supply chain transformation should be compelling.

5.3.2 The Foundation

Despite the slower than expected uptake in supply chain transformation, all the required foundation elements are now in place:

▶ Tremendous strides have been made in the art and science of **Supply Chain Management** as it has evolved from physical distribution and logistics to a more holistic focus on the management of upstream and downstream relationships with suppliers, distributors, and customers to achieve greater consumer value-added at less cost. A fundamental principle of supply chain management is that significant leverage can be obtained by working with suppliers and customers as if they were part of an integrated, seamless pipeline. In this way, considerable improvements in total delivered cost as well as customer satisfaction can be achieved.

▶ Supply chain management tools such as Continuous Replenishment and High Velocity Cross Docking delivered impressive results for customers and suppliers alike and led an entire industry to come together to develop more efficient supply chain practices. Launched in 1993, **Efficient Consumer Response (ECR)** has changed the whole trading partner focus from adversarial "win-lose" negotiation to collaborative trading relationships focused on removing inefficiencies from the total supply chain and delivering higher consumer satisfaction and value. Perhaps most important, ECR built trust and demonstrated the value of deeper collaboration across the supply chain, preparing these companies to fully leverage the powerful capabilities of the Internet.

▶ The dream of supply chain transparency and real time interaction with all trading partners became a reality with the arrival of the **Internet**. The Internet allows unprecedented, seamless and continuous exchanges across the supply chain. Significant efficiencies can be gained through linking the supply chain and removing unnecessary inventory, variation, cost and reducing cycle times to create an "extended enterprise". In an extended enterprise environment, the sharing of information leads to common goals, increased velocity of trade, and a meshing of business processes.

Because the Internet is a robust commerce platform, it shifts the emphasis from simply *connecting* partners, which is mostly transaction oriented, to *coordinating* inter-business processes. This is important because coordination is knowledge and process oriented and synchronization at this level creates more value across the chain.

5.3.3 The Opportunity

The real payoff from these three critical foundation elements: Supply Chain Management, Efficient Consumer Response and the Internet is enabling **Business Collaboration**. Collaboration occurs when companies work together for mutual benefit. It means that companies leverage each other on an operational basis so that together they perform better than they could separately. Collaboration can occur all along the value chain from design collaboration, through procurement and final distribution. This allows companies sharing information to dramatically shorten processing time, eliminate value-depleting activities and improve quality, accuracy and asset productivity. The overriding goal is to optimize the end-to-end supply chain for the benefit of the end consumer.

Collaborative Planning, Forecasting and Replenishment (CPFR) is a great example of a new, collaborative business process reflecting the evolution of an ECR supply chain practice (Continuous Replenishment) and a demand chain practice (Category Management). CPFR creates a "win-win" scenario, bringing demand and supply planning together in one process and tying the buyer and seller together so that their goals are compatible. By competing as one, buyer and seller form a **Value Chain** that will easily come out ahead of other buyers and sellers still focused on win-lose price negotiation.

The ultimate Business collaboration models emerging are called **"Value Nets"** and **"Virtual Enterprises"**. If you have ordered a computer over the Internet, you've come in contact with this model. It transforms the traditional linear supply chain to create differentiated capability and competitive advantage. Changing the way you do business is what it is all about!

The Value Net business model uses advanced supply chain and ECR concepts to achieve both superior customer satisfaction and company profitability. It links increasingly specific customer requirements to flexible, cost effective manufacturing and uses digital information to move products rapidly, bypassing costly distribution layers. It connects supply chain providers who work in concert to deliver tailored solutions. It elevates operational design to the strategic level and adapts to constant change.

As the name implies, it is no longer just about supply, it is about creating **Value** for customers, the company and its suppliers. It is also no longer a sequential, rigid, linear supply chain. Instead, it is a fast, flexible, high performance network of customer/supplier partnerships and information flows. The value net begins with the customer, allows him to design products from a menu and builds to satisfy actual demand, leveraging operations and customer choice to drive strategic advantage. Since the Value Net's product and service advantage is based on a collaborative set of relationships, it is also harder for competitors to replicate it.

Another powerful transformational model is the **"Virtual"** or **"Extended Enterprise"**, which changes the entire concept of what it means to be a company. In this model, each company performs just those processes at which it excels, leaving others to do the rest. A manufacturer, for instance, may concentrate on marketing and sales; its suppliers may collaborate to design the manufacturer's product; and a distributor may perform the actual assembly. Every participant in the virtual enterprise has a common focus: delivering the greatest possible value to the final customer at the lowest possible cost to the enterprise. To achieve this objective, information must be shared, redundancy eliminated, and opportunities for collaboration exploited. This in turn requires unprecedented cooperation, enterprise wide planning, alignment around common goals, and an inclusive culture.

5.3.4 The Challenge

The Value Net and Virtual Enterprise models offer a dramatic improvement in performance but also demand radical changes in thinking and behavior. There is no silver bullet. The key is good business process integration and customer focus. This requires clear consumer value identification of the business problem or opportunity; thinking externally and viewing your extended supply chain as a strategic differentiator; changing organizational structures-multifunctional and horizontal process teams, high commitment work systems, and flexible structures which can be easily modified. Traditional patterns of suspicion and mistrust must also give way to openness and sharing- collaboration is to be expected and rewarded. Finally, senior management's understanding and leadership are obviously critical to create the capacity for change and an environment for success.

In preparing for the transformation, companies must progress through various stages of supply chain competence:

▶ **Internal supply chain optimization:** typically a new organizational structure for product supply, metrics and internal communication system.

▶ **Network formation:** really beginning to work with supply chain partners and customers, removing barriers and sharing information.

▶ **Value network formation:** extensive use of extranets, collaborative planning and design systems and some process integration

▶ **Virtual Enterprise:** full network connectivity is achieved and the company becomes the nucleus of the extended enterprise.

Ultimately, the successful companies of tomorrow will be those that push the use of the Internet and supply chain partnerships more strategically than in the past, creating new revenue opportunities and achieving new levels of efficiency, customer loyalty and customer satisfaction. The message, then, is for companies to start building on and leveraging the transformational foundation now in place- it is time!

5.4 On the Road to the Network Economy – Developing an e-Transformation Roadmap for profitable Growth in the Consumer Goods Industry

Christian Koch, SAP AG
Dr. Gerhard Hausruckinger, Roland Berger Strategy Consultants

5.4.1 The Innovative Context

What keeps CEOs of consumer goods manufacturers and retailers awake at night worrying about the future of their companies? It is the search for sustainable and profitable growth – which is not that easy given the current state of the economy. Buzzwords such as globalization, innovation, brand (portfolio) management, supply chain excellence, and e-business are the main planks of strategy design today. In a recent study[3], manufacturers and retailers put the potential savings from a consistent e-transformation program alone at around 1-3%, and the growth potential at around 5% of their sales. The savings are seen mainly in the supply chain, in sales organization, and in improvements to marketing and promotional processes. The study found that this generates growth, mainly through better planning processes and through more effective promotions based on collaborative processes.

The entire economy is involved in a trend toward inter-company process optimization, shifting the focus away from purely internal process improvements. Innovation is firmly focused on manufacturers' interfaces on the sales side. For ECR Europe, as a joint initiative of manufacturers and retailers, this is nothing new. For a long time now, ECR Europe has been analyzing this potential and engaging in many projects and initiatives to create strategies for implementing it in practice. What we have found is that while the concepts are undoubtedly mature enough to be used in business, the technology available is unable to support them properly. Contrary to ECR's intentions, "enabling technologies" have thus become "disabling technologies," preventing the broad-based use of the proposed models. New technology can be a major driver of collaborative processes and help achieve quantum leaps in performance only if it dovetails with corporate strategies, core business processes, and the organizational framework.

In the consumer goods industry, projects are focused mainly on collaborative technology that is relevant to the sales side. Trade promotion management, advanced planning and scheduling, and Collaborative planning, forecasting, and replenishment (CPFR) are some of the hottest applications at present. In many ways, the Internet provides the basis for implementing processes in day-to-day business. Extranets, web EDI, and eBXML now offer communications opportunities that enable broad-based collaborative applications. Additionally, the emergence of marketplace technologies – driven initially by public exchanges, but seen increasingly as communications platforms for individual companies – has given the outsourcing efforts of the new economy a basis in reality, even in the post-new economy age. Innovative companies are turning

---

3   Source: Roland Berger Strategy Consultants, ECR Survey of 120 European manufacturers
    and retailers in the FMCG sector

to these technologies and trying to establish a sustainable competitive edge as "early adopters" or "smart followers."

An extensive portfolio of technologies is now available, with portal technologies and self-service applications in purchasing and internal administration. But even conventional approaches such as data warehousing and the associated reporting and analysis features have made considerable progress. The volumes of data that can be managed today are much larger than ever before, and at the same time, far more users are in a position to analyze them.

These technologies promise companies potential benefits across the board, but the question of what action to take, when, and how to do it still remains. To use a metaphor, it's all about using the right score to combine a large number of individual musicians and instruments into one orchestra playing melodious symphonies.

What makes matters worse is that, as the economy stands, short, transparent projects have a clear edge over long-term reorganization projects. Not knowing what resources will be available next year or what the economic climate will be like, people tend to focus on short-term improvements where the costs are foreseeable and the returns more or less immediate.

However, ensuring that this action maintains its long-term innovative momentum in the long term means embedding it in a long-term technology strategy. Otherwise it could meet the same fate as many e-commerce projects in the hype phase of their lifecycle. The cost of integrating stand-alone solutions into developing, and thus changing, IT structures in the long term can easily exceed the cost of introducing the solution in the first place, and so call its commercial viability into question. Or it may turn out that integration is not even feasible from a technological standpoint.

Managing Transition as a Planned and Actively Managed Total Process

To summarize the above, managing innovation successfully, both in technological and business terms, requires combining both levels into a single, total process. In real terms, this means

- ▶ Taking a cold, hard business look at the status quo

- ▶ Identifying the main weaknesses and potential for improvement (looking for short term, limited scope, and clear or measurable benefits)

- ▶ (Roughly) quantifying the benefits

- ▶ Examining existing solutions and technology options

- ▶ Putting options and potential into context

- ▶ Producing a project sequence (roadmap) for transforming the company within the network economy.

Systematically linking strategy, organization, business processes, and information technology also means bringing the right know-how into the complex process of roadmap development. That is why SAP and Roland Berger Strategy Consultants have joined forces to produce a master plan for the consumer goods industry, which can be used in designing company-specific e-transformation roadmaps to suit individual needs and aims. We will look at this more closely below.

5.4.2 Developing a Master Roadmap for the Consumer Goods Industry

Of course you can design a roadmap to help an individual company find its way to the network economy without using a ready-made template. The difference between the two is much the same as the difference between customized and standard software. Ultimately, customized software is rarely suited to wider applications, as the extra time and cost involved are disproportionate to the desired results.

However, as with standard software, adapting it to a specific segment or company is worthwhile and also significantly increases the value added. Here, the focus is on the FMCG (fast moving consumer goods) segment of consumer goods manufacturers. The roadmap is based on research conducted mainly in Europe, and so is inevitably Eurocentric. This must be taken into account when applying it outside of Europe.

The master roadmap consists of the following elements:

- ▶ Content

  - ▶ Industry trends
  - ▶ Specific IT solutions required
  - ▶ Roadmap specification

- ▶ Applications

  - ▶ Roadmap tool
  - ▶ Roadmap application model

In logical terms, the roadmap starts by defining and analyzing the main industry trends and environment, and then looks at what requirements these impose in terms of IT solutions. It then considers in detail what they actually mean in terms of technology and business management. The roadmap tool then puts these factors in the context of the individual company, customizing the approach efficiently and purposefully.

The complex nature of designing business processes in response to organization- and technology-driven innovation requires a clear guide through the multi-stage roadmap process. A simplified off-the-shelf approach is out of the question, if only because the changes we are looking at here will have a lasting impact on all aspects of a business. This is where the roadmap application model comes in, specifying a process model for using the e-transformation roadmap.

Using the roadmap is usually a multi-stage process that entails an increasing amount of detail at each new stage. In developing this tool, it was important to ensure that practical results could be achieved at relatively little cost in the initial stage. The roadmap tool is thus designed to work out key elements, in interaction with an FMCG company, based on an analysis period of just a few days, and to draw up the first draft of a holistic e-transformation roadmap with the help of the tool. The results obtained provide the foundations for the strategic renewal process, showing where innovation is particularly rewarding and promising. These results make it much easier to understand individual projects in the overall context and integrate them in medium to long-term planning.

They can then be further validated and worked out through a process of iterative improvement, in particular through continued use of the tool, both internally and together with external specialists.

The next steps in the roadmap application model involve progressively refining the results, with a view to internal communications as well as to implementing the projects identified.

5.4.3   Roadmap Content

As explained above, three main trends have become evident:

▶ Globalization

▶ Increasing efficiency

▶ Direct customer relationships

In this section, we will look at what this means in terms of the IT solutions required.

Requirements

What are the strategic consequences of these trends? It may be useful here to go a level deeper and examine what each of these main trends implies in detail.

Globalization requirements

This is a complex subject, and there is not enough room here to do more than skim the surface. Mergers and acquisitions have a particular impact on brand strategies in terms of creating a strong and consistent international image. Merging different corporate structures also touches upon many general elements, such as cultural and organizational aspects, IT systems landscapes, and supplier relations. Even with aggressive organic growth though, the question remains whether the business model and technology employed are scaleable. At present, many FMCG manufacturers are dealing with the question of how to organize themselves in response to key accounts with global operations, such as Wal-Mart, Ahold, and Carrefour, and to ensure prompt and meaningful global account controlling.

Efficiency requirements

There are two aspects that must be differentiated here:

▶ **Increasing efficiency in internal processes**
Although lasting improvements have been made in recent years, there is still a long way to go in speeding up and simplifying processes, focusing more clearly on the right processes, and creating an efficient communications environment. There is also a need to examine and classify processes in terms of their potential for being redesigned to accommodate an e-business approach.

▶ **Increasing efficiency in external processes**
In the business of the future, the key will be to form inter-company partnerships on the sales and procurement side and in the value creation process. Possible tools here include such solutions as CPFR, collaborative transport management, vendor managed inventory, and extranets.

Direct customer relationship requirements

In the consumer goods industry, the value chain must become even more tailored to consumer needs than it has been in the past. For manufacturers, this means intensifying relations with retailers, as they are the ones who ultimately sell things and who are in direct contact with consumers. On the other hand, web technology provides another option for getting in touch with end consumers directly, thus allowing greater proximity to them. A third possibility is to build up a flexible value network to give customers more value, whether by making products more individual or offering complementary services.

The e-Transformation Roadmap – an Action Program for Structured Decision-making

The overall trends in the industry imply a certain portfolio of business management solutions from which companies must choose the building blocks that will make the greatest contribution to their individual goals. Supporting this selection process is where the actual roadmap model comes in. It is based on the considerations elaborated above and provides specific recommendations on the selection and sequence of the projects to be implemented.

The roadmap is divided into four areas that can be seen as the steps a company takes to become a network economy player. However, if these areas were "steps" in the strictest sense of the word, which could be taken only in sequence, the model would have missed its mark. Rather, this step approach is designed to serve as an intellectual framework, in which various self-contained individual projects can be grouped together in a meaningful way. By taking the financial, technological, and organizational considerations of a specific business into account, the four areas can then be arranged to form an individual innovation plan: a customized e-transformation roadmap.

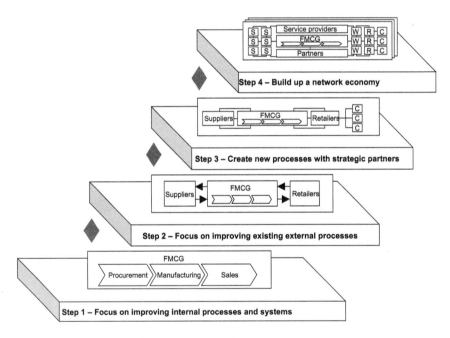

Exhibit 5.8 e-Transformation Roadmap for the FMCG sector.
Source: Roland Berger & Partner/SAP (C: Consumers, W: Wholesalers, R: Retailers)

The core areas of the roadmap mark out four steps in the development process, ranging from a more tactically oriented internal view, to collaborative processes in operations, to new value-creation approaches in a networked environment, and ultimately to redefining the business as part of the long-term vision of the network economy.

Each of these areas has its own processes and scenarios with their potential for innovation. Today, these processes and scenarios are more or less crucial to a manufacturer's innovation process. Therefore, the master roadmap also offers a master set of options from which a business can design its own specific action program, in terms of both content and chronological priority.

In **Step 1**, the focus is on optimizing internal processes and systems, doing the "homework," so to speak, to lay the groundwork for subsequent steps. This step is mainly about enterprise application integration (EAI) as a platform for technologies that enable automated communications and interoperability of various applications and business processes. This rather technical aspect of Step 1 should go hand in hand with a rigorous change management program, which could be managed by temporary business integration teams, for instance.

In **Step 2**, which can easily be run in parallel, existing external interfaces and processes are drawn into the optimization. Traditional issues such as EDI or – more recently – web-EDI are increasingly enhanced by implementing extra-nets, which enable flexible communications with a whole host of business partners. Also, advanced planning and scheduling (APS) systems, which address problems of forecasting, planning, and execution, are becoming increasingly popular. Global open standards form a common language for exchanging information of all kinds and play a key role in these issues.

Step 3 is based on the idea of a collaborative platform (collaborative hub) with five key features:

▶ Consumer/customer relationship management (CRM)

▶ Vendor managed inventory (VMI)

▶ Collaborative planning, forecasting and replenishment (CPFR)

▶ Supplier relationship management (SRM)

▶ Collaborative transport management (CTM)

This platform (see illustration) can be used to exchange information, products, and services via the Internet, and provides the basis for using the collaborative features above, integrating trading partners and service providers to the greatest extent possible. Due to space constraints, these features cannot be further specified here.

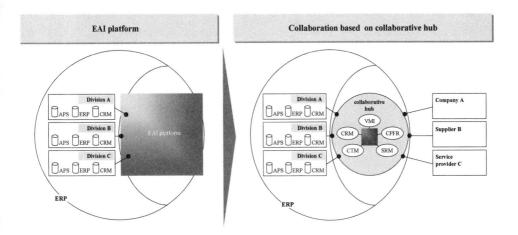

Exhibit 5.9 An EAI platform is an excellent base for running collaborative features. Source: Roland Berger & Partner/SAP

Step 4 marks the realization of the network economy, in which companies focus strictly on their core competencies and competitive advantages, work closely with all kinds of business partners on the basis of global industry standards and open, intelligent technologies, and create real value for their customers in the process.

If we consider the topics listed here in the light of the current debate, we find that the hottest topics, such as customer relationship management, supply chain management, and CPFR, are in Step 3, that is, developing progressive collaborative processes. Here, the desire to implement innovative processes is driven by the potential they can in theory unleash. Whether this potential can be achieved in practice, however, is another matter. It is of little use, for instance, to sit down with customers to work out joint plans for CPFR if unavoidable changes of plan in response to unforeseen events mean that production and distribution are unable to put such plans into action. Under these circumstances, it is best to identify where the greatest return can be achieved with the least effort, and to start there. The answer may be, not introducing CPFR, but rather improving processes that may be peripheral yet indispensable for smooth operations.

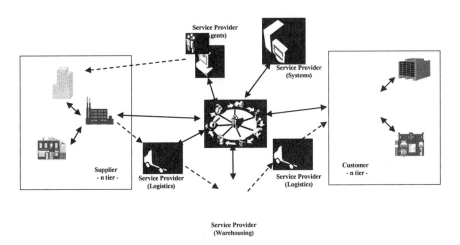

Exhibit 5.10 In the network economy, tier n trading partners will be linked via complex networks. Source: Roland Berger & Partner/SAP

The roadmap's real value added thus lies in considering the different development stages as a single whole. Put simply, it can be used to put the clean-up of the existing infrastructure – both organizational and technological – into the context of innovation that ensures enduring competitiveness. Securing and improving existing investments contributes directly to strengthening a company's competitive position without neglecting the medium to long-term effects whose potential for improving processes is, in fact, the actual starting point and ultimately also the goal.

In the next section, we will look at two process examples in greater detail to illustrate how the roadmap model can be used to develop a holistic innovation approach.

Process Example: Global Account Profitability

The process of globalization – or, more accurately, internationalization – in the retail industry is one of the greatest challenges consumer goods manufacturers face today. This trend is extremely evident in Europe in particular, and is magnified even further by the transition to a single currency, the euro. Increasingly, retailers are becoming multinationals and are keen to present a consistent image that transcends national boundaries. On the procurement side in particular, many retailers see potential for lasting efficiency improvement in uniform prices, supply structures and streamlined product ranges, and they want to tap this potential.

This trend presents both opportunities and risks for manufacturers. Those who can manage their customer relations actively and profitably in this context will be a step ahead of the competition. As always, here, too, the race will be determined primarily by the speed and flexibility with which manufacturers respond to the new conditions. The battle is not about size: it will be fast companies who win out over slow companies.

One of the fundamental requirements for success is that the profitability of customer relationships be transparent. This transparency makes it easier to decide with whom to work and on which areas to focus. If a manufacturer can determine and track how profitable his relationship with a given customer is, not only at the national level but also in the international arena, his negotiations with this trading partner will become much easier.

But how do we go about implementing global account profitability in a specific context? First, a detailed expert and technical analysis of the situation are needed. In many cases, the data is already available but is stored in multiple systems, or is difficult to consolidate because the structures are incompatible. In many cases, there are even systems available for use in calculating the indicators required. However, only the professionals and technology experts together can determine the details of the modifications, extensions, and new systems required.

This process was presented using the roadmap model for a consumer goods manufacturer. The results amazed everyone: the company already had virtually all the data it needed in its systems. All that was necessary to process it was to make proper use of powerful reporting and analysis tools. With this in mind, a data warehousing tool was selected and applied to consolidate and store data and to put the financial and controlling solutions already available at the company to greater use.

Process Example: CPFR

Today, CPFR is probably the most promising model for collaboration between retailers and manufacturers in the supply chain process. In some cases, it has resulted in a 5-10% improvement in service, more precise planning (50-80%), less capital tie-up through inventory reduction (30-50%), and lower supply chain costs (15 - 25%)[4]. Accessing the resulting potential is one of the most pressing tasks for both retailers and suppliers.

It doesn't always work, though, as shown by the example below. A well-known manufacturer, whose CIO was quick to recognize how useful CPFR could be, launched a number of pilot projects that tested different aspects of such a collaboration. Success was not slow in coming, and they decided to apply the processes right across the entire relevant product range. They soon found a solution provider and went to work. Some time later, however, after several attempts to link the existing systems to the new process element, they ultimately shelved the project altogether. So what went wrong?

Time and time again, the complex, incompatible data structures of the participating partners' systems, and the processes underlying them, resulted in the collapse of the collaborative process chain. Besides actually implementing the CPFR scenario, they had quite simply forgotten to address the necessary restructuring and harmonizing of the existing systems and processes. Even if this usually involves dry, abstract, detailed work in such "old-fashioned" but fundamental systems as sales, shipping, and billing, neglecting these matters could render the ultimate goal, namely the introduction of a complex process like CPFR, impossible.

---

4 Source: Roland Berger expert interviews and European studies

The real point that emerges here is the increasingly prominent issue of e-readiness. Not every company is in a position to implement the latest cutting-edge processes. In fact, it is often the more humdrum "homework" that promises greater success in the short term, paves the way for lasting process innovation in the middle term, and enables the company to survive in a competitive environment in the long term. However well the actual process itself may be reflected, it is only when it is used in conjunction with linked processes or, as in this example, associated systems, that additional value added can be realized.

With CPFR, this is especially true of the associated processes within the participating companies from the retail and consumer goods industries, where many functional areas are not yet ready to live with an increasingly flexible process chain. The outlook is better for the relationship between manufacturers and their suppliers, which is why many of today's successful CPFR projects can be found in this area. In some cases, multinational manufacturers have even used CPFR scenarios as internal process control tools. Thanks to past supply chain projects, most of the subsidiaries involved have already coordinated their processes and thus find it very easy to use the results of improved planning to boost the performance of their business operations.

5.4.4 Roadmap Application Model

Let's return for a moment to the question of what keeps CEOs of consumer goods manufacturers awake at night when it comes to the future of their companies. The answer, we said, was the search for profitable growth. How, then, can the e-transformation roadmap be used in reality? Can it be used to develop the basis for choosing the right innovation route for a company in the context of today's financial and technological environment?

The first point to note is that the master roadmap presented is not, in itself, capable of satisfying a demand of such great scope. It first needs to be adapted to the company's specific circumstances – in other words, an individual roadmap needs to be drawn up. Above all, it must include company-specific data regarding size, customer structure, and any organizational obstacles that exist.

What needs to be developed is thus a logical sequence of business cases that clearly show the individual steps along the way, quantify the steps in terms of cost, time, and expected revenues, and allow individual decisions. The holistic approach of the analytical model and the fact that projects are considered interdependent from the outset ensure that investments in individual projects are safe.

The dynamics of today's world, however, also demand a change management mechanism that will ensure that new developments and opportunities are included in the innovation plan as necessary. The name of the game is evolution, not revolution. Two key features of the roadmap make this possible: first, individual projects can be monitored separately, and are modular, so they can also be evaluated in terms of achieving the expected goals. This makes it possible to discern, in a timely manner, any revisions that need to be made to the strategy. Second, the projects are essentially independent of one another, so the strategy may be realigned at any time. For strategy revisions, an updated roadmap based on an extended master version is useful.

5.4.5 Prospects

The present approach provides a tool that enables consumer goods manufacturers to decide how best to transform themselves and evolve toward the network economy. A master roadmap supplies a portfolio of choices for this, drawn from best practices in the industry. Building on this, a company's strategic alignment and its organizational and technological constraints are taken as the basis for devising its individual innovation sequence. This provides top management with a tailor-made e-transformation roadmap laying out a sequence of business cases that can be implemented and decided upon on their own, plus a proposal regarding the timetable involved. Taken as a whole, these individual projects constitute a harmonious, compatible whole to ensure the company's short- and long-term competitiveness in the network economy.

At the end of the day, however, the success of the approach will have to be proven in practical applications. That is, after all, what it was designed for. The tool, with its combination of strategic and directly applicable implementation competence, has the potential to pave the way for strategic decisions in the holistic framework of the relevant technology context. This is undoubtedly what sets it apart from other, similar models, which either get too bogged down in strategy considerations or are too obsessed with technology to make a really convincing contribution to achieving profitable growth, a company's ultimate goal.

Unlike other approaches, this model's holistic aspect offers more potential than any partial approach such as supply chain management or customer relationship management models. The e-transformation roadmap blazes a trail through the jungle of options that companies have today when it comes to process innovation. It answers the question whether a given project makes sense in light of alternative value-creating projects, that is, if it identifies the "low hanging fruit" and shows the way toward more efficient, but also more sustainable, improvement.

In our opinion, this approach is a first step toward developing a collaborative innovation approach, combining strategic and operational process competence with extensive and technologically advanced IT expertise. In the future, a company's competitiveness will depend increasingly on its ability to establish a powerful innovation network. The task of this network will be to speed up the innovation in terms of decision-making and implementation, and to improve the quality of the process. Our aim is to ensure that IT really is the enabler so many strategic process models consider it to be.

A   References

Ahlert, D.: Vertikalisierung der Distribution – Die kundenorientierte Neugestaltung des Wertschöpfungsprozeß-Managements, in: Distribution im Aufbruch (edited by Beisheim, O), Munich 1999, p. 333-350.

Ahlert, D.: Distributionspolitik – Das Management des Absatzkanals, 4. edition, Stuttgart /Jena/New York 2001.

Ahlert, D./**Borchert**, S.: Prozessmanagement im vertikalen Marketing – Efficient Consumer Response in Konsumgüternetzen, Berlin/Heidelberg 2000.

Alvarado, U./**Kotzab**, H.: Supply Chain Management – The integration of Logistics in Marketing, in: Industrial Marketing Management, No. 2, 2001, p. 183-198.

Alves, R.: Integrierte Führung und Imitationsmanagement in Filialsystemen des Handels – Ein Beitrag zur Anwendung der Ergebnisse empirischer Erfolgsforschung, Frankfurt 1996.

A.T. Kearney Consulting/PAP Consulting: Assessing the Profit Impact of ECR – ECR Europe Study, Brussels 1998.

Bachl, T.: Category Management – Erfolgsrezept für den Handel?, in: Coorganisation, No. 3, 1995, p. 22-25.

Barth, K.: Betriebswirtschaftslehre des Handels, 4. edition, Wiesbaden 1999.

Barth, K.: Architektur der Kundenzufriedenheit und Kundenbindung: Die drei Säulen, in: KSA News – Kundennähe realisieren (edited by KSA), Düsseldorf 1997, p. 3-6.

Bastian, R.: Wachstum über Kundenbegeisterung, in: Marketing & Kommunikation, No. 1, 2000, p. 4-7.

Baumgart, G./**Bieber**, D.: Prozesskettenoptimierung vor dem Hintergrund sich verändernder Vertriebs- Informations-, und Logistikwege, in: VDI/VDE-IT: Schnittstellenoptimierung in der Distributionslogistik – Innovative Dienstleistungen in der Wertschöpfungskette, 2000, unpublished.

Behrends, C.: Category Management – Bestandsaufnahme und Perspektiven, in: Category Management – Neue Herausforderung im vertikalen Marketing?, Edition: Arbeits-/Dokumentationspapiere der Wissenschaftlichen Gesellschaft für Marketing und Unternehmensführung e.V. (edited by Meffert, H./Wagner, H./Backhaus, K.), Münster 1995, p. 5-29.

Belz, C./**Kramer**, M./**Schlögel**, M: Supply Chain Management: Probleme, Strategien und Lösungen, in: Thexis – Fachbericht für Marketing von dem Forschungsinstitut für Absatz und Handel, No. 4/1994, St. Gallen 1994.

Bertram, H.: Data Warehouse – Trends bei Wal-Mart, Sears & Co, in Dynamik im Handel, No. 7, 1999, p. 22-25.

Bickelmann, R.: Henkel's Unique Combined Use of EPOS & Panel Data, in: European Logistics and Supply Chain Management dated 05.01.1999, p. 8-9.

Biehl, B: Tesco nimmt Hersteller ins Boot – Tesco nutzt Industrie und Berater-Know how für sein Category Management, in LZ dated 27.03.1998, p. 46-48.

Biehl, B.: ECR noch lange nicht am Ende – Die 4. ECR-Konferenz befaßt sich in Paris mit dem Consumer Value, in: LZ dated 16.04.1999 (a), p. 38.

Biehl, B.: ECR und die Welt des Internets – Fünfte europäische Konferenz in Turin diskutiert EDI-Durchsatz und Global Commerce, in: LZ dated 31.03.2000, p. 58.

Borchert, S.: Führung von Distributionsnetzwerken – Eine Konzeption der Systemführung von Unternehmensnetzwerken zur erfolgreichen Realisation von Efficient Consumer Response-Kooperationen, Wiesbaden 2001.

Bösler, B.: Regeln für den Brückenbau zwischen Edifact und XML – Ausschuss des Deutschen Instituts für Normung verabschiedet Standards für den Weg vom klassischen zum Internet-EDI, in: LZ dated 3.11.2000, p. 62.

Brettschneider, G: Beschaffung im Handel unter besonderer Berücksichtigung von Efficient Consumer Response, Frankfurt 2000.

Brockman, B./ **Morgan**, R. M.: The Evolution of managerial Innovations in Distribution – What prospects for ECR, in: International Journal of Retail & Distribution Management, No. 10, p. 397-408.

Brown, P.G./**Visconti**, M.: ECR Europe 1996 Tracking Survey – Progress to Date and the Way Forward, Kurt Salmon Associates, presentation at second ECR Europe conference in Amsterdam 1997.

Bruce, R./**Ireland**, R.: CPFR: Only the beginning of Collaboration, in Supply Chain Management Review, Sept./Oct. 2000.

Buzell, R.D.: Is vertical integration profitable?, in: Harvard Business Review, No. 1, 1983, p. 92-102.

Cansier, A.: Efficient Consumer Response aus kooperationstheoretischer Sicht, Wiesbaden 2001.

CCRRGE (Coca-Cola Retailing Research Group Europe): Kooperation zwischen Industrie und Handel im Supply Chain Management, Essen 1994.

Centrale für Coorganisation: Managementinformationspapier CPFR, Cologne 2001.

Centrale für Coorganisation: Handbuch ECR Supply Chain Side, Cologne 2002.

Corsten, D./**Plötzl**, J.: Efficient Consumer Response – Integration von Logistiketten, Munich/Wien 2000.

Cooke, J. A.: CPFR: The countdown begins, in Logistics Management and Distribution Report, Nov. 1999.

Dantzer, U.: Was ist und was bringt "Efficient Consumer Response", in: LZ dated 08.11.1996, p. 82.

Dölle, C.: E-Procurement – Neue Perspektiven in der Beschaffung – B2B-Marktplätze werden mit Einkaufskooperationen konkurrieren, in LZ dated 3.11.2000, p. 63.

Doppler, K./**Lauterburg**, C.: Change Management, Frankfurt 1994.

ECR Europe: Introducing Efficient Replenishment, Brussels 1996 (a).

ECR Europe: Efficient Repenishment Techniques, Brussels 1996 (b).

ECR Europe: Efficient Repenishment Trials, Brussels 1996 (c).

ECR Europe: Introducing EDI, Brussels 1996 (d).

ECR Europe: Newsletter for European Retailers, Suppliers and Distributors – Amsterdam Conference Report, Brussels 1997.

ECR Euope: A Guide to CPFR Implementation, Brussels 2001.

Ester, B./**Baumgart**, G.: Cash Flow Aspekte bei der Supply-Chain-Gestaltung, in: Supply Chain Management (edited by Pfohl, H.-C.), p. 141-160, Berlin 2000.

Eierhoff, K.: Die Logistikkette als Wertschöpfungselement des Handels, in: Management der Logistikkette (edited by Pfohl, H.-C.), Berlin 1994, p. 129-147.

Eierhoff, K: Efficient Consumer Response (ECR) – Ein neuer Weg in der Kooperation zwischen Industrie und Handel, in: Informationssysteme für das Handelsmanagement (edited by Ahlert, D. et al.), Berlin 1998, p. 365-386.

Feld, C.: Category Management im Handel, Working paper No. 8 of the Faculty of Trade and Distribution, University of Cologne, Cologne 1996.

Feller, M./**Großweischede**, M.: Steht ECR am Scheideweg?, in LZ dated 09.04.1999, p. 55.

Fernie, J./**Sparks**, L.: Logistics and Retail Management, London 1998.

Figgen, B: Category Management und Efficient Consumer Response – Der Verbraucher steht im Mittelpunkt, in: Handbuch Efficient Consumer Response – Konzepte, Erfahrungen, Herausforderungen (edited by von der Heydt, A.), Munich 1999, p. 181-193.

FMI (Food Marketing Institute): Backgrounder: Efficient Consumer Response, in: http://www.fmi.org/media/bg/ecr1.html (Internet) dated 18.10.1999.

Friedrich, S. A./**Rodens**, B.: Wertschöpfungspartnerschaft "Handel/ Industrie" – Gemeinsam Werte für den Kunden schaffen, in: Das Neue Strategische Management (Hrsg. Hinterhuber, H.H./Ayad, A./Handlbauer, G.), Wiesbaden 1996.

Galloway, J.: EDI: Enabler of Business Process Re-engineering, in: Introducing EDI (edited by ECR Europe), Brussels 1996, p. 11.

GCI: VICS – Collaborative Planning, Forecasting and Replenishment, GCI Recommendation, 2001.

Glendinning Consultans: Der Verbraucher weiß, was er will – Glendinning Consultants untersuchen Warengruppen aus Kundensicht, in: LZ dated 16.04.1999, p. 41-43.

Günther, A.: Category Management und Efficient Consumer Response in der Kosmetikindustrie, in: KSA News – Kundennähe realisieren (edited by KSA), Düsseldorf 1997, p. 10-12.

Hahne, H.: Category Management aus Herstellersicht, Cologne 1998.

Hambuch, P.: Category Management: der Verbraucher steht im Mittelpunkt, in: Perspektiven ökonomischen Denkens (edited by Woratschek,H.), Frankfurt 1998, p. 41-51.

Hammer, M/**Champy**, J.: Business Reengineering, 5. edited, Frankfurt/New York 1995.

Heydt, A. von der: Efficient Consumer Response, 2. edition, Frankfurt 1997.

Hill, R.W.: Demand-Side Priorities & Vision, Andersen Consulting, presentation at second ECR Europe conference in Amsterdam 1997.

Hillemeyer, J.: Marktplätze als digitaler Brückenschlag – HIS-Tagung in Münster: Elektronische Kommunikation zwischen Handel, Industrie und Kunden, in: LZ dated 1.06.2001, p. 41.

Hinterhuber, H.H./**Friedrich** S..A.: Quo Vadis ECR? – Dated Effizienzstreben zur Kundenorientierung, in: Handbuch Efficient Consumer Response – Konzepte, Erfahrungen, Herausforderungen (edited by von der Heydt, A.), Munich 1999, p. 332-346.

Hinterhuber, H.H./**Friedrich** S.A.: Wettbewerbsvorteile durch Wertschöpfungspartnerschaft – Paradigmenwechsel in der Hersteller/ Handels-Beziehung, in: WiSt – Wirtschaftswissenschaftliches Studium, 1999 (a), No. 1, p. 2-8.

Hoffman, K. C.: The Vision: Suppliers, manufacturers, retailers collaborating as one, in: Global Logistics & Supply Chain Strategies, June 1998.

Holland, H./**Hermann**, J./**Machenheimer**, G.: Efficient Consumer Response, Frankfurt 2001.

Holmstström, J./**Hoover**, W.E./**Louhiluoto**, P./**Vasara**, A.: The other end of the supply chain, in: The McKinsey Quarterly, No. 1, 2000, p. 62-71, in: http://205.253.128.123/manuoper/oten00.asp (Internet) dated 24.04.2000.

Hughes, J./**Ralf**, M./**Michels**, B.: Supply Chain Management – So steigern Sie die Effizienz ihres Unternehmens durch perfekte Organisation der Wertschöpfungskette, Landsberg/Lech 2000.

Industry Directions/Syncra Systems: CPFR survey – Findings & analysis, April 2000, in: http://www.cpfr.org/WhitePapers/SurveyResults.pdf (Internet) dated 07.02.2002.

Jarillo, J.C.: On Strategic Networks, in: Strategic Management Journal, No. 1, 1988, p. 31-41.

Jirik, C. T.: Supply Chain Management – Gestaltung und Koordination der Lieferkette, in: WiSt – Wirtschaftswissenschaftliches Studium, 1999, No. 10, p. 547-550.

Johnson, M.: Collaboration data modeling – CPFR implementation guidelines, Syncra Systems publication, Reprint of 1999 annual conference proceedings of the Council of Logistics Management, in: http://www.cpfr.org/WhitePapers/CollaborationDataModelingA.pdf (Internet) dated 07.07.2002.

Joint Industry Project on ECR: Category Management Report, Washington 1995.

Joint Industry Project on ECR: Category Management II – Building Organizational Capability, Washington 1999.

Jordan, P.: Why do you need EDI for ECR, in: Introducing EDI (edited by ECR Europe), Brussels 1996, p. 2.

Kaas, P.N.: Efficient Consumer Response – Kooperation und Wettbewerb auf dem Lebensmittelmarkt, in: Perspektiven ökonomischen Denkens (edited by Woratschek, H.), Frankfurt 1998, p. 23-39.

Kalmbach, U.: ECR Europe und ECR Deutschland – Ein Überblick, in: Handbuch Efficient Consumer Response – Konzepte, Erfahrungen, Herausforderungen (edited by von der Heydt, A.), Munich 1999, p. 24-40.

Kaluza, B./**Kemminer**, J.: Dynamisches Supply Management und Dynamische Produktdifferenzierungsstrategie, Duisburg 1997.

Kapell, E.: WWRE launcht globales CPFR-Projekt im Juni – Marktplatz für weitere Händler und Hersteller offen, in: LZ dated 6.04.2001, p. 33.

Kansky, D./**Weingarten**, U.: Supply Chain: Fertigen, was der Kunde verlangt, in: Harvard Business Manager, No. 4, 1999, p. 87-95.

Kanter, R. M.: Collaborative Advantage: The Art of Alliances, in: Harvard Business Review, edition July/August, 1994, p. 96-108.

Kilimann, J./**Schlenk**, H., : Die ECR-Bewegung – Mehr Verständnis für den Kunden, in: Efficient Consumer Response – Strategische Waffe für Industrie und Handel (edited by Tienes, E.-C./Kilimann, J./Schlenk, H.), Stuttgart 1998, p.1-10.

Klein, H.L./**Lachhammer**, J.: Efficient Consumer Response – Die Aufgaben des Beziehungs-Managements, in: Absatzwirtschaft, No. 2, 1996, p. 62-66.

Kohl, M./**Zimmermann**, K.: Wie Continental eine ECR-Initiative steuert – Projekt Scorecard, in: Absatzwirtschaft, No. 6, 2001, p. 36-40.

Kolodziej, M.J.: Zur Kultur der Zusammenarbeit, in: Globales Handelsmanagement (edited by Zentes, J./Swoboda, B.), Frankfurt 1998, p. 429-448.

Koloszyc, G.: Retailers, suppliers push joint sales forecasting, in: Stores, Juni 1998.

Korpiun, M./ **Kohl**, M.: Supply Chain Management und Efficient Consumer Response als Herausforderung für ein effektives und effizientes Projektmanagement, in: Handelsforschung 2000/2001 – Kooperations- und Wettbewerbsverhalten des Handels, Jahrbuch der Forschungsstelle für den Handel Berlin (edited by Trommsdorff, V.), Cologne 2000, p. 217-238.

Kotler, P./**Bliemel**, F.: Marketing-Management – Analyse, Planung, Umsetzung und Steuerung, 10. edition, Stuttgart 2001.

Kotzab, H.: Distributionslogistische Kooperationsstrategien von Handelsunternehmen mit ihren Lieferanten in der Konsumgüterwirtschaft – Das Beispiel Efficient Consumer Response, in: ÖZV, No. 1, 1997, p. 58-67.

Kotzab, H.: Neue Konzepte der Distributionslogistik von Handelsunternehmen, Wiesbaden 1997.

Kotzab, H.: Improving Supply Chain Performance by Efficient Consumer Response? – A critical comparision of existing ECR-approaches, in: Journal of Business and Industrial Marketing, No. 5/6, 1999, p. 364-377.

Kotzab, H.: Management by ECR – Internationale Bestandsaufnahme und empirischer Vergleich der Umsetzung von ECR, in: Thexis – Fachzeitschrift für Marketing, No. 3, 2001, p. 29-33.

Kotzab, H./**Schnedlitz**, P.: The Integration of Retailing to the General Concept of Supply Chain Management, in: Journal für Betriebswirtschaft, No. 4, 1999, p. 140-153.

KPMG: Supply Chain Management-Studie, in: Logistik Heute, No.7/8, 1998, p. 57-58.

Krieger, W.: Informationsmanagement in der Logistik, Wiesbaden 1995.

Kruger, R. M.: Destination: Diapers – Category Management, in: Discount Merchandiser, No. 3, 1998, p. 57-58.

Kurt Salmon Associates: Efficient Consumer Response – Enhancing Consumer Value in the Grocery Industry, Washington 1993.

Kurt Salmon Associates: Quick Response, New York 1997.

Laurent, M.: Vertikale Kooperationen zwischen Industrie und Handel – Neue Typen und Strategien zur Effizienzsteigerung im Absatzkanal, Frankfurt 1996.

Lee, H.L./**Padmanabhan**, V./**Whang**, S.: Der Peitscheneffekt in der Absatz-kette, in: Harvard Business Manager, No. 4, 1997, p. 78-87.

Lord, S.: CPFR Inter-operability, White paper Procter & Gamble Maerz 2001, in: http://www.cpfr.org/WhitePapers/CPFRInteroperability.doc (Internet) dated 07.02.2002.

LZ Spezial: Die Viererbande auf einen Blick – CPGmarket, Global Net Xchange, Worl Wide Retail Exchange und Transora, in: LZ Spezial, No. 1, 2001, p. 16-17.

Margulis, R.: CPFR emergingfrom ECR's shadows, in IdeaBeat, June 1998, in: http://www.rampr.com/Articles.html (Internet) dated 17.02.2002.

Mattmüller, R./ **Tunder**, R.: Ein neues Selbstverständnis der Hersteller gegenüber dem Handel – Theoretische Hintergründe und Umsetzungsalternativen, in: Handelsforschung 2000/2001 – Kooperations- und Wettbewerbsverhalten des Handels, Jahrbuch der Forschungsstelle für den Handel Berlin (edited by Trommsdorff, V.), Cologne 2000, p. 3-26.

McAfee, A./ **Ashira**, M.: Syncra Systems, Harvard Business School Case Study, Boston 2001.

Meffert, H.: Einführung in die Problemstellung, in: Category Management – neue Herausforderung im vertikalen Marketing?, Edition: Arbeits-/ Dokumentationspapiere der Wissenschaftlichen Gesellschaft für Marketing und Unternehmensführung e.V. (edited by Meffert, H./Wagner, H./Backhaus, K.), Münster 1995, p. 1-4.

Meffert, H.: Zwischen Kooperation und Konfrontation – Strategien und Verhaltensweisen im Absatzkanal, in: Distribution im Aufbruch (edited by Beisheim, O), Munich 1999 (a) p. 407-424.

Merkel, H.: Logistik Managementsysteme, Munich 1995.

Merkel, H.: Firmenübergreifendes Prozeßdenken – Ein lohnender Ansatz, in: Efficient Consumer Response – Strategische Waffe für Industrie und Handel (edited by Tienes, E.-C./Kilimann, J./Schlenk, H.), Stuttgart 1998, p.35-52.

Meyer, M: Efficient Consumer Response – Eine kritische Betrachtung, in: Handelsforschung 1999/2000, Jahrbuch der Forschungsstelle für den Handel Berlin (edited by Trommsdorff, V.), Wiesbaden 1999, p. 297-314.

Mierdorf, Z.: Grundidee von CPFR ist ECR, Interview mit Zygmunt Mierdorf, Vorstandsmitglied der Metro AG, in: LZ dated 25.05.2001, p. 25.

Milde, H.: Category Management – die stille Revolution, in: Markenartikel – Zeitschrift für Markenführung, No. 7, 1994 (a), p. 343-346.

Möhlenbruch, D.: Kundenorientierung durch Category Management – Kritische Analyse eines Kooperationsmodells zwischen Industrie und Handel, in: Handelsforschung 1997/98 – Kundenorientierung im Handel, Jahrbuch der

Forschungsstelle für den Handel Berlin (edited by Trommsdorff, V.), Wiesbaden 1997, p. 113- 134.

Möhlenbruch, D./**Nickel**, S.: Kooperationsstrategien als Element der wettbewerbsstrategischen Konzeption von Einzelhandelsunternehmungen, in: Handelsforschung 1994/95 – Kooperation im Handel und mit dem Handel, Jahrbuch der Forschungsstelle für den Handel Berlin (edited by Trommsdorff, V.), Wiesbaden 1994, p. 3-22.

Moll, C.: Efficient Consumer Response, Frankfurt 2000.

Mouzas, S./**Araujos**, L.: Implementing programmatic initiatives in manufacturer-retailer networks, in: Industrial Marketing Management, No. 3, 2000, p. 293-303.

Müller-Hagedorn, L.: Der Handel, Stuttgart 1998.

Müller-Hagedorn, L./**Dach**, C./**Spork**, S./**Toporowski**, W.: Vertikales Marketing – Trends in der Praxis und Schwerpunkte der theoretischen Diskussion, in: Marketing ZFP, No. 1, 1999, p. 61-75.

Needel, S.P.: Understanding Consumer Response to Category Management, in: Journal of Advertising Research, No. 4, 1998, p. 61-67.

Olbrich, R.: Entwicklungsperspektiven des vertikalen Informationsmanagement zwischen Handel und Industrie, in: Handelsforschung 1995/96 – Informationsmanagement im Handel, Jahrbuch der Forschungsstelle für den Handel Berlin (edited by Trommsdorff, V.), Wiesbaden 1995, p. 39-50.

Picot, A./**Reichwald**, R./**Wigand**, R.T.: Die grenzenlose Unternehmung – Information, Organisation und Management, 4. edition, Wiesbaden 2001.

Porter, M.E.: Wettbewerbsvorteile – Spitzenleistungen erreichen und behaupten, 5. edition, Frankfurt/New York 1999 (a).

Porter, M.E.: Creating Tomorrow's Advantage, in: Strategische Unternehmensplanung – Strategische Unternehmensführung (edited by Hahn, D./Taylor, B.), 8. edition, Heidelberg 1999 (b), p. 944-952.

Pretzel, J.: Gestaltung der Hersteller-Handel-Beziehung durch Category Management, in: Category Management – neue Herausforderung im vertikalen Marketing?, Reihe: Arbeits-/Dokumentationspapiere der Wissenschaftlichen Gesellschaft für Marketing und Unternehmensführung e.V. (edited by Meffert, H./Wagner, H./Backhaus, K.), Münster 1995, p. 30-43.

Reda, M./**Harding**, P.: Demand Chain & Supply Chain Management, in: Supplement to Retail Info System News and Consumer Goods, edition May 1998.

Reda, S.: CPFR takes off, in: Stores, Feb. 2000, in: http://www.stores.org/archives/feb00cover.html (Internet) dated 07.02.2002.

Ritter, S.: ECR – Brücke zwischen Vision und Wirklichkeit?, in: Dynamik im Handel, No. 4, 1999, p. 39-40.

Rode, J.: Tesco ermöglicht Lieferanten Zugriff auf EPOS-Daten – "Revolution" per Internet, in LZ dated 27.03.1998, p. 48.

Rode, J: Trade Information Exchange: Workflow per Internet, in LZ dated 01.10.1999, p. 46.

Rode, J: Supply Chain als Top-Aufgabe – VICS Vision Summit – Chefs globaler Unternehmen diskutieren Zukunft des Handels, in: LZ dated 23.04.1999 (a), p. 44-45.

Rode, J.: CPFR – Zauberformel für Turbo-ECR, in: LZ dated 22.01.1999 (b), p. 14-15.

Rode, J: Drei Wege digitaler Daten – Metro wirbt Lieferanten für klassisches und WebEDI, in: LZ dated 12.05.2000, p. 44.

Rode, J.: Die digitale Handels-Revolution, in: E-Commerce – Das Web revolutioniert die Handelswelt (edited by LZ Spezial), No. 1, 2000 (a), p. 8-22.

Rode, J.: Schnelles Wachstum der B2B-Marktplätze – Handel größte Anwenderbranche, in: LZ dated 1.09.2000 (c), p.30.

Rode, J.: CPFR begeistert ECR-Konferenz, in: LZ dated 18.05.2001, p. 26.

Rode, J.: dm gibt POS-Daten frei – Extranet liefert Abverkaufs- und Perfomancezahlen, in: LZ dated 9.02.2001 (a), p. 28.

Rode, J.: B2B – Ein langer Weg für die Branche – CPFR, die IT-Integration der Marktplätze und globale Standards fallen nicht vom Himmel, in: LZ dated 25.5.2001 (b), p. 51.

Rode, J./**Weber**, B.: Die Viererbande – Vier Giganten wollen die Konsumgüterwirtschaft aufmischen: GNX, WWRE, Transora und CPGmarket, in LZ Spezial, 2001, p. 12-15.

Rode, J./**Wolfskeil**, J.: Planspiele im Web – Das Konditionsgerangel steht vor dem Aus, in: LZ Spezial, No. 1, 2001, p. 34-37.

Rodens-Friedrich, B.: ECR bei dm-drogerie markt – Unser Weg in die Wertschöpfungspartnerschaft, in: Handbuch Efficient Consumer Response – Konzepte, Erfahrungen, Herausforderungen (edited by von der Heydt, A.), Munich 1999, p. 205-221.

Roland Berger & Partner: Category Management Enabling Components Workshop, presentation at the second ECR Europe conference in Amsterdam 1997.

Roland Berger & Partner: Die große Unbekannte – Out-of-stock-Situationen kosten einige Umsatzpotentiale, in LZ dated 16.04.1999, p. 46.

Roland Berger & Partner: How to implement Consumer Enthusiasm – Strategic Consumer Value Management – ECR Europe Study, Brussels 1999 (a).

Roland Berger & Partner: Efficient Replenishment Project – "Working Three-Gether" – Transport Consolidation with the Involvment of Logistics Service Providers – ECR Europe Study, Brussels 1999 (b).

Roland Berger & Partner/The Partnering Group: Category Management Best Practises Report – ECR Europe Study, Brussels 1997.

Rotthowe, T.: Category Management Deutschland: Kurz vor dem Durchbruch?, in: Dynamik im Handel, No. 12, 1999, p. 49-51.

Rudolph, T./**Einhorn**, M.: Herausforderungen im europäischen Einzelhandel, in: Thexis – Fachzeitschrift für Marketing, No. 3, 2001, p. 2-7.

Runau, R.: Sicherheit im Datenmeer – Probleme und Risiken, in: LZ dated 3.11.2000, p. 66.

Schachtman, N: Trading partners collaborate to increase sale- CPFR brings companies together to share data, cut product cycle times, and reduce inventory, in: Informationweek, Oct. 2000.

Schmitt, D. / **Taplick**, N.: Elektronische Marktplätze – Mitmachen oder Abwarten? – WWRE und andere Branchen-Plattformen verändern die Geschäftsmodelle, in: LZ dated 3.11.2000, p. 58.

Schneckenberger, T./**Plötzl**, J.: Partner im Dilemma – Nutzen und Machtverlust beim Informationsaustausch – Ergebnisse einer Studie des Instituts für Technologiemanagement der Hochschule St. Gallen, in: LZ dated 14.05.1999, No. 19, p. 44-46.

Schröder, H./**Feller**, M./**Großweischede**, M.: Kundenorientierung im Category Management, in: LZ dated 17.03.2000, p. 60-61.

Schröder, H./**Geister**, S.: Internationales Category Management im europäischen Einzelhandel – Herausforderungen und Informationsgrundlagen, in: Thexis – Fachzeitschrift für Marketing, No. 3, 2001, p. 41-46.

Schröder, V.: Vertrauen und gemeinsamer Wille – Interview with Volker Schröder, Procter & Gamble Europe, about CPFR pilot projects, in: LZ dated 22.01.1999, p. 13.

Seifert, D.: Efficient Consumer Response – Exploiting Cost Saving Potentials, unpublished study for a major European consumer goods manufacturer, Budapest 1996.

Seifert, D.: Chance ECR: Zuerst eine grundsätzlich strategische Neuausrichtung – Strategische Unternehmensführung von Industrie- und Handelsunternehmen in Zeiten dramatischer Veränderungen im Absatzkanal, in: Markenartikel – Zeitschrift für Markenführung, No. 1, 2000, p. 40-43.

Seifert, D.: Efficient Consumer Response – Ein Instrument des Marketing Controlling zur Schaffung strategischer Wettbewerbsvorteile im Handel, in: Handbuch Marketing-Controlling (edited by Zerres, M.), Berlin/Heidelberg/ New York 2000 (a), p. 351-371.

Seifert, D.: Einzelhandel – wie er strategisch optieren muss, in: Harvard Business Manager, No. 4, 2000 (b), p. 22-27.

Seifert, D.: Wal-Mart hat die Metro weiter im Visier – Studie: Der Weltmarktführer im Einzelhandel ist in Deutschland auf Übernahmen angewiesen, in: Die Welt dated 07.08.2000 (c), p. 16.

Seifert, D.: On your Mark – Global Retailing, in: Chain Store Age – The Newsmagazine for Retail Executives, No. 10, 2000 (d), p. 72-74.

Seifert, D: Die Besten der Besten – ECR-Studie Deutschland, in: Logistik Heute, No. 5, 2001, p. 58-59.

Seifert, D.: Efficient Consumer Response – Supply Chain Management (SCM), Category Management (CM) und Collaborative Planning, Forecasting and Replenishment (CPFR) als neue Strategieansätze, second edition, Munich/ Mering 2001.

Seifert, D.: Efficient Consumer Response – Wie der Handel strategische Wettbewerbsvorteile erzielen kann, in: Handelsforschung 2001/2002 – Jahrbuch der Forschungsstelle für den Handel Berlin (edited by Trommsdorff, V.), Cologne 2001 (a).

Seifert, D.: Category Management Kompetenzführer im deutschen Handel und in der Industrie, in: Absatzwirtschaft, No. 8, 2001 (b), p. 55.

Seifert, D.: Die Kompetenzführer im Category Management – Ergebnisse der Efficient Consumer Response-Erfolgsfaktorenstudie Deutschland, in: Markenartikel – Zeitschrift für Markenführung, No. 6, 2001 (c), p. 24-28.

Seifert, D./**Gawlik**, T./**Kellner**, J.: Effiziente Kundenbindung mit CRM – Wie Procter & Gamble, Henkel und Kraft mit ihren Marken Kundenbeziehungen gestalten, Bonn 2002.

Seifert, D./**Ketels**, C./**Kracklauer**, A.: Kooperatives Kundenbindungsmanagement – Potentiale einer neuen Zusammenarbeit von Handel und Industrie, in Consulting 2002 – Jahrbuch für Unternehmensberatung und Management (edited by Breidenstein, F. et. al.), Frankfurt 2002, p. 125-131.

Seifert, D./**Kracklauer**, A.: Gemeinsam näher am Kunden – Wie Industrie und Handel kooperatives Kundenbindungsmanagement betreiben, in: Markenartikel – Zeitschrift für Markenführung, No. 3, 2001, p. 50-59.

Seifert, D./**Kracklauer**, A.: Category Management – Stellen Sie die richtigen Fragen, in: Absatzwirtschaft, No. 6, 2001 (a), p. 52-55.

Seifert, D./**Kracklauer**, A./**Mills**, D. Q.: Kooperatives Kundenmanagement, Wiesbaden 2002.

Seifert, D./**Kracklauer**, A./**Passenheim**, O.: Mutual Customer Approach – How industry and trade are executing Collaborative Customer Relationship Management, in: International Journal of Retail and Distribution Management, No. 12, 2001, p. 515-519.

Seifert, D./**Thiel**, E.: Optimierung innerhalb der Supply Chain, in: Distribution – Logistik in Warenfluss und Verteilung, edition No. 7/8, 2001, p. 26-27.

Sherman, R.: Collaborative Plannig, Forecasting and Replenishment – Realizing the promise of Efficient Consumer Response through Collaborative technology, in: Journal of Marketing – Theory and Practice, Special Issue, Vol. 6, No. 4, 1998.

Spaan, U.: Tesco TIE – ECR in Perfektion, in: Dynamik im Handel, No. 8, 1999, p. 26-27.

Spalink, H.: Erfolgsfaktoren bei der Einführung von ECR, in: KSA News – Efficient Consumer Response (edited by KSA), Düsseldorf 1996, p. 14-15.

Spalink, H./**Berten**, B.: Kooperation schöpft Markt besser aus – Studie von Kurt Salmon Associates belegt die positiven Effekte von CPFR, in: LZ dated 28.01.2000, p. 50.

Speer, F.: Verbraucherdaten als wesentliche Steuerungsgröße – Category Management – Wasch-, Putz- und Reinigungsmittel, in: Dynamik im Handel, No. 4, 1998 (a), p. 78-81.

Strüber, H.: Die neue Logistik – Hebel für mehr Effizienz, in: Efficient Consumer Response – Strategische Waffe für Industrie und Handel (edited by Tienes, E.-C./Kilimann, J./Schlenk, H.), Stuttgart 1998, p.53-68.

Swoboda, B.: Wertschöpfungspartnerschaften in der Konsumgüterwirtschaft – Ökonomische und ökologische Aspekte eines ECR-Managements, in: WiSt, No. 9, 1997, p. 449-454.

Swoboda, B.: Globale Transaktion und Wertschöpfung durch Electronic Commerce – Eine Herausforderung für die Hersteller-Handels-Beziehung?, in: Globales Handelsmanagement (edited by Zentes, J./Swoboda, B.), Frankfurt 1998, p. 349-384.

Täger, U.C./**Nassua**, T.: Der Einzelhandel in Westeuropa – Struktur und Entwicklungstendenzen, in: Globales Handelsmanagement (edited by Zentes, J./Swoboda, B.), Frankfurt 1998, p. 25-52.

Teuscher, H./**Engler**,G.: CPFR – Der nächste Schritt von ECR, in: LZ dated 18.05.2001, p. 35-36.

Thaler, K.: Supply Chain Management – Prozessoptimierung in der logistischen Kette, Cologne 1999.

Theis, H.-J.: Handelsmarketing – Analyse- und Planungskonzepte für den Einzelhandel, Frankfurt 1999.

Tienes, E.-C./**Kilimann**, J./**Schlenk**, H. : Efficient Consumer Response – Strategische Waffe für Industrie und Handel, Stuttgart 1998.

Tietz, B.: Kooperation statt Konfrontation – Kontraktmarketing zwischen Industrie und Handel, in: Handelsforschung 1994/95 – Kooperation im Handel und mit dem Handel, Jahrbuch der Forschungsstelle für den Handel Berlin (edited by Trommsdorff, V.), Wiesbaden 1994, p. 39-56.

Tietz, B.: Efficient Consumer Response (ECR), in: WiSt – Wirtschaftswissen-schaftliches Studium, 1995, No. 10, p. 529-530.

Töpfer, A.: Efficient Consumer Response – Bessere Zusammenarbeit zwischen Handel und Herstellern, in: Handelsforschung 1995/96 – Informationsmanage-ment im Handel, Jahrbuch der Forschungsstelle für den Handel Berlin (edited by Trommsdorff, V.), Wiesbaden 1995, p. 187-200.

Töpfer, A.: Das ECR-Konzept als Anforderung an Theorie und Praxis, in: Hand-buch Efficient Consumer Response – Konzepte, Erfahrungen, Herausforderun-gen (edited by von der Heydt, A.), Munich 1999, p. 362-375.

Tochtermann, T.C.A./**Lange**, E.: Analyse kommt vor dem Profit – Wie Her-steller mit Category Management profitieren können – Das McKinsey Modell, in: LZ dated 22.05.1998, p. 40-42.

Tomczak, T./**Schögel**, M.: Management globaler Hersteller-Handels-Beziehun-gen, in: Globales Handelsmanagement (edited by Zentes, J./ Swoboda, B.), Frankfurt 1998, p. 327-348.

Trommsdorff, V: Kooperation als strategische Option – Vorwort des Herausge-bers, in: Handelsforschung 1994/95 – Kooperation im Handel und mit dem Handel, Jahrbuch der Forschungsstelle für den Handel Berlin (edited by Trom-msdorff, V.), Wiesbaden 1994, p. V-XV.

Tucher, F.W. von/**Wiezorek** H.: Efficient Consumer Response, in: Management logistischer Netzwerke und Flüsse (edited by Klaus, P./Krieger, W.), Wies-baden 1998, p. 93-99.

VICS: Collaborative Planning, Forecasting and Replenishment Voluntary Guidelines, VICS publication, 1998.

VICS: Roadmap to CPFR: The Case Studies, VICS publication, 1999.

VICS: VICS CPFR XML Messaging Model, White paper VICS Juni 2001, in: http://www.cpfr.org/VICS_CPFR_XMLMessagingModel0601a.doc (Internet) dated 07.02.2002.

Vitek, S.: A Work in Progress – Category Management, in: Progressive Grocer, No. 5, 1998, p. 17.

Völlmecke, U.: ECR bei Karstadt, in: Dynamik im Handel, February 1999, p.62-66.

Waldmann, J.: Trends und Visionen in der Logistik – Das Spannungsfeld zwischen Industrie und Handel, in: LZ dated 01.09.1995, p. 68-71.

Walton, B./**Princi**, M.: From Supply chain to Collaborative Network – Case Studies in the Food Industry, in: http://logistics.about.com/gi/dynamic/off-site.htm?site=http%3A%2F%2Fwww.ascet.com%2Fdocuments.asp%3FgrID%3D134%26d_ID%3D266 (Internet) dated 07.02.2002

Weber, B.: Die Marktplätze der Branche müssen umdenken – Wal-Marts Extranet ist Vorbild, in: LZ dated 11.05.2001, p. 32.

Weber, B.: Die Schaltstelle – Der Handel braucht eine einheitliche Internetsprache für den Datenaustausch, in: LZ Spezial, No. 1, 2001 (a), p. 24-26.

Wehrli, H.P./**Krick**, M.: Mit strategischen Netzwerken Kundennähe realisieren, in: Absatzwirtschaft, No. 1, 1998, p. 62-68.

White, A. G.: The value equation – Value Chain Management, collaboration and the internet, White Paper Logility 1999, in: http://www.cpfr.org/WhitePapers/The_Value_Equation.doc (Internet) dated 07.02.2002.

White, A. G.: The rise and Fall of the trading exchange, White Paper Logility 2001, in: http://www.cpfr.org/WhitePapers/RiseandFalloftheTradingExchangeR1.doc (Internet) dated 07.02.2002.

White, A. G.: n-tier CPFR – A proposal, Whte paper Logility, May 2001, in: http://www.cpfr.org/WhitePapers/nTierProposal.doc (Internet) dated 07.02.2002.

White, A. G.: Collaborative data modeling – CPFR implementaion guidelines from the manufacturer's perspective, White paper Logility, in: http://www.cpfr.org/WhitePapers/CPFRManufacturersPerspective.doc (Internet) dated 07.02.2002.

Wiezorek, H.: ECR – Eine Aufgabe des Beziehungsmanagements, in: Globales Handelsmanagement (edited by Zentes, J./Swoboda, B.), Frankfurt 1998, p. 385-402.

Wiezorek, H.: Efficient Consumer Response – Kooperation statt Konfrontation, in: Informationssysteme für das Handelsmanagement (edited by Ahlert, D. et al.), Berlin 1998 (a), p. 387- 400.

Wildemann, H.: Kooperationen über die Wertschöpfungskette, in: Handbuch Unternehmensführung (edited by Corsten, H./Reiß, M.), Wiesbaden 1997, p. 743-765.

Wildemann, H.: Kundennahe Produktion und Zulieferung – Empirische Bestandsaufnahme und aktuelle Tendenzen, in: Kundenzufriedenheit (edited by Simon, H./Homburg, C.) Wiesbaden 1998, p. 97-126.

Zentes, J.: Strategische Allianzen: Neuorientierung der kooperativen Wettbewerbsstrategien im Handel, in: Handelsforschung 1994/95 – Kooperation im Handel und mit dem Handel, Jahrbuch der Forschungsstelle für den Handel Berlin (edited by Trommsdorff, V.), Wiesbaden 1994, p. 73-85.

Zentes, J.: Effizienzsteigerungspotentiale kooperativer Logistikketten in der Konsumgüterwirtschaft, in: Management der Logistikkette (edited by Pfohl, H.-C.), Berlin 1994 (a), p. 105-126.

Zentes, J.: Erfolgsstrategie ECR: Potentiale und Voraussetzungen, in: KSA News – Efficient Consumer Response (edited by KSA), Düsseldorf 1996 (a), p. 4-6.

Zentes, J.: Von Pull- und Push-Strategien zum kooperativen Wertschöpfungsmanagement, in: Markenartikel – Zeitschrift für Markenführung, No. 4, 1996 (b), p. 162-165.

Zentes, J: Trends im Handel – Chancen und Risiken zwischenbetrieblicher Kooperationen, in: Informationssysteme für das Handelsmanagement (edited by Ahlert, D. et al.), Berlin 1998, p. 345-351.

B   Contributing Authors

Joseph C. Andraski, Vice Chairman VICS-CPFR and Senior Vice President OMI International

Joe Andraski is a Senior VP for OMI International, and an adjunct professor at Michigan State and at Penn State University and serves as a member of the Senior Advisory Board of the Schulich School of Business Supply Chain Executive Program, York University. He spent 25 years with Nabisco as an executive responsible for supply chain management and customer marketing and is globally recognized as an expert in his field. He is a board member of the American Marketing Association and the Voluntary Interindustry Commerce Standards (VICS) Association and vice chairman of the VICS CPFR Committee. He has been involved in the development and evolution of CPFR as a global, leading edge business practice since its inception. He graduated cum laude from the University of Scranton.

Prof. Dr. Gerhard Arminger, Professor at the University of Wuppertal and Chief Scientist SAF AG

Gerhard Arminger is Professor of Statistics in the Department of Economics at the University of Wuppertal. He has taught at the University of California at Los Angeles, University of Arizona at Tucson, Indiana University at Bloomington, the Technical University of Vienna, Basel University and at the University of Salzburg. He has published 10 books and over 100 articles in scientific journals. He is co-founder and chief scientist of SAF-AG, a Swiss based company specializing in software for Simulation, Analysis, and Forecasting of demand and order building for retail and manufacturing. For SAF, he mainly works in the areas of micro-forecasting with self-learning systems and in optimization methods for order generation on all levels of the supply chain ranging from SKU-store to CPFR forecasts. Customers of SAF software for computer assisted ordering on the store level include dm-drogerie markt internationally and Metro Cash & Carry Germany.

Gunter Baumgart, Head of Strategic Sales Unit, Henkel

Gunter Baumgart is in charge of the international coordination of Supply Chain projects of Henkel with its trading partners in the fabric and home care department. Besides that he heads research projects sponsored by the German government in the area of Supply chain Management.

Greg Belkin, Senior Editor, MoonWatch Media's Supply Chain Alert[SM]

Gregory Belkin is a Senior Editor of Supply Chain Alert, which provides in-depth case studies and other original, factual reporting on how leading retailers, suppliers, and transportation companies are designing collaborative relationships with their supply chain partners. He is a graduate of George Washington University with a Bachelor of Arts degree in English.

Christopher A. Brady, Business Process Analyst, Safeway

Christopher A. Brady started with Safeway in 1983. He worked in retail operations for 13 years. Since 1998 he has worked in Supply Chain Management at Safeway. He earned his Bachelor's degree at the University of California at Davis and his M.B.A. at California State University, Hayward.

Robert Bruce, President, V.C.C Associates

Robert Bruce is a leading authority on the integration of corporate demand and supply chain strategies in the retail/CPG industry. He established VCC Associates to provide consumer value through strategic collaborative value chain advisory services. During his 18 years at Wal-Mart, he served as Vice President of Corporate Supply Chain Strategies, leading breakthrough initiatives in merchandising, replenishment, forecasting, supply chain and logistics optimizing decisions in a collaborative environment. He also led the development of VMI, CPFR and other collaborative supply chain initiatives with suppliers. He was also a Partner at Surgency, Inc. formerly Benchmarking Partners and a Director of Inventory Management and Replenishment for a division of Target Stores, Inc.

Ralph W. Drayer, Chairman, Supply Chain Insights and former Chief Logistics Officer, Procter & Gamble

Ralph Drayer is chairman and founder of Supply Chain Insights, a supply chain strategy consultancy. Prior to that he was Procter & Gamble's former Chief Logistics Officer. During his 32 years with Procter & Gamble, he held a number of distribution, logistics, customer service and Customer Business Development responsibilities, both domestically and internationally. As P&G's first Vice President of Customer Service/Logistics, he was instrumental in the development of P&G's industry leading supply chain capabilities. He has served as Co-chair of the Grocery Industry's ECR Best Practices Committee, Chairman of the GMA Distribution and Logistics Committee and on the Boards of The Uniform Code Council, VICS and The Council of Logistics Management's Executive Committee. He was also a founding member of the Global Commerce Initiative. Mr. Drayer is the recipient of the Grocery Industry's first Path Forward Award for his industry leading work on ECR and the Council of Logistics Management's Distinguished Service Award, the highest honor that can be bestowed on an individual for achievements in logistics.

Sergio Duque, Process Manager Trade and Sales Services, Henkel Spain

Sergio Duque is a process manager of the Trade and Sales Services Department of Henkel Ibérica, member of Henkel's CPFR Team and a member of the ECR-Europe working group on CPFR. He is an Industrial Engineer specializing in industrial organization.

Georg Engler, Manager, Accenture

Georg Engler is a Manager with Accenture. He is based in the Frankfurt Office, and specialized in Supply Chain Management and the development of CPFR solutions.

Dr. Birgit Ester, Head of Supply Chain Management, dm-drogerie markt

Dr. Birgit Ester joined the retail company in 1998. In 1999 she became head of Supply Chain Management. She is responsible for the optimization of the value chain from the suppliers to the point of sale. Prior to joining dm-drogerie markt, she worked in the areas of Logistics Consulting and Strategic Controlling at well-known pharmaceutical companies.

Lawrence E. Fennell, Vice President, Wal-Mart Stores

Lawrence E. Fennell has been with Wal-Mart more than twenty years. He served eighteen years in Store Operations, the last ten of those years as a Regional Vice President. In 1996 he was promoted to Vice President of Basic Inventory. Since 2000 he has been Vice President for Business Development and he is actively engaged in the implementation of Retail Link CPFR.

Julie Fraser, Principal & Director of Market Strategies, Industry Directions

Julie Fraser has 16 years experience as a manufacturing systems industry expert. Before joining Industry Directions, she held a position as Vice President of Marketing for Baan Supply Chain Solutions. Prior to that, she was the Senior Analyst on Manufacturing Execution Systems and Integration at Advanced Manufacturing Research (AMR). Fraser was the editor-in-chief of the *CIM Strategies* newsletter from the mid-80s to the early 90's, which built on her previous experience in production operations for a discrete industrial goods manufacturing.

Tom Friedman, President, MoonWatch Media Inc.

Thomas Friedman is founder and president of MoonWatch Media Inc., a global B2B events, publishing and advisory company. He is publisher of Retail Systems Alert Research Report, Supply Chain Alert Research Report and Top of the Net Weekly Update. He is author of some of the industry's most thought-provoking executive briefing papers, including Global Retailing in the New Millennium (1998), SupplyWebExchange: The Changing Supply Chain Landscape (2000), and Sorting Through the Standards Maze (2001, in conjunction with the Uniform Code Council). A magna cum laude graduate of Syracuse University, he continued his studies at London University, University of California, and Harvard University Extension. Mr. Friedman was recently selected by RIS News as one of the 25 most influential people in retailing

Esteban Garriga, Manager Trade and Sales Services, Henkel Spain and Co-Chair CPFR project (ECR Europe)

Esteban Garriga is the Trade and Sales Services Manager of Henkel Ibérica with 11 years of experience in the company. Involved in different international projects, Esteban is the co-chair of the ECR-Europe working group on CPFR and a member of the GCI-CPFR advisory group. Esteban holds an MBA degree from ESADE in Barcelona.

Peter Hambuch, Manager CPFR & Demand Process Excellence Germany, Austria, Switzerland, Procter & Gamble

Peter Hambuch has been with Procter & Gamble since 1980, where he held several management positions in the Customer Business Development. In recent years his main focus has been on the implementation of innovative concepts like Category Management and Efficient Consumer Response. His department is supporting multifunctional customer teams of Procter & Gamble Germany, Austria and Switzerland. He studied Mathematics at the University of Saarbruecken.

Dr. Gerhard Hausruckinger, Partner, Roland Berger Strategy Consultants

Gerhard Hausruckinger graduated from the University of Regensburg, Germany in 1988 where he then spent three years as assistant professor of marketing. After working for the German retailer Karstadt in the corporate development department, he joined Roland Berger & Partners in 1994. From 1998-2001 he headed the Consumer Goods/Retail competence centre in the UK, since August 2001 he is back in the Munich head office. His focus areas are Corporate Strategy, e-Commerce and ECR/Category Management.

Ron Ireland, Vice President, VCC Associates

Ron Ireland is an industry practitioner with a focus on best business processes and complementing – enabling technology. He has over 20 years of technical and functional experience. Ireland worked as a Manager of MRPII Application Development at Martin Marietta Data Systems, as Strategy Manager of Systems Application and Development responsible for replenishment and forecasting systems at Wal-Mart Stores and helped pioneer CPFR. Ron was also a Director of Systems Development at J.D. Edwards and a Partner at Surgency, Inc, formerly Benchmarking Partners.

Christian Koch, Director Marketing Consumer Industries, SAP AG

After completing his studies in physics and economics, Christian Koch joined the former DACOS Software company (now SAP Retail Solutions) in Germany to work in Consulting, Business Development and Sales for logistics and merchandise management solutions. In 1996, he moved to the SAP Industry Business Sector Consumer Industries where he has been concentrating on the worldwide rollout of SAP's solution for these industries. Since 1998 he has been responsible for SAP's international marketing activities in the Consumer Industries.

Christian Schick, Supply Chain Manager, dm-drogerie markt

Christian Schick heads the Continuous Replenishment/Vendor Managed Inventory at dm-drogerie markt. He is a member of the CCG (Centrale fuer Coorganisation) boards of Joint Forecasting and CPFR. He is deeply involved in the research and development of Supply Chain Management and CPFR at dm-drogerie markt.

Michael Seishoff , Project Manager, Centrale fürr Coorganisation (CCG)

Michael Seishoff has been a Project Manager at CCG since 1999. His focus is on ECR-Process-Management, with national and international projects in Efficient Unit Loads, Optimization of information and product flow in the consumer goods industry, forecasting, and CPFR. Before joining CCG, he worked for Bretzke Consulting and Klaus-Moers-Retail-Consulting. Mr. Seishoff studied Business Administration at the University of Duisburg.

Hans Teuscher, Manager Supply Chain Management, Accenture, Coordinator ECR Europe CPFR project

Hans Teuscher is a manager in Accenture's Supply Chain Management Line of Business, based in Barcelona. He is the coordinator of the ECR-Europe project on CPFR and serves on the CPFR Advisory Committee of the GCI. He has led various collaboration projects for clients in the retail and FMCG industry across Europe. Mr. Teuscher holds an MBA degree from IESE in Barcelona.

Saskia Treeck, Senior Project Manager, Centrale für Coorganisation (CCG)

Saskia Treeck has been responsible for national and international Supply Chain Management projects at CCG since 1997. Her main focus is on concepts like CPFR and ECR (Efficient Replenishment, Efficient Unit Loads and Efficient Replenishment Upstream). She also coordinates ECR Europe and ECR D-A-CH (Germany, Austria and Switzerland) committees. Prior to joining CCG she worked for UNIT Logistic Consulting and Thyssen Haniel Logistic. Ms. Treeck studied Business Administration jointly at the University of Dortmund and the Fraunhofer Institute for Product-flow and Logistics.

Index

T. Gawlik, J. Kellner, D. Seifert

Effiziente Kundenbindung mit CRM

Wie Procter & Gamble, Henkel und Kraft mit ihren Marken Kundenbeziehungen gestalten

Kunden werden immer anspruchsvoller. Sie entscheiden selbst, wann, wo, wie und unter welchen Umständen sie etwas kaufen. Die Herausforderung an das Management ist es, den Kundenwert langfristig zu erhöhen, indem die richtigen Kunden mit dem richtigen Angebot zur richtigen Zeit über den richtigen Kanal in bedient werden.

Das Buch zeigt, dass CRM ein strategischer Ansatz des Managements ist und nicht etwa eine neue Technologie aus dem IT-Bereich. Es präsentiert ein Zukunftsszenario für die durch Professionalität und extremen Konkurrenzdruck geprägte Konsumgüterbranche. Dabei dient es dem Leser zur Orientierung, Vorbereitung und als Leitfaden bei CRM-Projekten. Fallbeispiele namhafter Firmen wie Nestlé, Wal-Mart, Henkel u.v.m. dienen als Grundlage für eigene Ideen.

Galileo Business
216 S., 2002, geb.
29,90 €
ISBN 3-89842-246-1

Galileo Business